POWER TRAP

POWER TRAP

How fear and loathing between **New Democrats** and **Liberals** keep **Stephen Harper** in power— and what can be done about it

PAUL ADAMS

James Lorimer & Company Ltd., Publishers
Toronto

James Lorimer & Company Ltd., Publishers acknowledges the support of the Ontario Arts Council. We acknowledge the financial support of the Government of Canada through the Canada Book Fund for our publishing activities. We acknowledge the support of the Canada Council for the Arts which last year invested $24.3 million in writing and publishing throughout Canada. We acknowledge the Government of Ontario through the Ontario Media Development Corporation's Ontario Book Initiative

Cover images: iStockphoto

Library and Archives Canada Cataloguing in Publication

Adams, Paul, 1954–
    Power trap : how fear and loathing between New Democrats and Liberals keep Stephen Harper in power — and what can be done about it / Paul Adams.

Includes index.
Issued also in an electronic format.
ISBN 978-1-4594-0270-6

    1. Canada--Politics and government--21st century.
2. Political parties--Canada. I. Title.

FC640.A43 2012   971.07'3   C2012-903775-3

James Lorimer & Company Ltd., Publishers
317 Adelaide Street West, Suite 1002
Toronto, ON, Canada
M5V 1P9

www.lorimer.ca

Printed and bound in Canada

To my father, Dr. Paul V. Adams, who has always believed the path to grace is through the service of others.

Something is profoundly wrong with the way we live today. For thirty years we have made a virtue out of the pursuit of material self-interest: indeed, this very pursuit now constitutes whatever remains of our collective purpose. We know what things cost but have no idea what they are worth. We no longer ask of a judicial ruling or a legislative act: is it good? Is it fair? Is it just? Is it right? Will it help bring about a better society or a better world? Those used to be *the* political questions, even if they invited no easy answers. We must learn once again to pose them.

—Tony Judt, *Ill Fares the Land*

CONTENTS

CHAPTER 1
WHY PROGRESSIVES DON'T WIN

Why don't progressives win? Like a lot of Canadians, I have found Canadian politics immensely frustrating in recent years. Arguably, we have not had a government that could claim to be progressive since the ill-fated final Trudeau majority collapsed in 1984. The right-wing business columnist Neil Reynolds argued in the *Globe and Mail* that the country has been governed by essentially conservative governments since then.[1] But how could this be? The Progressive Conservatives were nearly annihilated in 1993. Stephen Harper's Conservatives have never quite managed even 40 per cent in an election and, according to the polls, often struggle to win the endorsement of even a third of Canadians. Their initial reaction to the 2008 financial crisis was complacent and ideology-bound. They were saved from themselves by the prospect of a Liberal-NDP coalition government, but once the political threat had passed they quickly relapsed. They squandered much of the fiscal surplus they inherited, and then they squandered the stimulus spending that was forced upon them in

2009–11. Since the mid-1990s, inequality in Canada has grown even faster than in the United States,[2] and the Harper Conservatives are hitting the accelerator instead of the brakes. They are cutting corporate taxes as they also set about cutting programs that benefit the poor. Under Stephen Harper, Ottawa has dropped the commitment to provide Canadians with comparable medical care wherever they happen to live.

Since winning a majority, the Conservatives have begun dismantling the collective structures that allow many ordinary Canadians to protect their interests from rampant markets, arbitrarily suspending the right of workers to bargain collectively and eviscerating the Canadian Wheat Board without consulting farmers, defying a judgment of the Federal Court. They have lashed Canada's economic future to an explosive development of the tar sands (or oil sands as they prefer) which raises the value of our dollar, increases our dependence on extractive industries, de-industrializes our economy and costs us jobs. And, speaking of the tar sands, the Conservatives' performance on climate change has been appalling, as they do nothing here at home, and help to thwart concerted action abroad.

They have systematically undermined checks and balances on executive power, whether it be at Statistics Canada, the Canadian Nuclear Safety Commission, the Military Police Complaints Commission, the Parliamentary Budget Office, conscientious public servants (like the Afghanistan whistle-blower Richard Colvin), or indeed parliament itself. Twice they have prorogued parliament for no other object than to save their political skins, and, girded with a majority, now ram legislation through parliament at breathless speed. Originally elected on a platform of accountability, they have undermined or ignored their own legislation and scoffed at its spirit. Ministers are not held accountable in parliament, because when one of them is in trouble the prime minister's junkyard dogs, John Baird and Peter Van Loan, answer for them. These Conservatives scoff too at knowledge, abandoning the mandatory census, turning their backs on pure science, and mounting an aggressive policy of incarceration without a whiff of evidence to support it. Not enough to dismantle the long-gun registry; the Harper government vandalizes the database, making it inaccessible to the police who remained adamant that it was a useful tool. Despite their tenuous electoral mandate, one of the Conservatives' goals is to use the instruments of power to change Canadians' underlying system of values and beliefs to something more like that of Republican America.

Yet it seems there are more of us than there are of them, so to speak; that the Conservatives' approach to the economy, the environment, and our social life is out of tune not only with most of the people we know, but, judging by the polls, perhaps even with most Canadians. But nothing, apparently, can be done about it. The main opposition parties, the New Democrats and Liberals, are caught in a power trap in which they each seek to reach government, not by defeating the Conservatives but by destroying their progressive rival. In the process, they secure Stephen Harper's grip on power.

For years now, the opposition parties have railed against the Harper government. But Stephen Harper's minority governments were sustained in power through literally scores of votes on matters of confidence in which one opposition party or another came to the government's rescue in some way. When it was in the NDP's interest to oppose a government measure, it was in the Liberals' interest to support it and avoid an election; and naturally the reverse also applied. Partisan interests took precedence over progressive policies or, for that matter, the public interest. In a desperate attempt to crowd the middle of the political spectrum, the opposition parties failed to develop or to present an intellectual challenge to the Conservatives' ideas, and now that their divisions have allowed a Conservative majority to be formed with a smidgen under 40 per cent of the vote, all the politicians who represent us can do is cavil. Cavil with the Conservatives and with each other, because the results of the 2011 election put the Liberals and the NDP into a mutual death-grip, each seeing their future prospects as dependent on hobbling or destroying the other's. As progressives, we have no agreed-upon platform or unifying vision, no leader who can claim undisputed primacy in the fight to dislodge the Conservatives. There is no party or alliance to shape our like-minded compatriots into an effective political force, much less to increase our strength by persuading new voters to join us.

Why can't progressives win? Because they too have been caught in the power trap. And what can they do about it? That is the subject of this book.

MY COUNTRY, RIGHT OR LEFT

Using a loose definition, you could argue that progressive-minded parties in Canada command the support of most voters. A clear majority of Canadians voted for a party with a progressive platform, not just in 2011, but also in 2008; and even in 2006, if you count the Bloc Québécois in the total. True, not every Liberal voter in the twenty-first century could be counted as a progressive. An EKOS poll in the spring of 2010[3] found that about one Liberal supporter in five listed the Tories as second choice, and some former Liberal supporters did desert to the Conservatives in 2011. However, the Liberal party invariably campaigns on a progressive platform, whatever it gets up to when in government. Support for the federalist progressive parties has remained remarkably consistent over the last generation. If you add together the Liberal, NDP, and, more recently, Green voters in the elections since 1984, their collective support has been much more stable than that of any individual party, ranging from a low of 47 per cent in 1984 to a high of 53 per cent in 2011.[4] This period includes two majority

Progressive Conservative governments, three majority Liberal governments, a Liberal minority, two Conservative minorities, and a Conservative majority. It also covers a period of profound transition in the party structure of Canadian politics, including the birth of Reform/Canadian Alliance, the Bloc, and the Greens, as well as the demise of the Progressive Conservatives and creation of the modern Conservative party. The presence of this level of stability through a period of tectonic change in the party system is remarkable. Of course, if you include the Bloc the progressive majority looks even more impressive.

Still, even these numbers do not prove that most Canadians are progressive. What they suggest is that the "universe" of voters available to progressive parties is usually quite large, and probably much larger than that available to conservatives. Over the last few years the Manning Centre for Building Democracy—a vehicle for the former Reform party leader Preston Manning—has published polls purporting to show that Canadians are growing more conservative. Even though these surveys are heavily skewed to get the result they want, they still show up stubborn facts about the progressive attitudes of many Canadians. By a margin of about two to one, a Manning Centre survey suggested, Canadians think government action is the best way to solve Canada's economic problems. And most of us think of poverty as a *social*, not an *individual*, problem.[5] One of the key economic issues in dispute between the Conservatives and the opposition parties in 2011 was the government's aggressive schedule of corporate tax cuts. When Harper won his majority, it ensured that those cuts would go ahead, but a poll taken just days after the election showed that a majority of Canadians opposed them.[6] Indeed, in the aftermath of the spectacular failure of financial markets in 2008, many Canadians became suspicious of the private sector's ability to regulate itself and wondered about the compensation its executives award themselves.

Meanwhile, Canadians have become increasingly concerned about the environment, driven by worries about climate change and revulsion at unnatural disasters such as the oil spill in the Gulf of Mexico and the meltdown at the Fukushima reactor in Japan. It's true that since we plunged into the Great Recession in 2008 worries about the economy have crowded out concerns about the environment, even among supporters of the opposition parties. But this is probably more a measure of peaking economic anguish, and despair at any government's taking action, than indifference to the environment. It may also be a comment on how timid the Liberals and NDP have been in rallying Canadians on the environment, since Stéphane Dion's ill-fated campaign for the "Green Shift." Nonetheless, outright climate change denial, which has flourished among US Republicans, has not found even shallow roots here in Canada.

Canadians have become increasingly tolerant of diversity. A Nanos poll in the summer of 2010 found that 65 per cent of Canadians felt that immigration was a "key positive feature of Canada" and 70 per cent thought immigration was a "key tool" for strengthening the economy.[7] This contrasts with the United States and Europe, where attitudes towards immigrants are moving sharply in the opposite direction. In fact, one researcher has recently referred to "Canadian exceptionalism," noting that multiculturalism is ranked near the top of what Canadians say makes them proud about their country. Calgary, of all places, has a Muslim mayor, Naheed Nenshi, the son of South Asian immigrants who came here from Tanzania. Ontario's Progressive Conservative leader, Tim Hudak, sabotaged his own campaign by referring to new Canadians benefitting from a provincial employment program as "foreign workers" during the 2011 provincial election. In general, Canadians have become much more cosmopolitan in recent decades, whether it is through business, travel, or a broader social consciousness. At the same time, Canadians are also more accepting of minorities such as homosexuals and their civic rights to marriage and adoption. When a million people show up for Toronto's Pride parade, as they did in July of 2010, with marchers who included the general manager of the Toronto Maple Leafs and the chief of police, it is hard to argue the pendulum is swinging hard to the conservative side. True, the new mayor of Toronto, Rob Ford, skipped the Pride parade the next year, but the fact that he portrayed it as a personal rather than a political or moral decision—a family get-together at the cottage—was in itself a measure of change. Even in Alberta what used to be regarded as "liberal" views are now mainstream: a survey commissioned by a conservative academic, Faron Ellis, showed that 74 per cent of Albertans supported same-sex marriage and 84 per cent supported women's choice on abortion.[8]

One Manning Centre study cited 60 per cent support among Canadians for the statement that abortion is "morally wrong" as evidence of conservatism. However, we know from other studies that many people who feel this way personally also believe it is nonetheless a woman's right to choose. When asked in another poll at about the same time whether they were pro-choice or pro-life, Canadians opted for the more liberal position by a margin of roughly two to one.[9] Interestingly, when Canadians were asked whether they'd prefer to see political leaders show stronger religious beliefs or keep their religion out of politics altogether, 68 per cent said keep them out—and this view was fairly consistent from eighteen-year-olds through to seniors.[10] This too is in contrast to attitudes south of the border. The Manning Centre also took the 89 per cent positive response to the statement "Nothing is more important than family" as a sign of conservatism even though, by definition, liberals, social democrats, and maybe even the odd communist must have agreed with it for the number to be so high. As the Sting lyric has it, "I hope the Russians love their children too."

So progressives have a lot to work with. Yet there certainly are areas where Canadians have become more conservative in the last decade. In the wake of September 11, many Canadians went wobbly on civil liberties. They were also ripe for a course-correction in their attitudes towards the Canadian military, embodied in the combative figure of General Rick Hillier. Outside of Quebec, Canadians tentatively accepted a transition from conventional peacekeeping to more robust peace-making and even war-fighting early in the twenty-first century. Even though that sentiment cooled as the Afghanistan war dragged on, it is striking how easily Canada slipped into the Libyan bombing campaign—an action that would have seemed "un-Canadian" to many voters a few decades ago. The Canadian nationalism of the late 1960s and the 1970s, which was bound up with medicare, tolerance at home, peacekeeping abroad, and modesty almost everywhere, has yielded ground to a more muscular patriotism represented by the likes of General Hillier and Don Cherry. We invited the world to participate in the Vancouver Olympics while simultaneously being determined to "own the podium," which meant elbowing our guests out of training time in Olympic facilities. The Conservatives have worked to sustain and broaden this new conservative nationalism, celebrating the War of 1812, reframing the development of the North as a military issue, and even reviving the monarchist brand in Canada. When my hometown Winnipeg Jets were reborn, the jetliner that adorned their old sweaters was replaced with a fighter-jet on a crest that looked very much like that of the (Royal) Canadian Air Force, and Harper was there to see the first puck drop.

The most fundamental challenge to progressives, however, is the widespread and fundamentally conservative conviction that no government can do much about the economic, social, and environmental problems we face. To a degree this reflects the failed hopes of 1960s progressive politics, as they encountered the bitter economic winds of the 1970s. Starting with the Mulroney government, Ottawa slashed spending to cope with rising deficits. Not only was government doing less because it was spending less, but much of what it did spend went, not to government projects and services, but to paying interest: Canadians were literally sending Ottawa more in taxes than they were getting back. When the Chrétien-Martin regime finally conquered the deficit in the 1990s, it began running large surpluses, meaning Canadians were still paying for more than they got in return. No one serious about government today—conservative or progressive—believes that the deficits of the 1980s and early 1990s were sustainable. But once those deficits were conquered in Canada, the Harper Conservatives chose to cut taxes and to make untied transfers to the provinces (sometimes used to cut provincial taxes!). Our industries, our jobs, our pensions and our children's careers are all less secure than they were a decade ago, but the federal government had precious little left over for all of that. Ottawa was less effective, in other words, because our political leaders chose to do less.

So, to a degree, disappointment in government was the inevitable result of the fiscal mess we had got ourselves into and the way in which our predominantly conservative governments worked their way out again. But anti-government sentiment has also been nurtured and propagated by conservative leaders who have "created facts." Many core elements of the conservative agenda since the 1980s, most notably deregulation and privatization, were only loosely related to government's fiscal problems. These trends were part of a deliberate policy of transferring the capacity to manage our economy and society into private, mainly corporate, hands. This was particularly true in areas touching on economic globalization. The vast expansion in international trade and communications was bound to weaken the hands of sovereign states as it created powerful transnational corporations whose activities could not be regulated, or even understood, from

the vantage of any single government. In trying to capture the
fruits of globalization, which were real, our governments sur-
rendered the power to manage its consequences. They fell over
one another trying to establish they had the most open borders
and the least stringent regulation. Business demanded "tax competitiveness," meaning governments, Conservative and Liberal,
needed to lower taxes primarily for corporations and the wealthy,
and to cut government spending. At a time when Canadians need
science, infrastructure, education, and training to help us compete, and income security for those who find themselves unable
to do so, Ottawa's cupboard is bare, and deliberately so. There is
no doubt that the expansion of trade since the 1980s has made
Canada a wealthier as well as a more cosmopolitan nation. It has
also made Canada a less equal one.

Canadians have generally gone along with all these changes.
They were frightened by the economic problems of the late 1970s
and early 1980s and baffled by the Trudeau governments' chaotic
response. They were convinced, slowly, that that deficit needed
to be conquered. And many simply came to accept that governments were powerless. This doesn't mean they all became fiscal
and economic conservatives. Some did, of course. Many others,
who should be in the progressive camp, simply gave up. Most
Canadians actually call themselves "centrists." But centrism is
not a policy, philosophy, or consistent set of beliefs. The centre is
constantly moving, as it has surely been in the last thirty years—to
the right on most economic issues, attitudes to government, and
perhaps also on security and crime, and to the left on many social
and moral issues such as abortion, gay marriage, and tolerance
for diversity. Where conservatives have had the advantage over
progressives in shaping this environment—at least since 2004—is
that they have had one house, one leader, and by and large one
message. They have usually sorted out their priorities internally,
and presented Canadians with a more or less clear proposal for

how they would govern. Canadians of a conservative bent know where to cast their ballot these days. Progressives do not.

SO, WHERE HAVE ALL THE PROGRESSIVES GONE?

Of course, many Canadians do not fall easily into the categories of conservative, progressive or even centrist. As the political scientists, Neil Nevitte and Christopher Cochrane have pointed out, some Canadians are socially liberal but economically conservative and vice versa—something that forces parties into complex calculations about how to present themselves.[11] Unlike American Republicans, who parade their socially conservative views, Stephen Harper has tried to tone down these elements in his own party in order to appeal to a broader public. In a rare act of insubordination, in the fall of 2011 a pro-life Conservative MP from Saskatchewan, Brad Trost, criticized the government's funding of Planned Parenthood, complaining that Harper had pushed social conservatives into a corner. Indeed, what Harper normally tries to do is send his socially conservative supporters symbolic signals, or speak to them through narrowly targeted channels of communications, so as not to turn off economic conservatives with more socially liberal views. Of course, some Canadians are just the reverse: economically progressive and socially conservative. It is perfectly possible to support generous social programs and also to oppose abortion-on-demand or gun control. A New Democrat friend who grew up, like me, in Manitoba, recently reminded me that the provincial NDP has a long history of electing MLAs who are ideological mavericks. In fact, Manitoba's most outspoken anti-abortionist when I was growing up, Joe Borowski, first came to prominence as the NDP minister of highways.

Still, the fact that many Canadians are hard to pin down ideologically doesn't mean that you can't define what a conservative or a progressive stands for. And it does not mean that advocates of these viewpoints don't struggle for the hearts and minds of

Canadians, or that they don't try to implement their ideologies when they hold office. Stephen Harper's conservatism is clearly built on a bedrock of neo-classical economics, stressing free markets, free trade, small government, low taxes, and unfettered competition, which means low levels of regulation. He sees the roots of crime and other social dysfunction mainly in individual moral failings rather than social conditions. And when he must make policy choices between traditional social and family values and more contemporary ones, he opts for tradition. This philosophy is not libertarian as such. Indeed, there is something of a disconnect between its economic and social components. It might be termed "defensive libertarianism," because at the core of its individualism is a desire not to have life impinged upon by government or society—which, paradoxically, may mean not being subjected to the sight of men holding hands or women wearing burkas. This explains why the ebulliently pro-immigration Jason Kenney also feels the need to unveil women when they take the oath of citizenship. Among Conservatives, there are philosophical variations and differences of emphasis, but this clump of ideas is recognizable to most people who follow politics.

And what about progressives? Do they have a similar clump of ideas? Because they are split among several parties and come from different social and political traditions, they may seem more difficult to define. Still, the outlines of a progressive worldview are similarly clear. Generally speaking, progressives are Keynesian in their economic views, see a positive role for the state in regulating and remedying some of the painful features of the market economy, and worry about the increasing level of inequality in our society. They are deeply concerned about the environment, particularly the potentially disastrous warming of the planet's atmosphere. They generally believe in social and political tolerance in moral and family matters, whatever their personal beliefs and practices. And they are inclined to see social factors such as poverty, inequality, and lack of education and opportunities as playing some role in the genesis of crime and other social problems.

In partisan terms, the progressives might include the small "Red Tory" wing of the old Progressive Conservatives, most (though certainly not all) Liberals, most New Democrats and Greens, and some, if not most, Bloquistes, as well as a significant number of non-voters. But thinking of them this way might actually be misleading. Canada, like many Western countries, has been undergoing what political scientists sometimes call dealignment. There may have been a time in Canada, as in Britain, when, as Gilbert and Sullivan had it:

> *That every boy and every gal*
> *That's born into the world alive*
> *Is either a little Liberal*
> *Or else a little Conserva-tive.*
> *Fal, lal, la!*

That time has passed. Fewer and fewer Canadians feel a life-long identity with a party, and if they do it is more like a brand loyalty to, say, Coke or Pepsi, than a religious affiliation as it once was. According to family lore, my grandfather's best friend—like him a lifelong Conservative—drew my grandfather near on his deathbed. "Grits are bastards, aren't they, Alex?" he supposedly whispered. My grandfather nodded and his friend passed away at peace. Is that kind of extreme unction even imaginable these days? Many, perhaps most Canadians, whether they are conservative, progressive, or sovereigntist, need to be rallied anew to the party each election. The inclination or habit of voting for a particular party is just that, and no more; it can be easily disturbed by some new leader, event, policy, problem, issue, perception, or tactical consideration. How else to explain the destruction of one of Canada's two great parties of state in the course of a decade, and the humiliation of the other? Or the emergence of new parties, such as Reform, the BQ, and the Greens, that among them have at times commanded the support of roughly half the electorate? The BQ both appeared and disappeared as the great indigestible fact of Canadian politics in a virtual flash.

I consider myself part of this motley collection of Canadian political wanderers, if a somewhat more politically engaged specimen of the kind. Because of the family tradition on my mother's side—and likely also due to something of a contrarian streak—at the age of thirteen I campaigned for the Progressive Conservatives in the 1968 election while the whole world was going mad for Pierre Elliott Trudeau. Strange as it may seem in today's more ideologically polarized atmosphere, it was possible in those days to be a PC and still consider yourself a progressive, feeling all of the social and political currents we associate with the 1960s. Looked at in the right light and from the right angle, the Tory leader, Robert Stanfield, could be seen as a kind of Disraelian one-nation conservative, who emphasized the obligations of the privileged to the society as a whole. He introduced the idea of a guaranteed annual income to Canadian politics, for example. John Diefenbaker before him had been a champion of individual rights, and had legislated Canada's first *Bill of Rights*—the forebear of Trudeau's constitutional *Charter of Rights and Freedoms.* As a practical matter, Dief also hastened the end of capital punishment in this country. In foreign policy, he took up the cause of blacks in South Africa. And he sold our wheat to China and the USSR! In the nationalist spirit of the 1970s I joined the Committee for an Independent Canada, some of whose prominent founders were PCs—and why not? Wasn't John A. Macdonald's National Policy the mother of all Canadian nationalist economics? In our little Manitoba PC Youth newspaper, we also called for the decriminalization of marijuana. And in May of 1970 we marched on the Manitoba legislature to condemn the killing of anti-Vietnam-War protesters at Kent State University—to no discernible effect, I am sad to say.

It wasn't that we thought the PCs as a whole were more progressive than conservative. But we could find a place for ourselves within the traditions of the party. This was possible because there really was a broad political consensus in Western societies born out of the Depression and subsequent world war that vigorous markets and active government were intertwined. It wasn't just Liberal and Labour and Democratic politicians building up social programs; "conservatives" such as Dwight Eisenhower, Harold Macmillan, and even Richard Nixon saw a role for the state in spreading the benefits of prosperity and giving new economic security to the ordinary man and woman. Markets and government were part of a functional whole; prosperity was not the opposite of justice and security, but a basis for them.

My biggest problem with Robert Stanfield was that he swallowed his reservations about Trudeau's invocation of the *War Measures Act* during the 1970 October Crisis in deference to the public mood. Nonetheless, I later worked as an assistant to an MP, Marcel Lambert, who was a francophone Tory champion of gun control from an Alberta riding—you don't see many of them any more. After that, I worked with Sidney Spivak, a brilliant and compassionate businessman who led the Progressive Conservatives in Manitoba at a time when the future media mogul Izzy Asper—then leader of the provincial Liberal party—tried to outflank the PCs on the right. To my astonishment and pleasure, Sidney revelled in a comment by a Winnipeg newspaper that if you put him and the NDP premier, Ed Schreyer, in a bottle and shook them up you would have trouble figuring out which was which. But in 1975 Sidney was thrown out as leader by Sterling Lyon, the tribune of an austere new conservatism, though we did not recognize it as such at the time: in fact, we wrongly viewed Lyon simply as paleo-conservative, a throwback to an earlier era. I worked for Sidney for one bitter year while he served in Lyon's cabinet, but Sidney and I were both more at home with the leftover NDP bureaucrats in our shop.[12] In the fall of 1978 I left Canada for graduate school in Britain—which would soon be Margaret Thatcher's Britain. It was in that place and at that time that the postwar political consensus was well and truly shattered by a new, radically individualist, pro-market, and anti-government ideology that swept and is still sweeping the world.

Since then, conservatives and their fellow travellers have systematically denigrated, diminished, and emasculated the public sector and its accomplishments while exalting the markets, inspired by a peculiar theory of extreme individualism that defies biology, anthropology, history, and psychology—and used to offend common sense. Its strange ideas gained currency in part because progressives had trouble addressing the economic problems that arose from a system they had created. As the new conservatism grew stronger, its critics were variously co-opted, cowed, ignored, or rooted in place. More specifically, it left progressives divided, and in this country divided among parties even if we are increasingly united on our goals: a more equal and human society and an environment that will not choke the life from our kids.

For former Red Tories like me, for Liberals of a progressive inclination, for New Democrats frustrated in their various attempts to collaborate with or dislodge the Liberals, for Green party supporters, and no doubt for some of those non-voters who stay home out of protest rather than indifference or ignorance, this is a difficult time. Ironically, in some respects our situation parallels that of Canadian conservatives in the 1990s.

DOING THE SPLITS

Jean Chrétien dominated Canadian politics for a decade partly because of his exceptional political skill, which embodied the traditional ideological adaptability of the Liberal party. He was assisted by the weakness of the NDP's leadership, the lingering effects of Bob Rae's unpopular government in Ontario, which suppressed the NDP vote there, and the emergence of the deficit as a significant issue in Canadian political life—something which did not play to the New Democrats' strengths. Chrétien was also a populist in his political style, if not consistently a progressive in government, something that his successors, the businessman Paul Martin, the academic Stéphane Dion, and the intellectual Michael Ignatieff could not match.

But, more than anything, Chrétien won because the forces of conservatism in Canada were deeply divided even as their ideology was growing more robust. They had created their own power trap on the right. Preston Manning created the Reform party because, as he saw it, the Mulroney Progressive Conservatives were not truly conservative, and did not adequately represent anglophones and the West in their approach to Quebec. He was certainly right. Although Mulroney's government was clearly more conservative than Trudeau's in its support of the objectives of corporate Canada, it was never as purist in its ideology as the Thatcherism or Reaganism that were flourishing elsewhere. In a sense, Mulroney represented a compromise between the liberalism of Pearson and Trudeau (medicare as "sacred trust," for example) and the more aggressive ideology of the conservative revolution that was by then well under way in Britain and the United States.

While Manning set out to purify conservatism, he recognized from the start that even his narrower movement needed to be a coalition. He pursued a strategy of uniting what he called fiscal conservatives, social conservatives, and populists. He understood that his job as leader was not only to conjoin these traditions but also to manage the tensions and conflicts among them. When the Reform party he created and shaped proved unable to win over the sturdier remnants of the Progressive Conservative party, he created a new vehicle, the Canadian Alliance, intended to broaden his movement further. Although it did not immediately succeed, and he was personally left by the wayside, these manoeuvres set the groundwork for the eventual merger of the Canadian Alliance and the Progressive Conservatives to form the modern Conservative party. What the merger did, in effect, was to extend the Manning coalition to include moderate conservatives (and former PCs) such as Peter MacKay and Jim Prentice, who then lost their own ideological voice. Interestingly, although this broader coalition was enough to bring the Conservatives to power in 2006, the new party has consistently won fewer voters than the combined total of the old PCs and Canadian Alliance.[13] (Progressives need to be realistic about this same possibility if the parties they support contemplate cooperation, coalition, or even merger.)

This failure to realize its full potential was likely due to two factors: the still unconstrained id of the party—its angry social conservatism—that scared off many Ontarians, and the lingering odour of the Reform party's hostility to Quebec. Together, these were crucial in Stephen Harper's inability to win a majority before 2011. Nonetheless, the new Conservative party has been able to dominate Canadian politics and government since 2006 largely because it has been more successful at aggregating conservative voters than any party has been at aggregating progressives.

Canada's increasingly peculiar first-past-the-post electoral system has also played an important part in this story, with its tendency to reward regional concentration and to punish parties whose support is thinly spread across the land. Because the Reform party and Bloc Québécois were both regional parties in the 1993 election, their popular strength was exaggerated in parliament. The Progressive Conservatives received more votes than the BQ and almost as many as the Reform party that year, but they were reduced to just two seats. The Reform party caucus was twenty-six times the size of the PC caucus, despite similar popular support. The BQ, in third place in terms of votes, became the official opposition.

While this first-past-the-post system continued to help the BQ until its collapse in popular support in 2011, it was an obstacle to the growth of the Reform party into Ontario and the Atlantic provinces. In these regions the stubborn residue of PC support made it impossible for Reform and, later, the Canadian Alliance, to overcome the Liberals. Indeed, this underlay the power trap in which conservatives found themselves in those years, and is the principal explanation for the Liberals' stunning ability to win all or virtually all of Ontario's seats in three elections running—even at a time when Ontarians were choosing a hard-line conservative government provincially, under Mike Harris. It was this feature of the electoral system that forced the Reform/Alliance and the PCs eventually to consummate a merger, which had been repugnant to large sections of each party throughout the 1990s.

There is an extremely important lesson here for those considering how progressives can optimize their impact. In a system of proportional representation, where party strength in parliament roughly reflects popular support, parties can vigorously represent their particular views at election time, get an accurate reflection of their popularity, and then collaborate or even form a coalition with like-minded parties in parliament. If there had been a pure proportional representation system in 2011, NDP, Liberal, and Green MPs would have been able to form a majority coalition government without the support of the BQ. That is one of the reasons why many third parties in first-past-the-post systems support electoral reform, as have the NDP and the Greens, who have usually been underrepresented in parliament in relation to their popular support. (This changed in 2011, when the NDP's representation in parliament somewhat exceeded its proportion of the popular vote.) It also explains why the Liberals and the Conservatives, who have had a duopoly on government since Confederation, have in the past usually opposed changes to a system that has benefited them.

But, for now, we have the electoral system we have. In our system, if Party X and Party Y, with slightly different points of view, respectively take 25 per cent and 26 per cent of the vote in a particular constituency they would together have a majority, but will lose to Party Z that they both oppose if it gets as little as 27 per cent of the vote. Canadian conservatives needed to merge their two parties—even at the risk of losing some of their combined strength—to overcome this obstacle. When they did that in 2003 they started to increase their share of seats in parliament, and eventually they won the 2006 election. Faced now with a united Conservative party, progressives in this country must either unite behind a single party or forge some sort of tactical alliance at the riding level that will present progressive voters with a single option rather than three, or even four. Progressives may maximize their raw vote total by offering the public different flavours in the form of the New Democratic, Liberal, and Green parties, but they will not maximize their number of seats or their impact in parliament or on government. In the absence of electoral reform, an electoral alliance or a merger of progressive parties is the best strategy, even if some votes are lost to the Conservatives in the process.

MY PARTY, RIGHT OR WRONG

Nothing seems odder to most Canadians than extreme partisanship, because most of them have left it so far behind themselves. No one except the tiny and shrinking minority who are party members has much time for parties as institutions, and frequently even they have time only for their own. The hyperindividualism of the modern era, which is a feature not only of the new conservatism but also of the cultural liberation of the 1960s and those who lived through it, and now of a younger generation, is poison to parties. Parties are quintessentially collective organizations. People of differing viewpoints come together to achieve shared political objectives, but in doing so they need to compromise. They may debate policy and fight each other in leadership contests, but at election time they are supposed to toe a common line. Candidates are expected to keep their views to themselves when they differ from those of the leader or the platform. Even if they are elected to parliament, caucus and cabinet solidarity require that they express their views in camera but tone their differences down in public. It is a matter of fact that fewer Canadians than ever are active participants in collective organizations, whether they be unions, churches, or political parties. And fewer still believe that participation requires them to adopt the views of the organization. In a day and age when practising Catholics think nothing of contradicting the pope on birth control, it seems strange to many voters that an MP would pay a price for expressing her views on, say, gun control or the Middle East. Not just "strange," it may even be seen as a form of hypocrisy.

Yet there is no example of a successful liberal democracy of the sort most Canadians would recognize and want for themselves without political parties. Attempts at one-party or non-party democracies in the developing world have usually decayed into authoritarianism. My own home province of Manitoba developed a robust anti-party ideology that dominated its politics for roughly a third of the twentieth century. When the United Farmers of Manitoba won the election of 1922 (defeating the Liberals), they were so loosely organized that they did not have a leader and they floated a proposal to have the premier's chair alternate between them and the opposition. The reason such uncompetitive arrangements rarely flourish for long is that no single political organization can represent all the important interests and viewpoints in a society. And, in many cases, political competition helps governments to avoid the twin temptations of atrophy and corruption. Parties are crucial for our system to function. They move ideas from think tanks and universities and talk on the street into political discourse. If their breadth is great enough, parties forge compromise between regions, interests, and social and economic groups. They engage tens of thousands of Canadians, as workers or donors, in the political process. And through their efforts they contact, cultivate, and, to a degree, engage, millions more at a time when engaging people politically is hard. They train future MPs and cabinet ministers in local campaigns, as staffers in MPs' offices, and at party meetings; and at the highest level they test their leaders by making them win elections inside their parties before presenting them to the wider public. (Who knows how much better Michael Ignatieff might have fared in the election if he had actually won a campaign for his own party's leadership?) In doing all these things, they narrow the political choices we have from the thousands intellectually conceivable to a manageable three or four.

For those outside the parties, it is hard to understand the depth of loyalty felt by those within. It is not just a commitment to certain ideas or interests—or indeed political ambition—that binds partisans together, though all of these are important. It is the experience of working intensely with others in pursuit of a common goal. There is an irrational, emotional, social factor at play here, as in the way fans (short form of "fanatics") of the Canadiens or Canucks feel a collective exhilaration in victory and disappointment in defeat. And, of course, fundamental to that aspect of the experience is the bitter rivalry: Oilers-Flames, Habs-Bruins, Habs-Leafs, Sens-Leafs. It is not just the feeling of communion that is irrational, but the antagonism to the "other." From the NDP perspective, the Liberals have long profited from stealing their ideas and then muscling New Democrats out of the way. From the Liberal perspective, the

NDP eats away at their left flank as they confront their true rivals for government on the right. Liberals and New Democrats think the Greens were invented to steal their votes, without a hope of electing enough Green MPs to make a difference. It is easier for any progressive party to gain votes from another progressive party than to win them from their common enemy. In this sense the game is not a struggle of ideas, but a contest among rival teams. And it leads straight into the power trap in which progressives find themselves.

During the 2011 election campaign, I spent a few days poking around Trinity-Spadina, a riding that stretches up from the Toronto lakeshore, from the CN Tower to the trendy Annex district. This seat has long been hotly contested between the Liberals and the NDP. Organizers for the NDP incumbent, Olivia Chow, complained that as many as fifty of their signs were being vandalized each night. The Liberals complained that bicycle and car tires were found slashed in the vicinity of election signs for their candidate, Christine Innes. A blog called "All Fired Up In the Big Smoke" and a Twitter feed called @wherestony2011 dished dirt on the business practices of Innes's husband, the former MP Tony Ianno, and made the case that he had been a right-wing Liberal—opposing same-sex marriage, for example. The Liberal campaign manager told me that there was a history in the riding of thousands of people registering to vote on election day, hinting that there had been electoral fraud. He told me the Liberals would have a lawyer posted at every poll, and said darkly that he had noticed a lot of activity at the Steelworkers' Hall on previous election days.

One night I went to an all-candidates meeting at St. Paul's Church, a gracious, originally Methodist church built in 1889 that is now multi-denominational and has a reputation for social activism. The candidates sat at a nondescript table, framed by a beautiful wooden altar and a gloriously large pipe organ. The pews on the main floor were filled, as were most of the seats in the balcony: several hundred people in all. The body language between Chow and Innes, who were seated beside each other, was decidedly chilly. But on everything from aboriginal affairs to urban development to social programs, their positions were virtually indistinguishable. They were joined at the table not only by the Conservative candidate, who seemed a sad sack next to these two articulate women, but also by the Green, Rachel Barney, who had grown up in the riding, and had gone on to teach philosophy at Harvard and the University of Chicago. Barney is now Canada Research Chair in Classical Philosophy at the University of Toronto. It seemed hard to believe that the mainly progressive-minded people in the hall wouldn't have been proud to have any one of these candidates representing them in parliament. I don't claim to have understood the dark passions running beneath the surface in Trinity-Spadina, but I could not help noticing that, while the candidates were attacking the Harper government and its policies in similar language, their workers were hacking away not at the Conservatives but at one another.

Notwithstanding the similarity of their appeals at election time, it isn't unusual for some Liberals and some New Democrats to insist that their party traditions are much too distinct ever to be combined. It is true that Liberals have tended to put more emphasis on individualism—the *Charter of Rights*, for example—and New Democrats on collectivism—unions and social programs. The Liberals have been more resolutely federalist, the New Democrats more open to asymmetrical arrangements, particularly with Quebec. Liberals have migrated more easily and frequently between business-oriented fiscal and economic policies and social reform. Many of my friends in both parties make this point the same way: unlike the Conservatives, who *re*-united in 2003 after a decade apart, Liberals and New Democrats have never been part of a single party or movement. Their point is that the chasm between the two parties is too wide to be bridged. I think this both understates the difficulties that conservatives had in getting together and overstates the differences between the progressive parties *from the perspective of voters.* The resistance of Progressive Conservatives to merger with Reform in the 1990s was not just tribal or institutional: many PCs were genuinely repelled by the social conservatism of Reform, its undertone of intolerance, and the rigidity of its pro-market and anti-government philosophy. Some lifelong PCs, including their two-time leader, Joe Clark, who had been steeped in the pragmatist tradition of the party back to Macdonald's time, believed the new party would traduce that tradition, which indeed to a degree it did. Clark retired from partisan politics rather than join the new Conservative party. Yet most PCs saw that their party and therefore their specific tradition was in twilight, and many saw the Harper Conservatives as closer to their views, and a better vehicle for their ambitions, than any of the alternatives.

I would not deny that the Liberals and NDP have separate traditions. Nor would I underestimate either the psychic pain of compromising those traditions, or, for that matter, of shedding the old uniform for a new one. But I don't believe that any of those feelings are broadly and deeply shared by those who vote for them. It is the party activists who cling to those differences, exaggerate their practical significance, and ignore the fact that they surface less and less visibly in the parties' election platforms—and the differences in any event mean little to the people who vote for the parties. Most of those voters would happily adjust to new names and colours, if only they could achieve a government that reflected their ideas and interests instead of those of the Harper Conservatives. If only they could find their way out of the power trap.

CHAPTER 2

WHY NOW IS THE TIME

You might be thinking: Hey, what's the rush? Why not take another election, and let things sort themselves out? Maybe 2011 was a fluke: the NDP might fade in 2015, and the Liberals re-emerge as the undisputed alternative to the Harper Conservatives. Or maybe the Liberals will wane, like the Progressive Conservatives eventually did, and leave a clear path for the NDP. Progressives will be in better shape, then, for the election of 2019—or, if the Conservatives are held to a minority in 2015, maybe even sooner. Any of these things *could* happen. No worries, then. But the experience of conservatives in the 1990s was that it took not one, not two, but three elections to get their act together and escape the power trap. The continuing competitiveness of two conservative parties prevented either one from effectively challenging for government.

Although it was cold comfort to the Reformers and Progressive Conservatives in the 1990s, they were running against a Liberal party under Jean Chrétien and his finance minister, Paul Martin, whose fiscal policies were not so fundamentally different from their own. Chrétien-Martin slew the deficit, attacked the debt, and eventually lowered tax rates, even if the Liberals were, from a conservative perspective, soft on social programs, crime, and same-sex marriage. Furthermore, the Chrétien-Martin governments may have talked a good game on climate change, but their policies were as passive as any tar sands producer might hope. On the economy anyway, the Chrétien-Martin governments could be described as Conservative Lite.

This is hardly the situation for progressives today. Stephen Harper is definitely not Progressive Lite, whatever his more astringent conservative critics may say. At a time when the market-worshipping policies of the last three decades have produced serial financial crises, slow-to-negative growth, growing inequality, and a financially stressed and anxious middle class, the Harper government's policy is to double down. Even after the market meltdown of 2008, the Conservatives showed no awareness that their economic model had cracked, and that tax cuts, program cuts, and trade deals with increasingly obscure trading partners would not equip us to address the economic problems we have now. And what about climate change? The science makes it clear that it will blight the lives of our children, and perhaps wreck those of our grandchildren. But the Harper government's approach is to stall on greenhouse gas emissions, promote "ethical oil" to our neighbours, and build pipelines to ship bitumen to Texas or to China.

The market philosophy of the Harper government is nothing new. In a sense his government represents the apotheosis of a trend that goes back to the 1980s. What is strange is that Canada would bind itself more closely to a conservative worldview today at the very moment that its practical failure is so obvious and its theoretical basis in academic economics is under withering attack. For more than three decades, conservative politicians, businesspeople, philosophers, and economists have had the dominant hand in shaping the system we have today in Canada and around the globe. But the system has created economic and environmental problems it cannot resolve—many of them urgent. Conservatives are too attached intellectually, politically, and often financially to the market orthodoxies that have failed us to find new solutions to our problems. Progressives shouldn't be taking their own sweet time to find a way out of the power trap in which their parties are now caught.

WHOSE ECONOMY IS IT, ANYWAY?

Let's start with the economy, and where we are today. Inequality has been steadily rising in this country[1] since 1989. As the business-oriented Conference Board reported in the summer of 2011, "average income has risen [in Canada], but that's due mostly to the top earners increasing their share of the economic pie at the expense of the rest." During the three decades of conservative, market-oriented policies, there has been economic growth, but only the top 20 per cent of Canadians have seen their share of the pie rising, while the remaining 80 per cent, including both the middle class and the poor, have seen their share falling. In fact, what the Occupy Wall Street supporters have said of the United States is also true here: most of the gains have actually gone to the super-rich—the top 1 per cent of income earners. Increasingly, even economists from such bodies as the Organisation for Economic Co-operation and Development (OECD), the International Monetary Fund (IMF), and the World Bank are raising concerns about the levels of inequality in Western societies and how they may impede economic growth.

This trend is at least partly a result of market-driven globalization. Rather than trying to manage these powerful forces and shape them to the collective benefit, politicians of various partisan stripes have adopted the policies advocated by the beneficiaries of globalization. Some of them, such as Margaret Thatcher and

Ronald Reagan, did so out of conviction; many others, out of fear and uncertainty about how the markets would react if they did not. The "liberation" of market forces led to collateral damage, such as the shrinkage of the manufacturing sector, the loss of low- and semi-skilled jobs, and downward pressure on wages. As well, at the urging of business groups and their supporters among academic economists and the media, governments adopted deliberate policies aimed to reduce the redistributive effects of government, or even to reverse them. In Canada, between 1976 and 1994, the net effect of taxes and government transfers was increasingly to reduce income inequality; since then, the reverse has been true.[2] Programs such as unemployment insurance have been slashed, and cover a much smaller percentage of the unemployed than they once did. Meanwhile, tax rates for high income earners and for corporations have been steadily cut, while new opportunities for wealth have been created for them through privatization and deregulation. The Harper government has opened up another flank on behalf of the wealthy with its campaign against organized labour.

These changes have most directly affected those at the lower end of the economic scale, whose jobs have disappeared, been downgraded in quality and pay, or become less regular. But as the economy sorts itself out into 20 per cent winners and 80 per cent losers, the solidly middle class are increasingly stalked by insecurity. My parents were children of the Great Depression. But by the time they were raising their family in the 1950s and 1960s, they had a reasonable expectation that their six children would be able to match the quality of life the family had achieved in the decades after the war. I don't think it ever occurred to them that sending us to the University of Manitoba for a general arts or science degree—tuition $450 per year—wasn't getting us off to a great start in life. Today, many middle class families sweat about their two or three children, whether they can get into the top-rated university programs for the multiple degrees they will need to guarantee a good job, and how on earth they will afford it all. As the divide between those who succeed economically and those who do not gets sharper, and the threshold gets higher, the stakes can seem overwhelming.

Many, perhaps most, Canadians still live a pretty good life. But even prior to the 2008 economic crash, it was clear that while Canada had become much richer over the previous three decades, as measured by Gross Domestic Product (GDP), the Canadian middle class wasn't feeling it. On the contrary, by all kinds of objective measures, economic life was getting worse. According to the CIBC's job quality index, which combines hours of work, compensation, and stability, there had been a more or less steady erosion in job quality in Canada since the 1980s.[3] By 2011, with the enthusiastic encouragement of the banks, Canadians who used to be savers rather than borrowers were racking up personal debt, often on their credit cards, to rival their American neighbours. Consumer bankruptcies—one crude measure of how we are handling all that debt—have increased sixfold since the mid-1970s. One broad statistical index of Canadians' economic security showed a steady fall over a quarter-century even prior to 2008.[4]

Of course, financial strains during the working years eat into our ability to save for our retirement. This has come at a time when the private sector is abandoning defined-benefit pension plans, and in some cases walking away from pensions altogether. Look at the pensioners of Nortel, once Canada's great high-tech globalized success story, left nearly penniless after its bankruptcy. Meanwhile, instead of being held up as models, defined-benefit pension plans in the public sector are under attack, presumably on the theory that old folks should be equally immiserated wherever they once worked. Many of the ordinary working stiffs the Conservatives purport to channel, who work hard and play by the rules, have reason to worry about the home economics of their own old age. In fact, poverty among the elderly is now rising after decades of decline.

These trends have affected most Western countries, though to differing degrees. Inequality in Canada is somewhat worse than it is in most Western European countries. It is not yet as bad as in the United States or the United Kingdom, but since the mid-1990s inequality in Canada has been rising at a faster rate. The reason for this difference may be that Canada, as we shall see, was slower to adopt the extreme pro-market policies of Margaret Thatcher and Ronald Reagan, which began with a deep plunge around 1980. However, Canadian policy under Mulroney and Chrétien-Martin gravitated steadily in the same direction. It was not for another quarter-century, though, that we got our very own version of Thatcher and Reagan in the form of Stephen Harper, and not until 2011 that he was unleashed with a majority.

"THERE IS NO SUCH THING AS SOCIETY"

In thinking about how we get out of this political and economic mess, progressives need to understand that the conservative wave that swept the Anglo-Saxon countries and eventually the globe over the last thirty years was reactionary in a literal sense. It was a reaction against a postwar economic model that had been shaped by liberal and social democratic values, and which seemed to fall apart in the 1970s. It was a *liberal* economist, John Maynard Keynes, whose ideas dominated economic and fiscal policy after the war. Internationally, he inspired the network of institutions, including the International Monetary Fund and the World Bank, erected to manage and stabilize the world economy. Domestically, he proposed a greater role for government fiscal policy in managing the ups and downs of the economy that had threatened capitalism itself during the Great Depression of the 1930s. According to Keynes, governments should smooth out the business cycle by stimulating demand through deficit spending during economic slowdowns and running surpluses during booms. Keynes thought that budgets should be roughly balanced, but over the business cycle rather than in any individual year. And his ideas were accepted, in many cases even embraced, by a business class that could remember the Great Depression and was enjoying an unprecedented economic boom in the postwar years.

At the same time, there was a powerful movement for governments to bring security and stability to the lives of their citizens through social reform. These were the years of the Beveridge Report in Britain, which created the foundations of the British welfare state on the pillars of national health and national insurance. In the United States, there was Lyndon Johnson's War on Poverty, which itself was a successor to Roosevelt's New Deal. And, of course, in Canada this was the period of national medicare, the Canada Pension Plan, and greatly expanded unemployment insurance. Some of these programs, such as unemployment insurance, fit neatly into the Keynesian model as "natural stabilizers," since spending on them would automatically increase in recessions and diminish in booms, helping to smooth out the business cycle of boom and bust. In 1965, Milton Friedman, possibly the twentieth century's greatest apostle of free-market economics, an eventual winner of the Nobel Prize, remarked: "We're all Keynesians now."[5]

But it was only a few years after Friedman's declaration that the consensus came undone. Liberated by Keynes from the shackles of balancing budgets every year, and by rapid economic growth that made last year's debts easier to pay off this year, governments became less and less disciplined about balancing budgets over the business cycle. For a while, this didn't seem to matter much. However, inflation took grip in the 1960s, perhaps as a result of Johnson's decision to print money, in effect, to fund the Vietnam War *and* the War on Poverty. In the 1970s, when the Organization of the Petroleum Exporting Countries (OPEC) cartel sent oil prices skyrocketing, Western governments confronted what was dubbed "stagflation." This was the phenomenon of inflation, normally a feature of booms, continuing even during a period of economic stagnancy. Stimulating the economy in the Keynesian tradition to encourage growth seemed likely to make the inflation problem— and thus the economic problem—worse. It wasn't really Keynes's fault, perhaps, but Keynesianism seemed to have produced a set of economic problems that it could not resolve.

As a student in the 1970s, I remember thinking that what the world needed was another Keynes; someone who, with a flash of insight, could create a model of economic policy that would address the issues that Keynesianism no longer could. Though I had read some of his writings at the time, it never occurred to me that this would turn out to be none other than Milton Friedman.[6] In the winter of 1978–79, I had just arrived in England as a graduate student at Oxford. It was a moment in history that would frame the global era of conservatism to come. I can recollect, in those first few months, a lorry drivers' strike, numerous train strikes, a garbage strike in London, coal miners' strikes, and walkouts in the auto industry. There was a gravediggers' strike in the north of England that prevented people from burying their dead and a health workers' strike whose pickets prevented the sick from entering hospitals. There were shortages of gasoline and sugar. There was a one-day national strike in support of the nurses, and there were stories in the papers (if and when they arrived) of union leaders at London's newspaper printing presses who pocketed the pay packets of supposed workers with names like "Mickey Mouse."[7] In many cases, the strikes occurred in industries, such as rail, steel, and coal, that had been nationalized by Labour governments after the Second World War. Nationalization had initially helped to rationalize these industries and produce some benefits of scale at the same time as improving the conditions of their workforce. However, they were severely undercapitalized by both Labour and Conservative governments, who treated them as cash cows rather than investments; now they were pinched between their rusted-out plants and their militant unions.

The British called it the "Winter of Discontent"—modifying the phrase from the first line of Shakespeare's *Richard III*—and it marked the demise of the postwar Labour party. The prime minister, James Callaghan, tried to impose a 5 per cent public-sector wage ceiling and asked businesses and unions in the private sector to respect that same limit. Watching the evening news, it seemed businessmen and labour leaders shuffled in and out of Number 10 Downing Street virtually every day. But neither business nor labour paid the prime minister much attention. It was a big, profitable, private-sector manufacturer, Ford Motor Company, which finally burst the government's balloon, by settling with its union for 17 per cent after a series of what Canadians would call wildcat strikes. All hell was let loose. Callaghan had tried to create a tripartite government-business-union approach to inflation, but it turned out that the government was the weakest of the three. The Labour party, which had fashioned a new set of social arrangements after the war that had brought a previously unknown degree of security into the lives of working people, and a previously unimagined degree of power to the unions that represented them, was simply unequipped intellectually and ideologically to address the problems generated by that very system. Labour was too tied to what it had done to imagine doing things differently. It had no plausible answer to what was becoming a social and economic crisis, except to muddle through. But someone did. In the election of May 1979, Margaret Thatcher's Conservatives ran a billboard ad designed by Saatchi and Saatchi that showed a long line of people queueing at the unemployment office under the slogan "Labour Isn't Working." It was right, and she won.

Thatcher's government became the prototype for what was to become a worldwide phenomenon. In November of the next year Ronald Reagan was elected president of the United States.

While Thatcherism and Reaganism diverged on important points, they had much more in common, and they both owed a huge intellectual debt to Friedman and the Chicago School of Economics he had led for three decades. At its core was an extreme individualism, whose radical nature was perhaps best captured by Thatcher's astounding remark, "There is no such thing as society." British Conservatives from Benjamin Disraeli to Edward Heath had acknowledged a duty of care for the well-being of the whole society. That was now dispensed with in favour of the conviction that if government simply stepped out of the way, the "invisible hand" of self-organizing markets would produce the best obtainable result. Skeptical of the ability of governments to address social problems (or in some cases skeptical of the problems' actual existence), both Thatcher and Reagan curtailed spending on social programs. Both also saw unions as impediments to the operation of the free market, and worked to limit their legal role as well as their economic and political clout. In both countries, but particularly in Britain where there had been a much greater scale of state enterprise, large sectors of the economy previously held in public hands were privatized (often at concessionary prices), which had the dual goals of reducing the size of government and inhibiting the influence of unions. Monetary policy was conducted on strict Friedmanite lines, with a rigorous focus on inflation and an indifference to unemployment.

In the United States, Ronald Reagan embraced the ludicrous "Laffer curve," which purported to show that government's tax revenues would rise if tax rates were cut, which they very much were. Ironically, while the experiment did not produce the hoped-for increase in revenues, it kicked off a classical Keynesian boom. Combined with rising defence expenditures aimed at crushing the Soviet Union, the tax cut provided a huge stimulus to the American economy, financed with debt. Paradoxically, the Republican party (or to be fair, its predominant wing, since there were always some dissenters) became the party of deficits and debt while the Democrats assumed the opposite role. This reached its pinnacle in the administration of George W. Bush, which began racking up deficits—like Reagan's, through a combination of tax cuts and military spending—after they had been eliminated during the Clinton years. Bush's former treasury secretary, Paul O'Neill, later wrote that the vice-president, Dick Cheney, had told him: "You know, Paul, Reagan proved deficits don't matter." (Because the US dollar is the world's reserve currency, he may actually have been right—for a while.)

In a sense, what Reagan and Thatcher were up to was remaking the world as they found it to conform more closely to the radically individualist economic models of the Chicago School: the models worked perfectly on paper, and so would the world if it could be made more like them. Increasingly, conservative policymakers travelled with a posse of outriders, economists whose recommendations were derived from these highly abstract and mathematized models. Although conservative politicians were very successful in promoting worthy values such as freedom and equality of opportunity, their specific policy prescriptions were more often derived from inscrutable calculations that were literally inaccessible to ordinary people—and to many politicians, in fact—but came with an aura of unchallengeable intellectual authority. Progressives had no credible account of the recent past or the near future with which to compete, and any social scientific authority they might once have claimed was in tatters by the 1980s. Indeed, progressives were split between those who refused to question the fundaments of their older faith, and those who simply wished to concede ground to the conservatives. Tony Blair's "New Labour" in the 1990s shed most of old Labour's ideological baggage—the preference for public ownership over private, for example. But despite its own socially progressive rhetoric, it also accepted many elements of the conservative consensus: preferring growth to equality, for example. Inequality grew apace under Blair and his Labour successor, Gordon Brown.

Internationally, this conservative phase developed into what was called the Washington Consensus. Named after the city in which it was forged, at the headquarters of the IMF, the World Bank, and the US Treasury, it was the extension of the Thatcherite/ Reaganite/Friedmanite view into international affairs. Governments, particularly in the developing world, that got themselves into economic trouble were put on a stringent regime of budget cuts and market liberalization in exchange for assistance from international institutions. Privatization, deregulation, tariff reductions, and the opening of international investment were prescribed for these countries, as they were already being adopted in the United Kingdom and the United States, though at the price of even more devastating human misery in many instances.

In Canada, the new conservative wave had already started to build at the provincial level. Bill Bennett was elected Social Credit premier of British Columbia in 1975, and two years later Sterling Lyon led Manitoba's Progressive Conservatives to power. Both in their ways foreshadowed the policies of Thatcher and Reagan. Later, in 1995, Mike Harris was elected in Ontario on policies that marked a stark departure from the traditions of the provincial Progressive Conservative party, which for a generation had deeply reflected the postwar Keynesian consensus. In Alberta, similarly, the Getty, Klein, and Stelmach governments could be counted as part of the trend, moving away from the activism of the Lougheed years.

At the federal level in Canada, the ideological shift that was sweeping the Western world did not occur with the same breathtaking speed that it did elsewhere. Trudeau's National Energy

Program, launched in 1980, was the last, purest expression of postwar liberalism in this country. However, there was already a rebellion stewing in his party among business Liberals, which exploded at the party's 1982 national meeting and eventually led to the selection of John Turner as party leader. Trudeau himself appointed the Macdonald Commission on the economy in 1982, which would later report to the Mulroney government with a strong endorsement of free trade with the United States, and which pushed for cuts to social programs aimed at greater productivity and economic efficiency. Mulroney was never as ideologically pure as Thatcher or Reagan, perhaps for practical political reasons. But, once he was elected in 1984, many of his policies of privatization and deregulation were similar to theirs. Of course his greatest accomplishment in office, the free trade agreement with the United States, was a near-perfect expression of the trend.

Although Jean Chrétien is sometimes thought of as a Trudeau Liberal, this was truer of his views on Quebec and national unity than it was of his economic and fiscal policy. Once he became leader in 1990, Chrétien organized the Aylmer conference in 1991, at which the Liberals staged a tactical retreat from John Turner's adamant opposition to free trade in the previous election. In the 1993 election, the Liberals promised to reduce the federal deficit to 3 per cent of GDP. But once in office, with Paul Martin as finance minister, the Chrétien government decided to eliminate the deficit altogether "come hell or high water," cutting deeply into social programs such as unemployment insurance, and chopping transfers to the provinces for health, education, and welfare. The Liberals also abandoned their campaign commitment to introduce a national system of daycare. (The Chrétien government did put some money back into social programs after the economy improved and the deficit had been eliminated, in child welfare, post-secondary education, and health care; and the Martin government had also made major funding commitments to child care and aboriginal peoples by the time it was defeated in 2006.) The Liberals were more cautious in deregulating the financial industry than their British and American counterparts. In retrospect, Martin's decision not to allow the big banks to merge in the 1990s looks even better than it did at the time. However, taken altogether, like Mulroney's government, the Chrétien and Martin governments are probably best understood as an ideological hybrid, which drew on some of the progressive traditions of the postwar period, but whose main energies were devoted to adopting the dominant conservative economic model with its emphasis on free markets, open trade, and limited government.

There's no doubt that these policies, replicated across the developed world, have created enormous wealth. When I visit central London today, with its glittering shops and bright lights, it is almost unrecognizable as the grey, decaying, garbage-strewn city of my student days, so redolent of lost empire. But this is more a function of the *distribution* of wealth than of its *creation*. Although conservatives sometimes style their policies as "pro-growth," as the economic historian Robert Skidelsky has pointed out, growth rates during the recent thirty years of increasingly market-driven economic policy have been lower than during the previous, Keynesian era.[8] Here in Canada, where the employment income of ordinary Canadians doubled in real terms between 1950 and 1970, it has flat-lined in the decades of conservative policy.[9] Prior to the 2008 market meltdown, recent decades were not, as many of us might assume, more economically volatile. Rather, because the same level of volatility has occurred with a lower underlying growth rate, the bottoms of business cycles have been more prone to dropping into negative growth or recession—with all the attendant consequences, particularly unemployment. Moreover, because the social safety net has been weakened, similar downturns create more distress among individuals and families now than was once the case.

That having been said, one of the features of the era of conservative economic policy has been an enormous growth in the
financial sector of the international economy and a crescendo
of financial crises. These crises, which were relatively unusual
in the postwar period, and largely confined to specific countries
or sectors, have come so fast and furious in recent decades that,
despite being worldwide in scope, they have become a blur: the
Black Monday stock crash (1987), the American Savings and
Loan collapse (1989–91), the Japanese asset price bubble collapse
(1990), the Black Wednesday crisis in which George Soros "broke
the Bank of England" (1992), the Mexican peso crisis (1994), the
Asian financial crisis (1997–98), the Russian financial crisis and
the subsequent collapse of the hedge fund Long-Term Capital
Management (1998), and the dot-com bubble crash (2001).
Since 2007, the financial world has, arguably, entered a period
of widespread, unremitting financial crisis that has included the
US housing bubble and subprime mortgage crash, the failure of
major financial institutions in the United States, the Irish and
Icelandic financial crises, a stock market crash and subsequent
volatility, large increases in government borrowing, debt crises in
Greece, Italy, and other European Union countries wrapped up
as the "Euro crisis," and so on, and so on.

Recently, some researchers, including David Moss, an economist at the Harvard Business School, have asked whether there
are causal links between financial deregulation, income inequality, and financial crises. Moss told the New York Times that when
he looked historically at the timelines, "I could hardly believe
how tight the fit was—it was a stunning correlation." By some
estimates, income inequality in the United States prior to the
2008 financial crisis was already the highest in 100 years. This is
not exactly the picture of an economic doctrine whose precepts
should be considered so sacrosanct that even progressives must
worship at its altar.

CAN'T STAND THE HEAT

So far, I have been talking only about those aspects of our world that the conservative worldview chooses to consider as relevant, such as economic growth. But the conservative worldview ignores as much as it comprehends. Conservatives have found it extremely difficult to bend their minds around what may be the greatest existential threat humankind has ever confronted: climate change. My nine-year-old daughter sometimes gets angry at me for inadvertently reminding her of an inconvenient truth—a friend is moving away at the end of the month, perhaps. This is a common psychological phenomenon and it can be remarkably robust even in extreme circumstances, for example when a spouse manages to deny their partner's alcoholism. This is what we are seeing in the climate science denial that has flourished in the American Republican party. There were tinges of denialism in Stephen Harper's original position on climate change. Though he eventually publicly accepted the science, there is no sign that it is an intellectual conviction, or, if so, that he has any inclination to turn that conviction to action. It is really hard when your worldview is built around economic growth and the glorification of the market to address an issue which fundamentally challenges both.

It doesn't help that conservatives rely so heavily on neoclassical economic theory, with its tendency to treat the unintended consequences of economic interactions as an afterthought. Technically, the emission of greenhouse gases, believed to be responsible for climate change, is an example of what economists calls a "negative externality." If I buy a pair of shoes, I expect to pay the costs of the materials, labour, capital, and distribution expenses as well as a profit to everyone involved. But if the shoe factory is polluting the air or the water, and getting away with it, neither I nor the shoemaker is paying the true full cost of making the shoe. That pollution is a negative externality. Ultimately, those costs may be borne by the municipality that must clean up the water, by individuals that need to move to another neighbourhood to escape the foul air, or simply by people living near the factory suffering the consequences in their health or quality of life. Sometimes, governments do try to deal with these negative externalities, but the simplest way is through some intervention in the market—a regulation, perhaps, or a tax. The factory might be required to clean the water before discharging it, or to pay a punitive tax designed to discourage pollution. Because these things will cost the shoe manufacturer money, the "negative externality" becomes incorporated into the cost of the shoe. Attempts by governments to manage negative externalities are interventions in the market. Because they put the interests of "society"—which Thatcher, remember, didn't think existed—ahead of the economic freedom of the individual embedded in market transactions, conservatives are as leery of them in principle as the shoe manufacturer is liable to be in practice. Quite naturally, businesses will fiercely fight any attempt by governments to make them pay for the damage they do.

The continued emission of greenhouse gases, with its effects on climate change, is a profound challenge to market ideology and to the profession of economics. In 2006, a commission appointed by the British government and led by Sir Nicholas Stern, a former chief economist of the World Bank, produced the most extensive report to date on the economics of climate change. In one section of the report, Stern specifically addressed climate change as a negative externality. He said it has a number of features that distinguishes it from other such externalities:

- It is global in its causes and consequences.
- The effects of climate change are longer-term and persistent.
- The uncertainties and risks are pervasive.
- "There is a serious risk of major, irreversible change with *non-marginal economic effects.*"[10]

Stern concluded that the standard approaches of contemporary economics were at best a starting point, and were inadequate to the task of dealing with climate change, *even from a narrowly economic perspective.* "Thus, climate change is an example of market failure involving externalities and public goods," he wrote. "All in all, it must be regarded as market failure on the greatest scale the world has seen." Remember, this comes from a former World Bank economist, steeped in the economics and public policy of the Washington Consensus years.

Stop and think about that. The potential climate catastrophe is a *market failure*—that is, an inability of the economic system that conservatives have promoted, implemented, and defended to address the most dangerous and deadly crisis of our time. The greatest challenge of our generation is, quite simply, hard for them even to think about using the intellectual apparatus they have constructed.

IRRATIONAL OLD ME

Of course, one of the problems with the obsession with markets, money, and growth is that it represents a pretty impoverished picture of human life. When I was at Oxford, one of my friends and roommates was doing his doctorate under Amartya Sen, the brilliant Indian economist who went on to win the Nobel Prize. Although I never came closer to Professor Sen than the back of a lecture hall, I spent many hours over pints of real ale listening to my friend expand on his thinking. One of Sen's many contributions[11] to economics was to draw attention to the dimensions of quality in human life that are not captured by traditional economic measures. Sen, who had done groundbreaking work on the economics and politics of famine, was concerned that the standard economic yardstick—the Gross Domestic Product (GDP)—badly misstated the experience of people in the developing world. A Pakistani academic and close friend of Sen's, Mahbub ul Haq, came up with the idea of creating a Human Development Index (HDI), which would measure things like literacy, life expectancy, and child welfare, following Sen's insight that it was "silly" to equate raw economic growth to development.

At first, Sen was skeptical. "I told Mahbub that it's vulgar to capture in one number an extremely complex story, just as GDP is vulgar," Sen told the *New York Times.* "And he called me back and said: 'Amartya, you're exactly right. What I want you to do is produce an index as vulgar as GDP but more relevant to our own lives.'"[12] Although the HDI has hardly displaced GDP in the way we think about the world, it has become increasingly influential in assessing developing countries, where burgeoning wealth may sometimes be more than counter-balanced by soaring inequality or deteriorating conditions of life for ordinary people.

This perspective, although it comes as an offshoot of traditional economics, is deeply subversive of the currently dominant market philosophy. No market on earth has ever created a system of universal primary education, for example, even if markets have greatly benefitted from general literacy and sometimes helped create the conditions within which it was possible. The same is also true, for example, of child and maternal welfare; women's equality; and the socially legitimate distribution of land, income, and wealth. Although markets have sometimes played a role in delivering these social goods, governments are almost invariably the central force in their organization.

A new stream of research has extended these insights to Western societies, by examining the issue of inequality and its relationship to social or individual well-being.[13] The conservative argument over the last thirty years has been that while tax cuts, deregulation, and the curtailing of social programs may initially seem to favour the better-off, the benefits ultimately "trickle down" to improve everyone's lot by encouraging investment, growth, and job creation. There is some truth to the conservative mantra that the best social program is a job. However, not only has growth been slower in the period of the conservative consensus, but unemployment has been higher. And inequality did not simply grow in the short term while these policies were first being adopted. Higher than historic levels of inequality have persisted as a feature of this new economic regime. What researchers such as Richard Wilkinson and Kate Pickett have demonstrated through comparisons among developed countries and among the American states is that high levels of inequality are associated with all kinds of social dysfunction, including homicide and other violence, teenage pregnancy, mental illness, and even obesity. One of their most striking findings is that even those of us who are better off show higher levels of dysfunction in less equal societies. The poor gain most from greater equality, but everyone gains somewhat; it is not a zero-sum game. This is not as startling as it may sound at first, since most of us value neighbourhoods in which we know our neighbours, enjoy their company, and feel safe to walk the streets at night. In fact, the more prosperous devote a considerable portion of their extra incomes to escaping the effects of inequality: investing in alarm systems, moving to monocultural suburbs, sending their kids to private schools, even buying SUVs to protect them as they get around the urban jungles.

Treating the performance of the market and our place in it as the measure of human life leads us astray in terms of public policy. Not all economic activity is inherently good: rising tobacco and alcohol sales, or a boom in the private security industry, wouldn't fit on the positive side in any meaningful measurement of wellbeing, though they would in the GDP. But, more importantly, for most of us quality of life is defined in significant part by such non-economic factors as our relationships with our family, friends, and neighbours. It is connected with a sense of security about our lives: that we will be able to find satisfying work when we leave school, that if we lose our job we will be able to survive until we find another, and that we will not be forced to live in penury when we are old. We want to know that if we are sick we will be cared for, and not at the cost of financial ruin. We want communities in which we can enjoy the company of others in public spaces and not be ever-fearful of drugs and crime. We want our children to attend good schools and we don't want to leave them a world crackling in man-made heat. We want the freedom to choose (or refuse) the comforts of religion, the solace of literature, or the joy of learning without the coercion of others. And we want Team Canada to win every international hockey tournament. Some of these good things can be partly captured by narrow economic measures, but many cannot.

Even the psychological assumptions of traditional economists are now coming under serious attack from within the profession. The image of *homo economicus,* the rational, self-interested individual who seeks to maximize his advantage towards self-defined ends, which is at the philosophical heart of modern economics, particularly of the Friedmanite school, looks increasingly shaky. Some people have argued that *homo economicus* most closely represents the behaviour of those decidedly unrepresentative creatures, economists themselves. One study suggested that while economics majors are already more selfish than other students at the time they enrol in university, students who major in another subject but take an economics course actually become more selfish by the time they graduate![14] As it happens, at the very moment that the conservative consensus was about to take hold, Daniel Kahneman and Amos Tversky published a seminal paper[15] that used the insights of psychology to modify the traditional image of a perfectly rational and fully informed economic actor to something more human. They and their followers demonstrated that human beings have structures of mind that lead them to be satisfied with less than adequate information to make choices, to be overconfident, to make specious comparisons, and to act in ways that on the surface may even seem weird. Human beings will turn down the offer of a free ticket to a football game worth $100 if it is pouring rain, but will trudge to the park despite the weather if they've paid for the ticket themselves. *Homo economicus* wouldn't see the difference. Human beings will allow a phone or a cable company to add a service at a fee without their explicit consent—negative-option billing—even though they would not have chosen to subscribe. Believe it or not, some people will sign up for mortgages with interest rates that soar to the wildly unaffordable after two years. And, incredible as it may seem, sophisticated investors, including banks, will buy bonds composed of these loans and treat them as if they pose no more risk of default than regular mortgages.[16] We systematically fail to make rational judgments about matters of probability once the numbers get large enough: the mechanism by which lotteries entice us to spend our money at terrible odds, for example, and the way terrorists frighten us well beyond their capacity to do us harm. I happened to be a reporter in Israel at the height of the Palestinian suicide bombing campaign in 2001–2. The Israelis diverted police officers from their notoriously deadly highways to combat terrorism, even though the chances of dying on the road remained higher than those of being killed by a bomb.[17] Unlike traditional economics, that assumed that these kinds of "mistakes" or deviations from rationality were evenly distributed and thus cancelled each other out, behavioural economics has shown that they are systematic.

This rich research, which eventually won Kahneman the Nobel Prize,[18] has been exploited by marketers, and has begun to seep into the formulation of public policy at the margins.[19] But its intellectually corrosive effect on the ideas underlying market economics has yet to be fully understood at the popular or political level. One of the central insights of behavioural economics is that individuals cannot reliably perceive their own self-interest, or reliably calculate how to advance it. One of its "discoveries" is that it is easier to see the flaws in the reasoning of someone else than in your own—something every watermelon knows, as they say in the Middle East. The obvious implication of this finding is that we need the help of friends, family, and society to help us avoid the pratfalls of our minds—and that they need us. The libertarian impulse behind Friedmanite economics, that each of us should be allowed to get on with choosing our own goals and pursuing them, since we invariably know our own interests better than anyone else, is not only simplistic; it is mistaken. We are all better off when we care for one another.

The point I am making is that the economic thinking underlying much of our public policy of the last thirty years was already under serious intellectual scrutiny before it encountered the twin challenges of climate change and financial crisis.

ALAN GREENSPAN TO WORLD: I GOT IT WRONG

The seductiveness of the market theories promoted by conservatives lies partly in their claim to be "natural." Markets are presented as self-ordering and self-regulating—managed by an *invisible hand*—if only governments would get out of the way. Perplexingly, this idea still has enormous power over our society even after the failure of the markets to do any such thing was so spectacularly revealed in the 2008 financial crisis. Markets are created by human beings and operate according to rules they construct. As Bernard Harcourt has argued,[20] these rules—which may come in the form of laws of incorporation, legal responsibilities to shareholders, royalties, professional qualifications, registration of brokers, chartering of banks, rates of taxation on capital gains, and so on—inevitably distribute wealth. And the rules as they have been reconstructed in the last thirty years have proven to be spectacularly inadequate to the job.

After the housing bubble had broken, the subprime mortgage

market had imploded, and Lehman Brothers, Bear Stearns, and AIG had collapsed, Alan Greenspan, who had been chairman of the Federal Reserve from 1987 to 2006, was called to testify before a Congressional committee. There had been no more influential or effective policy-maker in the articulation, implementation, and application of the conservative consensus, both domestically and internationally. At the hearing, a Democratic congressman, Henry Waxman, quoted back to Greenspan some of his comments in his time as chairman of the Fed, including his oft-repeated claim that there was nothing about government regulation that made it superior to market self-regulation.

> Greenspan: *I made a mistake in presuming that the self-interest of organizations, specifically banks and others, were such that they were best capable of protecting their own shareholders and the equity in the firms…So the problem here is that something that looked to be a very solid edifice and indeed a critical pillar to market competition and free markets did break down and I think that, as I said, shocked me. I still do not fully understand why it happened and obviously to the extent I figure out where it happened and why, I will change my views. If the facts change, I will change.*

> Waxman: *You had an ideology. You had a belief… Do you feel your ideology pushed you to make decisions you wish you had not made?*

> Greenspan: *Well, remember what an ideology is, is a conceptual framework with the way people deal with reality. Everyone has one. To exist you need an ideology. The question is whether it is accurate*

*or not, and what I am saying to you is yes, I found
a flaw. I don't know how significant or permanent
it is, but I have been very distressed by that fact...I
found a flaw in the model that 1 perceived is the
critical functioning structure that defines how the
world works, so to speak.*

Waxman: *In other words, you found that your view
of the world, your ideology was not right. It is not
working.*

Greenspan: *Precisely. That's precisely the reason
I was shocked, because I have been going for forty
years or more with very considerable evidence that it
was working exceptionally well.*

The point is not that Greenspan was a fool. Far from it. He brilliantly applied a powerful economic model that generated enormous wealth. At the Fed, he was a shrewd and delicate manager of the system over which he presided, steering the United States, and to a degree the world economy, through an unusually sustained period of growth. But, like all models, this one had limits that were impossible to anticipate from within its own confines.[21]

Much more dramatic than Greenspan's sudden moment of ideological doubt, however, were the actions of his intellectual soul-mates still in office. In September of 2008, as the grandiose edifices of Wall Street seemingly crumbled, George W. Bush, now in the final months of his presidency, stood on the White House lawn to announce that he was proposing the most massive bailout of the private sector in history and a plan to tighten regulations in the financial industry. As if to say that this had not been his idea, Bush surrounded himself with some of the closest guardians of the conservative flame: Henry Paulson, the Treasury Secretary and former CEO of Goldman Sachs; Christopher Cox, Chairman of the Securities and Exchange Commission (SEC) and former Reagan aide; and Ben Bernanke, former chairman of Bush's Council of Economic Advisers and by then Greenspan's successor at the Fed. "Our system of free enterprise rests on the conviction that the federal government should interfere in the marketplace only when necessary," Bush said. "Given the precarious state of today's financial markets and their vital importance to the daily lives of the American people, government intervention is not only warranted, it is essential." Throughout the remainder of his time in office, Bush seemed to have trouble internalizing what he had done, often talking about his decisions as if they had been made out of deference to advisors rather than personal conviction. Paulson's own wrenching ideological struggle was by this time much further along than Bush's. "Government owning a stake in any private US company is objectionable to most Americans, me included," Paulson commented. "Yet, the alternative of leaving businesses and consumers without access to financing is totally unacceptable."

CRISIS? WHAT CRISIS?

As Robert Lucas, a prominent member of the Chicago School and also a Nobel Prize winner, somewhat bitterly remarked at the time, "I guess everyone is a Keynesian in a foxhole." However, in Canada this was not at all instantly clear. Well after Bush had been driven to his desperate measures, and a week before the 2008 Canadian election, in what was apparently a considered comment, Stephen Harper described the gut-churning drop in the stock market as a "buying opportunity," and told the CBC's Peter Mansbridge that, "I think there are probably some gains to be made in the stock market." A month and a half after the election, in late November, Harper's finance minister, Jim Flaherty, delivered an economic and fiscal statement to the House of Commons that makes, if possible, even more astonishing reading now than it did at the time. It acknowledged the international economic crisis, but said mildly that Canada was not completely insulated from what was happening elsewhere. It predicted that the Canadian economy would continue to grow, albeit modestly, in 2009. (The economy actually contracted in 2009, as most economists were predicting at the time, by about 2.5 per cent.) It described previously announced tax cuts as stimulus, and so declined to add anything new. It laid out a plan for continued balanced budgets, though it conceded that the government's "best efforts" might not be enough to keep a small surplus on the books.

The Harper government, unlike almost all its international counterparts, did not seem to realize that it was in a foxhole. In retrospect, the most generous interpretation of Harper's and Flaherty's reaction to the international financial crisis may have been that they believed Canada was better placed than other countries to weather it, particularly because our more tightly regulated banks did not appear to be under threat the way American, British, and European banks were. This was generally true. The government may also have been relying on fiscal stimulus in the United States and elsewhere having a spillover effect in Canada's highly export-driven economy. And Harper and Flaherty may also have believed that stimulus undertaken here in Canada would, obversely, be largely dissipated because of the openness of our economy. All that having been said, it seems likely that it was Harper's ideological commitment to the conservative consensus crumbling around him that led the government to close its eyes to the scale of the looming economic downturn, and to turn its face against the mounting international wind for a classical Keynesian stimulus to combat it.

It is hard to say what would have happened here in Canada had Harper and Flaherty not committed an astounding tactical blunder in that same economic statement. Under the transparent guise of belt-tightening, the government announced its intention to cut the $1.95-a-voter public subsidy enjoyed by all the parties. The result was the short-lived and ill-fated coalition attempt forged between the Liberals and the NDP. After parliament was prorogued for nearly two months, Flaherty returned with an avowedly stimulative budget, including tax cuts and an infrastructure spending program financed with large deficits, which the Liberals, now under their new leader, Michael Ignatieff, decided to support.

Who knows what kind of budget the Harper government would have presented in the winter of 2009 if it had had a majority, or had it not faced the threat of ouster by coalition? Very likely, it would have been a minimally stimulative document accompanied by significant spending cuts in recognition of rapidly deteriorating tax revenues. This is what Flaherty was saying in November. It certainly appears that the Conservatives changed their approach to the budget because of politics, not economics. It did not represent an ideological *volte-face* by the Conservatives, as some have argued. Rather, it seems to have been a tactical manoeuvre demanded by the Conservatives' minority status. There is no indication that Harper and Flaherty ever considered themselves to be in a fox-hole, much less that they converted to Keynesian economics in a moment of terror. They did what they had to do to stay in power, not what they believed was necessary from the perspective of their own economic doctrine. That's why the anguish so visible on the faces of George Bush and Hank Paulson was not so apparent on Jim Flaherty's and Stephen Harper's mugs.

Indeed, it wasn't so very long afterwards, as host of the G8 and G20 meetings in the summer of 2010, that the Harper government returned to preaching its old-time religion of deficit reduction, spending cuts, and smaller government. In sum, the Conservatives have not seen either the 2008 financial crisis or the rolling crises since as reasons to re-evaluate the tenets of their dogma.

BACK TO SCHOOL

Whether or not we yet recognize it, the last decade has been disastrous for conservative ideas. Many crucial years have been lost
in confronting a looming environmental disaster of unknowable
scale. The economy has given us greater inequality and uncertainty, without the reciprocal benefits of jobs and reliable growth.
As Thomas Kuhn, the American historian and philosopher of
science, argued[22] almost fifty years ago, it often takes generational
change for new knowledge or discoveries to percolate through
the universities and become fully accepted. And the same is true
with the social sciences. The lessons of these recent years will take
time to work their way into the psyches of the policy-makers and
the public. But some of our problems can't wait. In the wake of
the financial crisis, the ever-inventive George Soros founded the
Institute for New Economic Thinking, which is intended to jump-
start this intellectual process, and it has identified many promising
avenues of thinking, even if it falls well short today of providing
any coherent rival to the Chicago School. The Occupy Wall Street
movement, if nothing else, has focussed the media's attention on
inequality for the first time in a generation. Progressive economists like Joseph Stiglitz, Jeffrey Sachs, and Paul Krugman have
found a more public audience. But their ideas fall well short of
forming a "progressive school." The Obama-era reforms to bank-
ing and market regulation have at best played around the edges of
the problem, and in Canada the response has been that, since we
emerged from the crisis with our banks relatively unscathed, there
never was much to fix. Our thinking should now go beyond the
tenets of Blairism or Clintonism, which were essentially attempts
to moderate the conservative consensus at a time when it was at its
height. These approaches introduced an element of pragmatism
into left-centre politics, but they were also deeply implicated in
the failures of the conservative era, including the financial collapse
of 2008 (not to mention the Iraq adventure in which Tony Blair

enthusiastically joined). Progressives have an opportunity now to develop a clear and comprehensive alternative to the conservative consensus while retaining the practical bent to their politics that was the best of Blair and Clinton.

We cannot assume that the failures of the conservative consensus mean that conservatives are the inevitable losers of the current intellectual and political struggle. There are a lot of smart people embedded in our academic, bureaucratic, business, media, and political organizations who have a powerful interest in that consensus, enormous resources to draw on, and who should be expected to be just as vigorous in trying to adapt their ideas as progressives are in trying to consolidate and elaborate their own. In the decisive moments of late 2008 and early 2009, the Liberals under Stéphane Dion and Michael Ignatieff were able at best to mount a tactical challenge to the Conservatives— never a fundamental challenge to their ideas. Moreover, the Conservatives have been more successful in tapping the energies and resentments of evangelicals and small businesspeople, for example, than the Liberals, NDP, or Greens have been with, say, social activists, community groups, the unions, and environmentalists. Ominously, south of the border we see the explosion of a yet-more-radical individualist conservative politics, expressed in the emergence of the Tea Party movement and the soaring sales of Ayn Rand's canonical libertarian books. Progressives may take comfort in divisions on the American right, but we should also heed the warning that this is sometimes a more vibrant part of the political landscape than we occupy.

CHAPTER 3
WHY CONSERVATIVES WIN

Just five weeks after his victory in the May 2011 election, Stephen Harper was in Calgary speaking to supporters at the beginning of Stampede week. He looked more comfortable in his cowboy hat than he had sometimes done, and his face was decorated with an uncharacteristically broad grin. On election night, at his campaign headquarters only a few kilometres away, he had given his familiar, unctuous pledge to govern for all Canadians. But now it was time to strip off election-night pieties and say what he really thought. "Conservative values are Canadian values," he said. "Canadian values are Conservative values."

"Under our Conservative government, Canada is more united than it has ever been. My friends, I think something has changed. I believe the long Liberal era is genuinely, truly ending. As with disco balls and bell-bottoms, Canadians have moved on…We are moving Canada in a Conservative direction, and Canadians are moving in that direction with us…Canadians have found through a costly forty-year experiment with liberalism that big government is not an instant answer to everything."[1]

The crowd laughed and cheered.

Harper was not just doing a victory lap after the humiliation of the Conservatives' historic nemesis—the Liberal party. He was declaring victory in an ideological war. That may seem strange for a prime minister who had won his parliamentary majority with a tick under 40 per cent of the vote. But the truth is that the Harper Conservatives have not simply been the passive beneficiaries of a split opposition and an electoral system that presents a distorted mirror of public sentiment. They represent the culmination of a decades-long conservative trend that has affected politicians of every partisan stripe, including Liberals, New Democrats, and Greens. Their ideas, founded in the Thatcher and Reagan revolutions of more than thirty years ago, are literally outdated. They have ready answers to problems we no longer face—high taxes, high crime, and unions supposedly throttling the economy. They have no idea how to address the problems of today—economic stagnancy, inequality, a shrinking middle class, bank-driven consumer indebtedness, serial international financial crises, and climate change. And yet, with the resources of a majority government behind them, they will continue to reshape our institutions in their image, and if they can, deepen their penetration into our collective psyche. Stephen Harper's ambition has never been simply to change the government, but to change Canada.

The Conservatives' ideological dominance lies behind their electoral success, in particular the slow, steady advance in Ontario and among some minority communities, which produced the current majority. It also lies behind their ability to get the public—and even the opposition parties—to accept some of their most problematic choices as unremarkable. The most obvious example is the supine reaction of the Liberals and NDP to the Conservatives' commitment to eliminate the deficit in the middle of an economic slowdown.

A lot was made of Harper's plodding, safe, front-runner's campaign in 2011, famously deaf to the shouts of Terry Milewski from behind the media barrier. On the day he called the 2011 election, Harper framed it around themes he had sedulously cultivated since just a few weeks after the previous one: "On May 2, we will choose between stable national government and a reckless coalition; between a low-tax plan for growth and a high-tax agenda that will stall our recovery, kill jobs and set families back." In the end, the campaign dynamics that reshaped the world of the opposition parties made little difference to the Conservatives, who finished the campaign with about the same support as they began. The Conservatives have developed a core constituency with broadly shared values that distinguishes it from all of the opposition parties. A post-election Environics survey indicated that most Conservative voters in 2011 *did not even consider* the other parties.[2] This is not to say that Harper's Conservatives are immune to the mood swings of a less-and-less-partisan electorate, but they are less susceptible than any of the progressive parties, who must fight amongst themselves for the rest of the electorate. It is sometimes said that Harper aims his appeals at the Tim Hortons voter—though the Conservatives' micro-targeting of demographic groups is actually more sophisticated than that. Harper's policies are, if anything, more oriented to the benefit of a small corporate and economic elite than those of Brian Mulroney. But he has managed to identify his government socially with the ordinary guy. This apparent paradox is at the heart of his success, and progressives need to understand it if they want to combat it.

Harper's Conservatives have also harnessed a much more effective political organization at a technical level. They turned the permanent election campaign in parliament that is inevitable during minority governments into a permanent election campaign on the airwaves as well, and a much more one-sided campaign at that. They know better than the other parties who their supporters are—not just generally, but as individuals. They understand better what motivates them. As someone joked, if the long-gun registry database is destroyed, the Conservatives will be the only ones left with an accurate list of gun-owners. Conservative supporters are not only disproportionately drawn from social groups more likely to volunteer, vote, and give money—older people, men, Protestants, anglophones, and the economically better-off—the party also has superior channels of communicating with them. And it raises a lot more money—often more than all the other parties combined.

IT'S THE ECONOMY, STEPHEN

In the 2000 election—the last before Harper became leader—the Canadian Alliance won sixty-six seats, only two of them east of Manitoba. In 2011, Harper's Conservatives won exactly 100 more than that—166. Nearly three-quarters of that growth occurred in Ontario, and more than 90 per cent in Ontario, Quebec, and the Atlantic provinces. Although the merger of the old PCs and the Canadian Alliance, which took place just before Harper's first election in 2004, obviously played a role in this growth, it is not the whole story. Only about a third of the total growth under Harper occurred in that first election. The newly minted Conservative Party of Canada gained about four percentage points over the old Canadian Alliance, to reach just under 30 per cent of the popular vote. Since then, the party has gained another ten percentage points, to just under 40 per cent. In other words, Harper has not succeeded only because he united conservatives and faces split opposition. He has persuaded a substantial number of voters in Central and Eastern Canada to set aside their reservations about what began as the Reform Party and vote for him.

Let me remind you of Preston Manning's approach to building the Reform party. He intended to unite three groups: economic conservatives, who believed that Mulroney's PCs were not sufficiently orthodox on balancing budgets, and reducing government and taxes;[3] social conservatives, unhappy with abortion, homosexuality, and immigration from developing countries; and populist conservatives, who advocated changes to the structure of Canadian politics, including not only senate reform, but also mechanisms of direct democracy such as plebiscites, recall of unpopular MPs, and more autonomy for MPs to represent the views of their constituents. Although he was less explicit about this in describing his tactics, Manning also tried to channel anger towards Quebec, fiercely opposing both the Meech Lake and Charlottetown Accords[4] and the Trudeau-Mulroney bilingualism policies. In the 1997 election, at Manning's insistence, and against the wishes of some of its own MPs, Reform ran candidates in Quebec for the first time. Nonetheless, when Manning saw his prospects in the West slipping mid-campaign, he unleashed the most explicitly anti-Quebec ad in living memory, showing pictures of Jean Chrétien, PC leader Jean Charest, BQ leader Gilles Duceppe, and Quebec premier Lucien Bouchard, each with a red slash across his face, and the message that Canadians had for too long been governed by Quebec politicians.

Although many people have correctly observed that the 2003 merger of the PCs and the Canadian Alliance could be seen as a Reform "takeover" of the conservative movement, Harper's party is very different from Manning's. Harper, after becoming leader, curbed or eliminated many of the distinctive features of Reform party politics and focused on a simple message: small government and free markets. Manning himself seemed ambivalent about Reform's democratic populism, which he had supported in principle at the same time as he was imposing hierarchical discipline within the party. Under Harper, this ambivalence was dispensed with, replaced with some of the strictest top-down party and caucus discipline ever seen in Canadian politics. In this respect, the

Reform party tradition lives on only in the government's intermittent enthusiasm for a watered-down version of senate reform.

Harper also decided to circumscribe his party's social conservatives, which he did decisively at the Conservatives' highly orchestrated first policy convention, in 2005. The convention was preceded by a series of regional conferences, which one of his advisors, Geoff Norquay, described to the journalist Paul Wells this way: "It was people at the microphones, arguing about policy…And it was people saying, to anyone who got too far out, 'Hey asshole, I think I'd like us to be government. Why don't you take that and stuff it.'"[5] Abandoning their leader's earlier flirtation with opposition to same-sex marriage, Harper's supporters successfully argued at the convention that the party should advocate a free vote in the House of Commons, effectively killing the controversy. Under Harper, issues that primarily involve individual morality, such as abortion and homosexuality, would play little part in official policy. The government might no longer fund a Pride parade, but it would not attempt to curb established rights. While these strictures produce occasional splutterings of rage from backbench MPs, they have largely held because they are the price the Harper party pays to appear mainstream in Central Canada.

Under Harper, the party's social conservatism has generally been narrowed to issues where it could be expressed as a limitation on government[6]—something not easy to do with abortion or homosexuality. The abolition of the long-gun registry and the mandatory long-form census questionnaire fit neatly into this category. The same could be said of the Conservatives' decision to abandon the Liberals' plans for a national system of child care in favour of small monthly cheques. Even the decision to strip pay equity provisions from public-service legislation was portrayed as deference to the market—in this case, "free" collective bargaining. The Conservatives also set about defunding organizations, agencies, and programs that promoted government involvement in social life, whether it was the Court Challenges Program or women's groups.

The big exception to the general rule that Harper is more inclined to pursue social conservative objectives when they represent a limitation on the state is obviously criminal law, where Harper has pursued an aggressive policy of incarceration. It seems paradoxical to the progressive mind that conservatives are lyrical in their praise of freedom with this one magnificent exception. But this simply reflects American conservative thought that the free market needs a sturdy barrier of punishment of deviant behaviour to protect it. Tough criminal laws are the walls that protect the free space inside. It is well established that crime rates have fallen substantially in Canada over the last half century,[7] but in 2010 one of Harper's ministers, Stockwell Day, famously claimed that crime statistics cannot be trusted because the rate of unreported crime is rising—a logical conundrum he was unable to explain. In any event, with a majority in hand, the Harper government set about implementing its tough-on-crime agenda, whose core is longer prison sentences. This appeals not only to social conservatives, but to many urban and suburban voters who are affected by crime or the perception of it in their communities. Moreover, outside of Quebec, there is no substantial constituency against longer sentences.

Nowhere was Harper's reformation of the Reform agenda more striking than on two issues closely linked to Manning's socially conservative appeal: Quebec and immigration. That 2005 policy convention endorsed official bilingualism and supported the notion of a *fiscal imbalance*—code words for saying Quebec was not getting its fair share of federal dollars. Under Harper, Manning's hostility to Quebec would be replaced with what Chantal Hébert called Harper's "French kiss,"[8] wooing Quebecers through a combination of promises to increase federal transfers to the province and symbolic gestures large and small. Not only would Harper officially acknowledge the Québécois as a "nation," he personally started every press conference in French. This helped the party to gain a political toehold in Quebec, where it won ten seats in both 2006 and 2008.[9] Equally important, it mollified Ontarians who had seen the Reform party as a threat to national unity. Once he had a majority, Harper did begin loosening the strictures of official bilingualism, appointing a unilingual Supreme Court justice and Auditor General. But this was at most a minor relaxation rather than a reversal of the Trudeau-Mulroney policy.

Harper also took his party on a historic U-turn on immigration. In the late 1980s and early 1990s, fury at the idea of Mounties in Sikh turbans had contributed to the rise of Reform. The nativist streak in Reform was fundamental to its early appeal under Manning. But by 2011 Stephen Harper was happy to be filmed wearing a Sikh headdress himself, speaking in a Sikh temple. As I'll discuss below, this also played a critical role in his success.

Harper was able to take his party on these wrenching reversals because he had obtained a magical political substance that had once belonged to the Liberals: the elixir of power.

WHAT'S THE MATTER WITH THE GTA?

Nearly a decade ago, the American journalist Thomas Frank asked, "What's the Matter with Kansas?" Why, he wondered, did people in the economically distressed state of Kansas support the Republican party, with its policies of low taxes, deregulation, and smaller government? In many of the poorest counties in the state people voted for this Wall Street agenda by overwhelming margins. Frank's answer was social conservatism. Abortion, school prayer, gun rights, same-sex marriage—these were the issues that Frank said had redirected populist anger away from the corporate elites towards cultural and media elites. "Cultural anger is marshalled to achieve economic ends," Frank wrote. "And it is these economic achievements—not the forgettable skirmishes of the never-ending culture wars—that are the [conservative] movement's greatest monuments."[10] In the United States in 2004, Bush's campaign guru Karl Rove promoted state and municipal referendums on hot-button issues such as same-sex marriage, in a successful attempt to drive social conservatives to the polls, where they would also vote for George Bush's re-election.

In a way, though, the puzzle here in Canada is greater than the one Frank was trying to explain down in Kansas. Here in Canada, Harper has tried to disarm the very debates Karl Rove tried to nuke up. When Harper takes on cultural issues, he uses them surgically, as with the long-gun registry and hostility to the CBC, to move votes or raise funds among narrow constituencies. Gun-owners, church-goers, supporters of the death penalty are all disproportionately likely to support the Conservatives.[11] But Harper's fundamental message, and that of his government, is economic. It may not seem surprising, then, as pollsters Darrell Bricker and Keren Gottfried wrote after the 2011 election, that "put simply, the more money you make, the more likely you were to vote Conservative."

However, when you think more deeply about it, in an economy where the benefits of growth accrue only to the top 20 per cent or so of the population, there must be some more complex answer to the Conservatives' success: there just aren't enough economic winners in Canada today to add up to the nearly 40 per cent support Harper took in 2011. No surprise that the Conservatives do very well among managers, but how come they do so well among bus drivers and truck drivers? Of course petroleum-enriched Calgarians vote Conservative; but why Scarborough Centre? Why is it that high-school- and college-educated Canadians are more likely to vote Conservative than those who have university degrees? At first it may not *seem* surprising that the Conservatives do well among seniors: after all, the older you get the more conservative you get, right? Actually, seniors used to be solidly in the Liberal camp, and that too made perfect sense. Once you retire, you are more dependent than ever on the state. The Canada Pension Plan, old-age security, and medicare were all quintessentially progressive programs, associated with the Liberal party, which used to harvest the votes of their beneficiaries.

Part of the explanation for this apparent paradox is that the deepest cuts to income-support programs such as unemployment insurance and welfare actually occurred under the Mulroney and Chrétien governments. Moreover, the Harper government has been careful to squelch serious debate about medicare at the federal level. It hopes to ratchet down health spending through arcane changes to the funding formula, not by a direct assault on the principles of medicare. Predictably, as the government has done less and less for its citizens over the last three decades, fewer people perceive its role in their lives as important. Bricker's explanation of the "new tectonics" in Canadian politics is that the Conservatives have become a party of *taxpayers*. To the degree that this is true, what the Conservatives have done is to persuade large numbers of Canadians that they should think about their relationship to the government primarily through the narrow lens of taxes. You may have been born in a public hospital, been educated in public schools, gone to a publicly funded university with government-backed loans, and you may drive to work on a public road or take a publicly subsidized train. If it weren't for government regulation your eyes would be watering from smog, your cell phone wouldn't work properly, and you'd be a lot more concerned about the money in your bank account. But, despite all that, you might be one of the 40 per cent who support the "taxpayers'" party.

Although the Conservatives' tax policies may not be sound according to the experts, they are ingeniously devised. In Harper's first campaign, in 2004, the party had a complex proposal for changing tax brackets which was not easily understood, and was deftly countered by the Liberals. By the time he had his next crack, in the 2006 election, Harper had fixed those problems. His showcase promise was to take one percentage point—and eventually two—off the GST. Although it would be hard to point to a single Canadian whose life was substantially improved as a result, it sent a signal that everyone could understand that the Conservatives cared about the routine tax burdens of everyday life. It also had the happy, though unmentioned, effect of trimming $12 billion annually in government revenue, helping make the case for further spending cuts.

The Conservatives employed psychographic analysis to identify small constituencies of potential support, and target policy, especially tax policy, directly at their heads. Strategists embodied the psychographic categories in fictional characters to make them easier to think about. "Dougie"—a twenty-year-old single man working at Canadian Tire; "Steve and Heather"—fortysomethings with three kids; "Eunice"—a Protestant senior on a small pension, who owned her home. And so on. There were also characters like "Zoe," a sprouts-eating, yoga-doing, twenty-five-year-old living downtown, who was never going to vote Conservative anyway.[12] From this process sprung a series of tax promises aimed, not at addressing social problems, much less reforming the tax system, but at connecting the Conservatives' low-tax agenda to particular groups of Canadians. Much like my wife and me, "Steve and Heather" no doubt find themselves having to dig into their wallets several times a year to find the $400 or $500 for soccer or hockey fees.[13] Hey! Presto! A child fitness tax credit. Dougie might benefit from the apprenticeship incentive grant, and later, from the tools tax deduction. Eunice got an increase in the amount of pension deduction eligible for tax credits. At a time when the economic system is failing to produce benefits for a broad swathe of Canadians, these trifles at least seem like something.

The practical effect of these tax giveaways is almost certainly negligible, both at the individual and the social level. I don't think anyone has even tried to demonstrate an increase in the number of children playing organized sport, for example, as a result of the child fitness tax credit. My wife and I were going to enrol our son in hockey regardless; now we get a tax credit. Across the street from where we live in central Ottawa there is a public housing development. Before the tax credit, the kids living there never crossed the threshold of the rink they pass every day on their way to school; after the tax credit, they still do not. There may, of course, be a few people at the margins for whom the credit was decisive in putting their kids in sport. But that was never the point. The point was to send a message to Steve and Heather that the Conservative party understood their lives and the ordinary things that pinched them month to month. Maybe the Conservatives weren't the wild-eyed Reform crazies from out West; and maybe they weren't the silk-tied double-breasted emissaries of Bay Street, as Mulroney's PCs so often seemed to be. Maybe the Conservatives are just the sort of people I'd bump into at the rink. Not only did these signals from the Conservatives break down barriers to middle- and lower-income voters, particularly in Ontario, but they also helped create bonds to their tax-cutting agenda. Ordinary people tolerate the cuts in corporate tax rates because they believe they, too, are benefitting from the low-tax agenda. The idea that there was something in this for each of us was expressed metaphorically in an astonishing series of government-funded TV ads: they showed tax credits floating in the air over the heads of ordinary Canadians, who would literally reach up and grab the one that applied to them.

You don't have to buy into the hyper-individualism of this approach, or accept the wastefulness or policy incoherence it entails, to recognize that progressives have been less successful in connecting themselves to the lives of ordinary voters. In the campaign for the 2006 election, Paul Martin's aide Scott Reid famously dismissed the Conservative proposal to issue small monthly cheques for day care, because, he said, the money would be quickly gobbled up for beer and popcorn. This was a classic "Kinsley-gaffe"[14]—a gaffe precisely because it was true. Unlike the Liberals' national scheme for building and enhancing institutional childcare, which was about to find its footing, the Conservative proposal would do absolutely nothing to improve the well-being of children. The small cheques would be incorporated into the household finances with barely a ripple. But Reid's comment made a negative emotional connection with ordinary Canadians just when the Conservatives were making positive connections.

The Liberals, under Paul Martin and Stéphane Dion, each in his way a high-flying strategic thinker, were simply not very good at putting themselves round the table at the Tim Hortons after the game. Michael Ignatieff tried dropping his *g*'s, but never had much to say. Jack Layton came closer with his attack on credit card rip-offs by the banks, something that did connect. But progressives in general simply have not been as good as the Conservatives at relating their policies to the struggles of ordinary, middling Canadians.

"THE PERSONIFICATION OF THATCHER'S ASPIRATIONAL CLASS"

There is probably no other area where the Conservatives' focus on an economic message has been more effective than among minority communities.[15] A few weeks before the 2011 election, a Conservative party memo on "ethnic" voters was leaked to the media.[16] One slide, labelled *Take Away*, had three points in stark white on black relief:

- There Are Lots of Ethnic Voters
- There Will be Quite a Few More Soon
- They Live Where We Need To Win

Another slide, labelled *Target Ridings—Very Ethnic*, listed ten seats with an "ethnic group" making up 20 per cent or more of the total population. In the 2008 election the Conservatives hadn't taken any of these seats, most of which were in the Toronto area and in the lower mainland of BC. Eight had been won by Liberals in 2008 and the other two by New Democrats. On election night 2011, the Conservatives took seven, the NDP once again took two, and the Liberals just one. The significance of this shift is twofold. First, it represents a historic failure by the Liberals to hold voters that were fundamental to their grip on Canadian politics over the previous half-century. Second, it is a tribute to Stephen Harper and his acolyte, Jason Kenney, in transforming their party.

One of the Liberals' greatest ideological accomplishments during their long reign was a definition of a national identity with which Canadians who were neither British nor French in their origins could identify. Although the Liberals initially had reservations about the idea of multiculturalism (Pearson had created a royal commission on bilingualism and biculturalism, remember), Trudeau appointed the first secretary of state for multiculturalism, the child of Polish immigrants, Stanley Haidasz. More importantly, Liberal immigration policy, with its heavy emphasis on family reunification, helped cement the loyalty of generations of new Canadians, who became a Liberal cornerstone in urban areas, particularly in Montreal, Toronto, and Vancouver. The party's emphasis on individual rights, enshrined by Trudeau in the *Charter of Rights and Freedoms*, was also crucial here. Most Canadians today would have trouble remembering such figures from the Chrétien years as Rey Pagtakhan, a cabinet

minister born in the Philippines, Raymond Chan, the first Chinese-
Canadian to enter cabinet, or Herb Dhaliwal, the first Indo-
Canadian in cabinet. But I travelled with these people to the
countries of their birth on Chrétien's Team Canada trade mis-
sions and can attest to the sensation they made there and the
reverberations that had on their communities back home in
Canada. Of course, the prominent Liberal politicians from older
immigrant communities, such as Italian-Canadians, were so
numerous as to go almost unnoticed.

To a degree, the Liberals succeeded with new Canadians
through a system of patron-and-client politics. Leaders of minority communities were welcomed into the Liberal fold partly
because they were able to provide what the late-Victorians called
"voting cattle."[17] Anyone who has covered Liberal nomination
meetings over the years can recall many instances of hundreds of
Greek, Lebanese, Ismaili, Sikh, or other minorities, on occasion
speaking little or no English or French, being herded into meetings to vote for candidates whose names they had never heard
before.[18] The community leaders who organized this would be
rewarded with party influence and government patronage, which
in turn would help consolidate their hold on the communities
they led. These ethnic networks could be connected and coordinated by some especially shrewd politicians like Joe Volpe, who
not only had deep roots in his own, older, Italian-Canadian community in Toronto, but also cultivated the Jewish community in
his constituency, and was able to link up with leaders of many
other minority communities, not just in Toronto, but across the
country—a capacity that he used twice to great effect in Paul
Martin's runs at the national leadership.

But, even within the Liberal party, frustration with this kind of
politics could sometimes boil over. At a Liberal party convention
in Vancouver in 2009, one black delegate complained that "we
are tired of being taken for granted at election time," to which

the Indo-Canadian Liberal MP Ruby Dhalla added that new Canadians "can no longer tolerate" being bused out for nominations and fundraisers but otherwise ignored. Dhalla, whose seat was on the Conservatives' ethnic target list, was defeated in 2011 by the Conservative Parm Gill, a businessman who was also born in India.

While researching this book, I went to visit David Smith, a Liberal party warhorse, who sat in Trudeau's cabinet but played his biggest role in the life of the Liberal party as a back-room organizer. He was a protégé of Pearson's (who took to him in part because, like the prime minister, he was a son of the manse) and Pearson's campaign guru, Keith Davey. Smith was part of John Turner's successful bid for the Liberal leadership in 1984 and of Jean Chrétien's in 1990. He engineered Chrétien's three successive near-complete sweeps of Ontario. He is a senator now and his office walls are decorated with a half-century of photos of him smiling beside prominent Liberal politicians, and a stunning collection of antique lithographs of British and Canadian political figures, as well as the odd Hogarth and Millais that would not be out of place in a London gentlemen's club. Despite his background and tastes, his career has allowed him to observe the rise and the fall of Liberal fortunes among ethnic minorities and new Canadians.

"There was a time when most Catholics were Liberals," Smith remarked in his unusual voice, which manages to be both gravelly and a little high-pitched. "Not just in Quebec. Italians... Portuguese and so on, all gravitated to the Liberal party. Jews [as well]. Protestants were mostly Conservatives, though Scottish Presbyterians were an exception to that. I have a theory that the Scottish Presbyterians, like the Catholics, didn't like the English who tended to dominate, so they had a common enemy. But the Liberal party has lost its quasi-monopoly on those groups."

For Smith, the Liberals began losing their grip well before

the Conservatives' campaign to pick off minority voters. "New Canadians loved Trudeau," Smith said. "Turner didn't connect in the same way. Chrétien did relatively better—the little guy from Shawinigan—but then Paul [Martin] and Stéphane [Dion] were less successful…In some of these communities, people are maybe a little more prosperous, so they identify with a different kind of politics. Civil rights are not as important to them as they are to earlier generations."

In Smith's view, in other words, the Conservatives did not create the Liberals' problems with minority communities, which have been much longer in the making. Indeed, as he saw it, the Conservatives have only recently begun to exploit a Liberal vulnerability that was already there. Although Preston Manning was not personally racist, his anti-immigration thematics attracted supporters that unquestionably were. In the middle of the 1993 election campaign, I was on Manning's tour when he was confronted at York University by a student journalist asking about one of Reform's Toronto candidates, John Beck. In an attempt to squelch the story, Manning's aides rushed the travelling press corps to the airport to board a long flight to Edmonton, giving us little time to file. As the plane rolled out for take-off, we were handed a press release saying that Beck had been fired as a candidate. As we flew, however, Beck's words were being broadcast and laid into print. Complaining about the Mulroney government's immigrant investor program, Beck had said: "You have a $150,000 guy there coming to buy a citizenship into Canada to create a job. Fine, he's bringing something to Canada. But what is he bringing? Death and destruction to the people."[19] He told one reporter: "We're all being hooked on booze and drugs and we're going to end up just like the Indians." Part of Manning's problem was that, while he didn't want his candidates talking like this, he seemed to covet the votes of people who felt that way.

Once Harper was installed as leader of the Canadian Alliance,

he began the transmogrification of the party with the assistance
of Calgary MP Jason Kenney. Eventually appointed minister
of immigration and multiculturalism, the irrepressible Kenney
became as relentless as any Liberal ever had been, devouring
pappadums and perogies with equal enthusiasm. He could cram
meetings with Macedonians, Portuguese, Coptic Christians, and
Hindus into a single weekend—and made dozens of such trips
every year. In its bid for the votes of new Canadians, the Harper
government made many symbolic gestures, apologizing for the
Chinese head tax and for sending back the Sikhs aboard the
Komagata Maru in 1914. The government stopped calling Macedonia "the former Yugoslav republic of Macedonia"—a burr in
the community's side. Most important, the Conservatives main-
tained high immigration levels—higher, in fact, than those of the
Chrétien years—while all the time sounding tough on queue-
jumpers and refugee claimants.

It is important to recognize that, unlike the Liberals, the
Conservatives have never tried to appeal to minority voters *in
general* or to win them over as a bloc. The measure of their success is not whether they become the party of immigrants per se,
as the Liberals once were, but whether they become competitive
among groups of voters who at one time would not even have
given them the time of day. Although the Canadian Alliance
under Stockwell Day attempted to appeal to some minority
communities on the basis of conservative moral values—something Harper dabbled with early in his leadership—the Harper
Conservatives have primarily appealed on economic grounds.
"You observe how these new Canadians live their lives," Jason
Kenney once remarked. "They are the personification of
Margaret Thatcher's aspirational class…They're all about a
massive work ethic…striving to get their small business going,
strong family values, respect for tradition."[20]

One of the Conservatives' earliest successes was in attracting

Jewish support. In the postwar years, Jews had voted Liberal in much larger numbers than one would have predicted based on their growing prosperity. A classic example was Izzy Asper, who was born in rural Manitoba into a humble family that had fled pogroms in Ukraine. Although he became a tax lawyer, and eventually a multi-millionaire media mogul, with the views on government that one would pretty much expect, he was a Liberal for most of his life, and led the provincial party for a time. His attachment to the Liberals was founded on its openness to minorities and its belief in individual rights. People like Asper were naturally suspicious of the Reform party with its subterranean racism even if it cleaved closer to their own views on taxes, spending, and regulation. By purging the Conservative party of some of its nativist legacy, by opening it up to immigration, and of course by becoming the fiercest supporter of Israeli government policy in the Western world, Harper made his party an increasingly appealing option for Jews.[21] But in a sense he merely liberated the Jewish community to vote more along the economic lines one would otherwise have expected. The success of the Harper Conservatives in wooing Jewish voters is all the more striking because American Republicans have been working in this same vein much longer but to less effect.[22]

To a greater degree than the Liberals ever did, the Conservatives have targeted specific ethnic communities,[23] and specific sub-groups within those communities. They have obviously made a calculated choice between Jewish and Muslim voters, for example. They aim their messages primarily at people who share their entrepreneurial, free market orientation, so that the Chinese and Korean communities get more attention, for example, than do Tamils or those from the Caribbean. Because they are not making a general appeal to all minorities, they have been able to develop an ingenious policy that appeals also to nativist sentiment among old-stock Canadians. In the 2011 election, the

Conservatives ran ominous ads raising the menace of human smuggling and bogus refugee claimants. What the Conservatives understand is that many new Canadians—certainly those to whom they hope to appeal—make a sharp distinction between legal immigrants and illegal refugees, and so don't feel targeted by these ads. Old-stock Canadians, on the other hand, tend to be blurry on the difference, and some of their supporters connect with the xenophobic undertone.

Some commentators have remarked that the Conservatives still do somewhat less well among Canadians born outside Canada than they do with those born here.[24] That's missing the point. The Harper Conservatives are doing far better than Reform or even Mulroney's PCs ever did. In the 2011 election, besides winning a majority of Jewish voters (52 per cent versus 40 per cent of the general population), they won a plurality among Cantonese-speaking and many South Asian communities. According to a massive post-election survey by Ipsos-Reid, the Conservatives had their greatest success among foreign-born voters who had been in Canada longer than ten years: in other words, those who were more economically established. These successes have corroded the Liberal party and helped build the Conservative majority. And they are fundamental to the party's future. The Conservatives' core includes some dwindling demographic groups, such as rural voters and regular church-goers. Their ability to extend into more dynamic elements of society, such as well-established and prosperous members of minority communities, gives them a chance to break out of that demographic trap.

WE KNOW WHERE YOU LIVE

When I was a kid, if someone sneaked into the photocopier room at school and made an image of his bare butt, it circulated for a few days, got a few laughs, and then disappeared into a landfill somewhere. We are only slowly coming to terms with a world where if our children do something similar it becomes part of the public record, more or less permanently, on Facebook or in some mysterious digital archive. At any time, someone or something may be tracking my mouse-clicks unbeknownst to me, and it is no longer remarkable that when I go onto Amazon it knows my predilection for political biographies, photography books, and Raymond Chandler. The fact that digital technologies are also changing retail politics only occasionally impinges on public consciousness, usually when it goes wrong: when an Irish-Canadian with the last name Park gets a Korean New Year's card from the Conservative party, perhaps. Or when a robocall tells a Liberal his polling place has changed when it hasn't. But the new technology is a critical element in the success of the Harper Conservatives.

The academic and former Harper strategist Tom Flanagan once remarked to me that the Liberal party's organizational professionalism was historically one of the Liberal party's "natural advantages." But that has utterly changed. And at the heart of that change is a database called the Constituency Information Management System, usually written CIMS and pronounced "sims." Flanagan, who has a flinty, dry look to him, has had a somewhat curious career as an academic and political operative. He is a charter member of the so-called Calgary School of conservative academics, based at the University of Calgary, where Harper studied. Like Margaret Thatcher, a disciple of the Austrian philosopher Friedrich Hayek, Flanagan is also an expert on Louis Riel and a devotee of game theory. He worked as Harper's campaign manager on a number of occasions, but has been a sometimes acerbic critic since leaving his inner circle. In 2003 and 2004, he was at the organizational heart of the new Conservative party. The Canadian Alliance had had chronic problems tracking its supporters, so the new party adapted a system used by the Ontario PCs. "There was a voter ID management system," he later wrote. "We wanted to go further by incorporating financial data into CIMS."[25] The system was designed so that data was available to party workers at both the national and the local level. When the party sold a membership, local organizers could use that information to seek out a volunteer or perhaps erect a lawn sign.

"Well, every time a Conservative party worker knocks on your door at election time, and you talk, CIMS is collecting data," Flanagan told me. "Is Paul Adams sympathetic to the Conservative party? Is he undecided? Is he decidedly hostile? What about the issues? Maybe Paul is a traditional Liberal voter, but offside with his party on gun control or abortion. Perhaps he leans Conservative but is put off by what he perceives as the party's conservative agenda on moral issues such as abortion and gay marriage."

Whenever someone writes to a Conservative MP's office on gun control, say, or government regulation, this can be entered into CIMS. Conservative MPs have used so-called "ten percenters"— publicly funded mail-outs to voters in the ridings of Liberal or NDP MPs—not only to target vulnerable opponents, but to identify sympathizers. They might be invited to mail in a coupon to register their support for the Conservative position on gun control. The data is sucked right into CIMS.

The novelty and power of CIMS was not just its high degree of integration—with access to upload or download by local party workers, MPs offices, and national headquarters—but its role in the party's fundraising. Over time, the Conservatives came to wield this cyber-weapon to great effect. CIMS became the database for direct-mail and phone-bank fundraising by the national party. Knowing which "hot button" to push with a potential donor—whether gun control, the mandatory census, or the CBC—was critical. Although the party's initial CIMS-based fundraising campaigns cost more than they produced in revenue, the database was streamlined in the process. People who gave could be approached again; time wouldn't be wasted on those who repeatedly declined. CIMS not only uses information on individuals, but makes indirect inferences from the data as well. Are men more inclined to be generous than women? Are people in certain regions more motivated by special appeals on crime or taxes? The core of the Conservative technique is to address targeted audiences through direct mail and reinforce these appeals directly by phone calls. People won't necessarily give on the phone, Flanagan told me, but the calls reinforce the message of the direct mail. The Conservative machine sometimes places thousands of phone calls on a single night.

Ironically, CIMS prepared the Conservative party to adapt much more effectively than their principal rival, the Liberal party, to the new financing regime established by Jean Chrétien in his final days as prime minister. The Chrétien legislation banned both union and corporate donations to political parties, and capped individual contributions; in compensation, there was a system of public subsidies to the parties based on their vote total in the most recent election. The Liberals had been the most dependent of any party on corporate donations, with the NDP drawing on union support. But the Reform/Canadian Alliance/ Conservatives had always been reliant principally on numerous small donations from individuals. CIMS was designed precisely for this task. Even after the new law was passed, the Liberals continued to rely on a relatively small number of wealthy people willing to max out their donation limit. This was initially $5,000 a year, but was reduced to $1,000 by the Harper government, putting a further squeeze on the Liberals and enhancing the value of the Conservative fundraising machine, powered by CIMS. After winning their majority, the Conservatives began phasing out the per-vote public subsidies, screwing the vise yet tighter. The interim Liberal leader Bob Rae put it succinctly: "The corporate sugar daddy is gone; the government sugar daddy is gone."

The raw facts are brutal. In 2007 and 2008, the Conservatives raised almost four times as much money as the Liberals, who barely raised more than the NDP. By 2010, in the run-up to the last election, the Liberals had improved, but still lagged far behind their main rivals, raising $6.4 million to the Conservatives' $17.4 million. Equally telling is the difference in the number of contributors. The Conservatives had ninety-five thousand individual contributors in 2010, compared with just thirty-two thousand for the Liberals and twenty-two thousand for the NDP. They had about a third more individual contributors than the Liberals, NDP, BQ, and Greens combined, and took in about a third more revenue. When you consider that Conservative support on election day was about a third *less* than those other parties combined, it gives you a measure of their superiority as fundraisers. The Conservatives have been able to use this wild discrepancy in financial resources to special effect outside of election campaigns, when the law doesn't limit spending in the same way. When the party mounted TV ads to frame Stéphane Dion as "not a leader" and Michael Ignatieff as a self-serving political adventurer, the Liberals simply didn't have the cash to reply, much less reply effectively.

The Liberals' inability to adapt to a regime their own government introduced was rooted in the history of the party. Under John Turner's leadership, the Liberals had greatly decentralized their administration in reaction to Trudeau's highly centralized approach. Then, for more than a decade, in the Chrétien-Martin years, the party's most capable organizers devoted their energies to an internal leadership struggle rather than to the challenge of the other parties. At times the national party itself actually could not pry data on memberships from some of its own provincial associations, who in any event stored the information in various incompatible ways. In some Atlantic provinces, members joined "for life," so there was no way of knowing whether they were still supporters, or even whether they were alive or dead. Losing candidates routinely took the data they had accumulated during an election campaign with them, leaving the candidate in the next election to start from scratch. When the Conservatives started using CIMS to target Jewish voters in Toronto—a traditionally Liberal constituency—the Liberals discovered to their dismay that they had no comparable data that would allow them to respond. According to Steve MacKinnon, a former director of the Liberal party, in the run-up to the 2011 election, the Liberals were "ten years behind" the Conservatives in managing their data.[26]

In 2009, the Liberals did acquire software from the Voter Activation Network in the United States that has been widely used by Democrats, including Barack Obama. The new Liberal system, called Liberalist, was intended to allow the party to close the gap, and the local campaign workers I talked to during the 2011 campaign were enthusiastic about it. But the Liberals' problem is rooted in the lack of historical data. Some new data was collected in 2011, but, in a ramshackle, losing campaign, it was nowhere near enough to close the gap with CIMS.

This is a huge issue for fundraising because direct mail is a high-volume, low-margin business. "You need to have clean data," Flanagan told me. "It's like selling food in a supermarket. You need to sell a lot because of the small margins, and you have to keep your costs down...If you send out a thousand pieces of mail, at a dollar a pop, and maybe support this with phone calls, you need to get thousands of dollars back to justify the expense... At first, with a list that isn't 'clean' you are going to waste a lot of money contacting people who have moved, are dead, have migrated to another party, or lost their jobs and can't give any more." Flanagan also argues the Conservatives have a natural advantage in small-donation fundraising. The Conservatives' core is white, English-speaking men, he said, "who also happen to be the demographic most likely to have an ethic of voluntary giving, are easy to contact because they have reasonably stable homes, have landlines and speak English, and also more likely to hold views that lend themselves to 'hot-button' approaches...So you can get them on the phone and they can afford to give."

The Liberals, he said, "are a watered-down version of the vic-tim party: francophones, new Canadians, women, youth...This coalition works in electoral politics but it is a harder coalition to manage in fundraising terms." Non-English-speakers are more likely to throw away mailers without looking at them, he said. Aboriginals and new Canadians have less money to give. Asians and Mediterraneans "don't have a tradition of civic voluntarism." Young people have no money and are hard to reach. Franco-phones give less than anglophones. Women, he said, are also less likely to give. "Waiters always shudder when they see a table of women [because they are bad tippers]." The CIMS approach, he says, wouldn't necessarily work as well with these groups as with the Conservatives' core.

If you take away Flanagan's characteristically caustic tone, MacKinnon essentially agrees. The Liberals' own hot button con-cerns, such as abortion rights, are about defending the status quo, he told me—harder to raise money around. The Conservatives, many of whose supporters feel beset with "enemies," whether the CBC, the courts, the arts community, gay or feminist groups, or government more broadly, are more easily moved to give out of anger.

"WE'RE ALL CONSERVATIVES NOW"

How do you recognize an ideological triumph? One way is to see whether a set of ideas becomes "common sense." When that hap-pens, it is difficult to criticize without seeming to impeach your own judgment and credibility. It is not so long ago that it was hard to argue that blacks shared full humanity with white men. Even Abraham Lincoln, in his famous debates with Steven Douglas, would say: "I, as well as Judge Douglas, am in favor of the race to which I belong having the superior position." Lincoln wished to curb slavery, but he would not challenge what was to his audience obvious, that whites and blacks were inherently unequal. Today, that view is almost unthinkable, and certainly unspeakable. Common sense has changed, and in this case that is a good thing. But I would argue that important elements of the conservative economic worldview have penetrated our politics so completely that they appear like common sense, which is making it hard for us to think our way out of our economic and ecological crises.

With the world economy still reeling from the market meltdown two years earlier, Canada hosted a G20 summit in the summer of 2010. As chair of the meeting, Steven Harper had considerable influence over the agenda and successfully pushed for a resolution that industrialized nations should cut their deficits in half within three years. In its own budget, the Harper government went beyond that, pledging to eliminate the deficit completely by 2015, even in the face of sluggish growth and stubbornly high unemployment.[27] With the government already committed to a schedule of corporate tax cuts, this would inevitably mean substantial cuts to program spending, including the end of the infrastructure program launched under opposition pressure in the 2009 budget at the height of the crisis. So, what was the response of the opposition parties? Of course they reacted in outrage, you may think. Ridiculous to make balancing the books a priority with the economy as shaky as it has been in living memory—especially when Canada's fiscal situation is relatively sound by international standards. Surely unemployment was the top priority, not deficit reduction. Concerted action to cut deficits by all the industrialized countries, irrespective of their fiscal circumstances, as Harper was urging, would dampen the international recovery from the Great Recession. The Liberals and New Democrats would rightly reject this folly on orthodox Keynesian grounds, you might reasonably imagine.

But if that's what you think, then you are wrong. The Liberals and New Democrats not only accepted the Harper government's objective of slashing the deficit; they put it in their election platforms. The Liberal platform called deficit-reduction the "anchor" of the party's fiscal policy, pledging to reduce the deficit to 1 per cent of GDP (from 3.6 per cent) within two years, with rolling targets to get to zero after that. The NDP platform simply repeated the Harper government's pledge, entirely uninflected. Indeed, a post-election poll suggested that while Conservative voters were somewhat more likely to support a balanced budget, more than 80 per cent of both Liberal and NDP voters shared that view.[28]

In this country, the sacralization of deficit reduction has played a particular role in the dominance of conservative ideas. In the 1988 election campaign, which was fought on free trade, Brian Mulroney made nary a mention of the deficit, and it had no place in the PC party platform. However, immediately afterwards, his finance minister, Michael Wilson, began a major public relations campaign to convince Canadians that we were "living beyond our means." As a matter of fact, it was absolutely clear that the cumulation of Trudeau- and Mulroney-era deficits, and the rising interest payments that entailed, was unsustainable. The issue was what to do about it. By framing Canada's economic woes around the deficit, the Mulroney government was able to justify major cuts in public spending—including unemployment insurance, for example. Wilson also undertook a significant reform of the tax system, eliminating many corporate tax breaks but adding a huge off-setting drop in the corporate tax rate, from 36 per cent to 28 per cent. More significantly, he abolished the manufacturers' sales tax (MST), replacing it with a new goods and services tax (GST). At the time, Mulroney and Wilson argued that the replacement of the MST with the GST was "revenue neutral"— that is, the new tax would not take in any more money than the old one. While this may have been true in the short term, as they well knew, revenues from the GST—a tax on consumers—would grow much more rapidly over time than the MST—a tax on Canada's shrinking manufacturing sector.

Despite all these changes, whose net effect was to reduce public services and shift the tax burden from corporations to individuals, the Mulroney government was unsuccessful in reducing the deficit. But the Liberals, within less than a year of being elected, decided to eliminate the deficit completely, "come hell or high water," as Paul Martin famously put it. Within a few years, the Liberals had accomplished this goal through a combination of spending cuts, temporary tax increases, reneging on their promise to replace the GST, and, luckily for them, unexpectedly robust economic growth. It is important to recognize that the Liberals inherited a genuine fiscal crisis from the PCs: by the time they took office interest payments were eating up a third of the budget, and rising. The Liberals' progressive bona fides, and the seeming reluctance with which they came to deficit cutting, helped persuade many Canadians to endure the consequences. The fact that their principal opposition in English Canada was now the Reform party, which almost bizarrely attacked the Liberals for not moving aggressively enough on the deficit, helped greatly. The NDP at this point had lost official party status and was groping ineffectually for a credible response to the deficit. Indeed, one of the most remarkable aspects of this story is how effectively the Liberals were able to persuade Canadians that the pain was necessary. Amazingly, Paul Martin emerged more popular than he began.

As part of his fiscal program, Paul Martin adopted and publicly promoted what he called the no-deficit rule. This was a deliberate rejection of the Keynesian notion that governments could and should run deficits to stimulate the economy in slumps.[29] "One of the most important aspects of the no-deficit rule," Martin wrote in his biography, "was that it implanted in the public's mind the need for a sound fiscal policy so that politicians would pay a price at the polls if they started to stray. In fact the growing public support for the no-deficit rule was crucial to our success." Martin later argued that his rule was never meant to prohibit governments from stimulating the economy in a *deep* recession, but this certainly wasn't something he dwelt on at the time. Canadians were encouraged to feel that the deficit had been conquered once and for all and that any return to deficit was contrary to good fiscal hygiene. In this way, public opinion has become the enemy of clear thinking about when and in what circumstances the federal government should run a deficit.

The no-deficit rule helped shape the debate in the aftermath of the 2008 financial crisis. At first, the Conservatives resisted the suggestion that they would run a deficit at all, even in the face of collapsing revenues. Once they recognized that it was inevitable, they conceded only that they would run a small, near-term deficit. They were eventually forced to reverse that policy and plan for a large deficit only in the face of the coalition threat by the opposition parties. Even at that point, however, with financial markets and the world's economy in crisis, the Liberals under Ignatieff were unable to free themselves from the grip of the no-deficit ideology they themselves had promoted. In a perceptive article after the 2011 election, Paul Martin's former pollster and campaign manager, David Herle, remarked that the Liberals' "unwillingness to veer from conservative economic orthodoxy meant they could not propose any measures that would have a meaningful impact on the circumstances of people clinging to their middle-class lifestyles." Although Herle did not mention it, he had been among a number of Liberals prior to the election who had tried privately to persuade Ignatieff to loosen the party's commitment to balancing the budget in the short term.

But Ignatieff seemed strangely uninterested in the wider meaning of the financial and economic crisis once he got his stimulative budget out of Harper in 2009, and was thus utterly incapable of mounting any sort of economic critique. Not only did he effectively endorse the Conservatives' proposed track to a balanced budget, he declared that he was opposed to "big government"—a phrase he must have picked up during his years in the US and the UK—and "passionate" about making corporate tax cuts, even if he did think Harper was making them too quickly. Ignatieff did not question the assumptions underlying the Harper economic policies: rather, he suggested incremental variations on that policy, which he defended on tactical grounds.

Meanwhile, the NDP also steered clear of presenting a broad critique of the faltering conservative economic model. One senior New Democrat in a position to know told me that the NDP held back from doing so as a matter of communications strategy, fearing that the media—that great champion of conventional wisdom—would paint it as radical and unrealistic. In Ignatieff's case, to the extent he ever thought about economics, he seems to have been an unreflective supporter of the conservative fiscal consensus of the previous decades, a testament to the penetration of the ideology. In the NDP's case, it seems more like a timidity in taking on what had become a pervasive view.

One of the reasons that some columnists have been able to claim credibly that Harper is more a pragmatist than a conservative is that his opposition has drifted so far in his direction. No one ever said "we're all conservatives now," but to a surprising degree it was true.

THE PERMANENT CAMPAIGN

There seems to be an assumption among many progressives that the Harper Conservatives will come to an inevitable downfall. It is just a matter of time. And, when they fall, we will inherit the earth. This was, more or less, the strategic approach of the Ignatieff Liberals. And it was a dismal failure.

It is true, of course, that Canadians may tire of Stephen Harper and his party by the next election, in 2015, by which time it will have been in office nearly a decade. It is possible that in their transformation from a populist, movement party to the most disciplined, centralized and professionalized party in the political system, they will lose some of their vital energy on the ground. Perhaps a full term in majority government will stifle the anger that seems to fuel the ardour of their core. It is true as well that the Harper Conservatives always seem to limp a little in the polls between elections. This gives progressives hope, even though it may be not much more than an artifact of the way polls are conducted.[30]

But the fact is that Harper's party has grown in every election since he became leader. It has penetrated into communities that were unavailable to its predecessors, the Reform party and the Canadian Alliance. It has considerable strength among minority Canadians, among Ontarians, and even urban voters, most notably in that electoral honeypot, Toronto. It now has at its disposal the powers of a majority government to consolidate and extend those inroads through public policy. It is reshaping the symbols of nationality and raising the profile of the monarchy and of the military, as well as embedding its low-tax, small-government philosophy in the psyches of many Canadians. It has the financial resources to run a permanent campaign of advertising against its divided and less-well-funded opponents. The Harper Conservative party actually has room to grow—in parts of British Columbia, which will have more seats in 2015 and where it has not yet matched the performance of Reform and the Canadian Alliance; in Toronto; and even, perhaps to a limited extent, in Quebec.

The Harper Conservatives may drop to the ground in 2015 like overripe fruit, ready to be gobbled up by some combination of the four opposition parties they currently face in the House of Commons. Possibly. Or, they just might become the new natural governing party, as Harper has long hoped. That is at least partly up to the way progressives decide to conduct themselves between now and then.

CHAPTER 4

WHY THE NEW DEMOCRATS BROKE OUT

I got the news at eleven minutes past seven on Wednesday evening, the twentieth of April, with just ten days left in the election campaign. A journalist friend had just spoken to a senior New Democrat, who had himself heard the news not long before. The Dips, as journalists call them, were as stunned as anyone. As perpetual also-rans, the NDP targeted their polling on the thirty-six ridings they held across the country, and a roughly equivalent number they thought they had a shot at. In Quebec, where the party had only one seat before the election—its most ever—it had targeted three or four more. Brad Lavigne, who was running the NDP campaign, was in his office in Ottawa that day, talking on the phone, when one of his colleagues walked in and held a sheet of paper up against the window with the not-yet-released poll numbers from the CROP organization in Quebec emblazoned in marker: "NDP 36%, Bloc 31%, CPC 17%, LPC 13%." He acknowledged the numbers with a hand gesture and casually finished his call as if nothing had happened. But he knew that it had. "The breadth of the advance was unknown at the time," Lavigne later acknowledged. This changed everything.

Soon after I learned the news about CROP, I also heard that EKOS (where I had once worked) was scrambling to get its latest numbers out quickly—telling a similar story about Quebec, and providing an arresting picture of what was happening in the rest of the country. I emailed a high-ranking member of the NDP campaign team to see whether he had heard that EKOS had something coming. He sent me back a note. "Looks like 31% and leading in Quebec, and just shy of 25% and thus statistically tied with libs nationally. Romanow used to say that you can usually expect one big thing to happen in any election campaign. Perhaps this is it. Wow!"

And then, a few hours later, it hit the news with full force. The numbers were breathtaking enough, but when EKOS published a seat projection that suggested the NDP could win a hundred seats, the cognitive dissonance was simply too great. One of Canada's most serious and thoughtful journalists, the conservative *Maclean's* columnist Andrew Coyne, who kept a close watch on the numbers, rubbished the projection as preposterous. The prospect of an NDP wave of that scale was unbelievable—until it wasn't. Just a week and a half later the NDP surged to 103 seats, more than half of them in Quebec. In many cases, the new Quebec MPs had barely campaigned, if at all, having simply put their names on the ballot as a gesture, or perhaps as a favour to a friend. Jack Layton had won fifty-nine seats in the province—more than Lucien Bouchard or Gilles Duceppe had ever done, and equalling Brian Mulroney's first sweep of the province in 1984.

The seemingly incomprehensible breakthrough in Quebec may even have understated the scale of the NDP's success in the 2011 election. The party increased the number of its seats outside Quebec more modestly: from thirty-five to forty-four, a gain of just nine. But it was now the second-place party in every English-speaking province except Prince Edward Island. In fact, nearly two-thirds of the 4.5 million votes the NDP received were from outside Quebec. The party more than doubled its percentage of the popular vote nationally and more than doubled the number of seats in which it ran either first or second to 224.[1] It had comprehensively replaced, not only the Bloc as the main party in Quebec, but also the Liberal party as the principal alternative to the Conservatives in the rest of the country.

THE MAKING OF INSTANT SUCCESS

The shock of Jack Layton's death only weeks after the election, the reaction to his deathbed call to Canadians for hope, and that long, startling, awkward moment at his funeral when Conservative ministers waited for Stephen Harper to decide whether they should join a standing ovation for his commitment to social democracy, both burnished Layton's reputation and somewhat obscured the nature of his accomplishment. At the time, some journalists suggested that Harper felt he had no choice but to offer a state funeral for Layton, in anticipation of the outpouring of public grief. That strikes me as unlikely. Much more plausible that Harper rightly saw this as a chance to help institutionalize the NDP, to help bring it, culturally, from the political margins to replace the Liberals as one of the country's two great parties. This has long been a goal of many Conservatives, who see the NDP as the weaker opponent. Indeed, the theatre of Layton's funeral—Olivia Chow's sombre stoicism, Stephen Lewis's full-throated celebration of Layton's social democratic values, and yes, that hesitant standing ovation—created the first occasion on which most Canadians ever felt deeply about the NDP. If it was too much to say that we were all New Democrats that day, most Canadians could at least imagine the best part of being one.

Jack Layton came from an extended line of politicians, of both liberal and conservative stripe. A great-great-uncle on his mother's side, William Steeves, was a father of confederation from New Brunswick, and a Liberal. His grandfather Gilbert Layton had been a cabinet minister in the provincial Union Nationale government of Maurice Duplessis. His father, Robert, was a federal Liberal turned PC who held a junior post in Brian Mulroney's cabinet, and who chaired the PC caucus for a time— perhaps a source for Layton's caucus management skills. As a young man, Layton moved to Toronto from the Montreal area where he had grown up. I first remember him from the time I was a reporter for CBC-TV posted in Toronto in the early 90s. Layton, then a city councillor, was a lefty gadfly, a skinny, shaggy-haired, moustachioed man who turned up at demonstrations and press conferences on his bicycle, wearing a backpack. When he had had his say, usually opposing the council's latest developer-driven project, he hopped back on his bike and pedalled off. He seemed like a well-meaning publicity hound. He struck a more mature image when he ran for mayor of Toronto in 1991, and came a surprisingly strong second to his right-wing opponent.[2] Later, he had a stint as president of the Canadian Federation of Municipalities, in which he developed collaborative skills and learned to combine his idealism with practicality.

Layton came to the leadership of the NDP in 2003 at a time of confusion and disarray for the party. Ten years earlier, the party had fallen to just nine seats in parliament—short of what it needed to receive official recognition. After a brief and modest improvement in 1997, it had slumped back to just thirteen seats in the 2000 election. It wasn't just journalists and political opponents who thought the party might be over. A group of left-leaning NDPers, including Libby Davies, Peggy Nash, Jim Stanford, and Judy Rebick, embraced something called the New Politics Initiative, which called for the NDP to disband and regroup in combination with anti-globalization, feminist, and environmental groups that had a vitality the NDP conspicuously

lacked. Though the idea was defeated at the party's 2001 convention, it managed to get 40 per cent support. Layton had not joined
the initiative, but he was regarded as a sympathizer when he ran
for the leadership, and he relied for his support on some of the
same people. His campaign had a made-in-Toronto feel, emphasizing the concerns of urban activists over the party's prairie and
union roots. But he focused much more on "party renewal" than
on ideology.

As it turned out, those who thought he would move the party
to the left were mistaken. He sharply attacked the Paul Martin
government as taking the Liberal party to the right, and took
populist shots at Martin and his shipping business for sailing
under foreign flags to avoid Canadian taxes. But he unceremoni-
ously dumped the NDP's opposition to NATO and NORAD in
2004, and moved the party's position on deficits and balanced
budgets increasingly towards that of the dominant conservative
consensus. Though the party did not score a breakthrough in
Layton's first three elections, it steadily increased in both seats
and popular vote. By 2008, Layton's third election, the NDP
had doubled its share of the popular vote and took thirty-seven
seats. More often than not, polls suggested that the NDP was the
most popular second choice for those supporting other parties,
particularly the Liberals. Increasingly, the NDP's policies differed
from those of the Liberals mainly in the conviction and populist
style with which they were expressed—barring a few conspicuous
exceptions such as NDP opposition to Canada's military mission
in Afghanistan. In keeping with the party's role for a half century,
its positions were often the source of policy ideas later adopted
by the Liberals.

At the same time, Layton gathered a team of organizers around
him, including Brian Topp, a rumpled former Montrealer, whom
I first met when he was Roy Romanow's advisor during the constitutional negotiations for the Charlottetown Accord. Topp was

the consummate backroom boy, deeply involved in Romanow's political strategizing and the organization of the Saskatchewan NDP. He had an unusual mix of social democratic conviction, government experience, and political savvy, telling the CBC after the 2011 election, "The trick to growing up is keeping your idealism after you've lost your innocence" (a quotation from Abbie Hoffman, he later told me). After leaving Saskatchewan he had worked for the credit union movement and later as an executive of ACTRA, the actors' union. He became a part-time advisor to the NDP, except during elections when he dropped everything else. Layton also recruited Brad Lavigne, a British Columbia New Democrat who had come out of the Canadian Federation of Students. Lavigne would move from a communications role to overall direction of the campaign in 2011. The third member of the inner circle was Anne McGrath: a communist in her youth who had later become a New Democrat, she served as president of the federal NDP before becoming Layton's chief of staff. As the years passed, while Topp retained a strategic role, Lavigne and McGrath became increasingly important to Layton, and certainly closer to the day-to-day direction of the 2011 campaign.

Under Layton's leadership, this group would substantially alter the structure of the federal party. Before this time, the federal NDP had essentially "rented" its resources—everything from workers to office space to lists of supporters—from its provincial counterparts. In provinces where there was a history of provincial NDP government—BC, Saskatchewan, Manitoba, and, to a degree, in Ontario—the feds played second fiddle to their provincial cousins. Under Layton, however, the federal party built up its own parallel structure, with dedicated regional staff in seven offices across the country. Meanwhile, they bulked up their national headquarters in Ottawa. In contrast to the Liberals, who had an unwieldy, highly decentralized party structure, and the Conservatives, who ran extremely centralized campaigns, the

federal NDP was something of a hybrid. In some ways it paral-
leled the structure of the epically successful Obama campaign
machine of 2008: a strong central organization that could manage a focused national campaign, but at the same time support
activists at the community level who worked with considerable
autonomy. It was an attempt to adopt some of the techniques
of elite, professionalized parties like the Liberals without losing
the local energy of a populist movement party. Among other
things, this structure allowed NDP-affiliated unions to support
the campaign without becoming formally part of it, something
necessitated by changes to electoral law.[3]

Surprisingly, perhaps, the New Democrats did as well as, and
sometimes better than, the Liberals (though not nearly as well as
the Conservatives) under new party financing legislation passed
in the final days of the Chrétien regime. Because the new public
subsidies to the parties were based on the votes they won, the Liberals and the Conservatives obviously benefited more. However,
the ban on corporate donations hurt the Liberals more than the
ban on union donations hurt the NDP. In the months before the
legislation took effect, the New Democrats had convinced many
of their union backers to bundle up their contributions for the
next few years, allowing the party to buy its Laurier Street headquarters in Ottawa outright. This gave the party equity against
which it could borrow at election time. And, since it was not
carrying as much debt as the Liberals to begin with, the NDP was
actually *more* stable and secure financially. Meanwhile, the NDP
rivalled the Liberals, and sometimes exceeded them, in raising
money from individuals, something on which the new system
put a premium. In the 2008 election campaign the NDP spent
the legal limit on its national campaign for the first time in its
history, while the Liberals, hesitant to borrow on the prospects
of Stéphane Dion, spent about $5 million less than they were
allowed.[4] Jack Layton's insistence that he was running to be prime

minister often sounded hollow to reporters—and to many voters. But the NDP was actually at the grown-ups' table when it came to national campaigns.

Almost exactly a year before the 2011 election, I met Brad Lavigne at a Bridgehead coffee shop on Bank Street in Ottawa, a few blocks from party headquarters. I have discovered over the years that Ottawa New Democrats will walk past a half dozen Starbucks and Second Cups to get to a Bridgehead—"fairly traded, organic and shade-grown coffee from small-scale farmers," its website boasts. Lavigne, an intense, thirty-something man with closely cropped hair, then national director of the party, leaned across the table, and, speaking over the din of the busy café, made me the same pitch he had made to many other journalists over the years. The NDP was serious, he said. It had reorganized. It had learned how to raise money in the new era of party financing.

"You have to give people an incentive—an excuse—for people to raise money." He described a recent scheme in which local NDP associations in ridings held by other parties were offered fifty cents for every dollar they raised over a sixty-day period, up to $10,000. One hundred and sixty associations had signed up, he told me, and they raised a half-million dollars for the party in just two months. Unlike the Liberal party, whose supporters had few hot-button issues that would send them reaching for their wallets, the New Democrats, he said, were succeeding in direct mail campaigns, backed up by phone and internet, on topics such as unemployment insurance and sheer antipathy to Stephen Harper. NDP supporters were, quite simply, angrier than Liberals. The NDP was out-raising the Liberals on small donations, with the Liberals depending more on their traditional $500-a-plate dinners, drawing heavily on lawyers, businesspeople, and lobbyists. Lavigne said the party expected an election in the spring of 2011 (a prospect I doubted at the time). His enthusiasm and confidence were so strong—the voice of a salesman who truly believed in his product—that I was unsure whether to be swept away or to be completely dismissive.

Among other things, Lavigne told me that the NDP, like the Conservatives, were eating into the Liberals' traditional base among new Canadians and visible minorities—not the most economically successful immigrants, in the NDP's case, but those for whom the Canadian dream remained elusive. "Layton is winning over people on economic grounds—for example, people with trades or professions they can't practise here, who can't reach their full potential." I have to say I was skeptical that the NDP could be as effective as the Conservatives in dissecting this element of the Liberal base. I was wrong.

I asked Lavigne who the party's main target would be in the coming election.

"The Conservatives. Of the next twenty seats we're after, fifteen are Conservative, four Liberal, and one Bloc. The next tier is mostly Tory."

JACK AND GILLES

Lavigne wasn't being entirely straight with me. The party was targeting a few Conservative seats—Oshawa and Edmonton East, for example, neither of which it ultimately won. It wanted to convey the image of a party that was aiming to slay Stephen Harper. But the NDP campaign was actually targeting "Layton Liberals": swing voters who could yield the party mainly Liberal-held seats in Toronto, British Columbia, and the Atlantic provinces. If the party succeeded, the NDP strategists thought, they would do so mainly by eating the Liberals' lunch: they just couldn't say so. Lavigne's professed optimism about the 2011 campaign turned out to be amply justified. But the party would not succeed in winning even the first tier of seats he had identified to me. Nor would it win all that many of the Liberal seats it was actually going after—most of which were in English Canada. The NDP would do OK outside

Quebec, but no more than that: a gain of nine seats.

The other 58 seats the party picked up came where the party had sown its seed for years but had never harvested much of anything. When the NDP was founded in 1961, bringing together the prairie populism of Tommy Douglas and the political heft of the recently united Canadian Labour Congress, it had high hopes of attracting Quebecers. The platform language on federal-provincial relations, for example, was largely written by and for Quebecers. While many Quebec intellectuals flirted with the NDP, including none other than Pierre Elliott Trudeau, it was the provincial Liberal party under Jean Lesage that captured the exhilarating spirit of the Quiet Revolution. Then, as politics in the province increasingly turned on a polarizing debate about federalism and sovereignty, Quebecers found their contrasting champions in Trudeau and René Lévesque. It left precious little oxygen for the NDP, even if it did share many of the Quiet Revolution's values. Ed Broadbent, who led the party in the latter part of the 1970s and the entire 1980s, proved to be the most popular leader the NDP ever had, probably including Layton. Under his leadership the party had some heady months in first place in the national opinion polls in the mid-eighties. Broadbent was tireless in cultivating Quebec, devoting his summer vacation to travelling through the province and many months working on his French, which ultimately achieved that special fluency of Canadian politicians that anglophone reporters find much easier to follow than their francophone colleagues. He was popular in Quebec, as he was across the country. Still, in 1984 Broadbent won only 30 seats, none of them in Quebec. The NDP was tantalizingly close to the Liberals at 40 seats, but laughably distant from the Mulroney PCs at 211. Broadbent's best shot at governing came in the "free trade election" of 1988 when, unfortunately for him, Quebec enthusiastically supported the Mulroney policy. He took the party to 43 seats, its highest-ever total prior to 2011, but again, none was from Quebec, where the party won just 14 per cent of the vote.

In the next three elections, the party failed to take more than 2 per cent of the vote in Quebec under its barely bilingual leaders, Audrey McLaughlin and Alexa McDonough. Layton had picked up some French working summer jobs in Montreal as a young man, which perhaps gave him an ear for the language. But a public servant who attended an immersion French course with him at Jonquière shortly after he became leader told me his French was still far from perfect—something that was evident in his 2004 debate performance. Layton's subsequent fluency, and the image he later cultivated as a native Québécois, was something acquired by hard work and practice after he became leader.

The NDP's performance in the province in Layton's first three elections was only modestly better than under his immediate predecessors—almost 5 per cent in 2004, 8 per cent in 2006, and 12 per cent in 2008—but still less than Broadbent had managed. In 2007, however, the NDP won a by-election in the Montreal riding of Outremont. Thomas Mulcair, an articulate, impeccably bilingual former provincial Liberal minister with a reputation as a maverick, won nearly half the vote in a riding that had long been a rotten borough for the Liberals, by sucking away support from both them and the Bloc Québécois. For the first time, the NDP had a highly visible Quebec lieutenant. Of course, by-elections are by-elections and often turn out not to mean much. But in 2008, Mulcair held his seat in a general election, something no New Democrat had ever done in Quebec.

None of this even remotely prepared the party, the province, or the country for what happened in 2011. In most of Quebec, the party had no organization. It had only two personalities—Layton and Mulcair—who were known across the province, and a few candidates with a local reputation, such as Françoise Boivin, a former Liberal MP running in Gatineau, and Romeo Saganash,

Quebec's first Cree lawyer, who ran in a huge, heavily native riding in northern Quebec. Parties with national aspirations like to be able to say they are running a candidate in every constituency in the country, and they go to great efforts to persuade people to put their name on the ballot even where they have no hope of winning. In the rural Alberta riding of Crowfoot, for example, the Liberal candidate was a Omar Harb, a second-year business student at the University of Calgary, who was unable to campaign much because of exams.[5] In the Manitoba riding of Churchill, the Greens ran Alberteen Spence, who had no background in politics, no agent or campaign manager, and was tied down from campaigning in the vast northern riding by her job as an addictions worker.[6] And so it was that Ruth Ellen Brosseau, a twenty-seven-year-old Carleton university pub assistant manager with imperfect French, was persuaded by a friend working at NDP headquarters in Ottawa to put her name forward for the riding of Berthier-Maskinongé, near Trois Rivières, a place she had never visited. No one ever got on Harb's case or Spence's, because they never had any chance of winning. But Brosseau became a national celebrity of sorts when suddenly, in the midst of the campaign, it looked like she just might win, and she turned out to be vacationing in Las Vegas. That didn't bother the voters of Berthier-Maskinongé. Brosseau, who had not attended a debate, knocked on a single door or made a single phone call, and never did visit the riding, won by a margin of nearly six thousand votes. Less spectacularly, but just as tellingly, another of the new crop of NDP MPs, Charmaine Borg, just twenty years old, *had* been campaigning—except not in the riding in which she was a candidate, Terrebonne-Blainville, north of Montreal, where she quite reasonably assumed she had no chance. Instead she worked for Mulcair in Outremont until almost the end of the campaign.

For several years, the respected columnist for the *Toronto Star* and *Le Devoir* Chantal Hébert had been among a small number

of commentators arguing that the Bloc Québécois' *château fort*
was an empty shell disguising the waning sovereigntist ardour
of the province.[7] The seemingly irreducible fact that the BQ
would take nearly fifty seats each election, frustrating the hopes
of national parties and confounding the arithmetic of majority
government, appeared more fragile to her than it did to others.
The BQ had long ago lost its original *raison d'être:* the plan in
1991, when the party was founded, was to disband after the next
referendum on sovereignty in Quebec, which occurred just four
years later. In 2000, Jean Chrétien managed to win more votes
in Quebec than the BQ, though fewer seats, and the BQ seemed
to be on the wane. But the BQ was revived in the 2004 and 2006
campaigns, not by sovereignty, but by the sponsorship scandal,
which was most devastating in Quebec, where it was centred, and
where the proceedings of the Gomery Commission, mostly in
French, played out as a teledrama from the fall of 2004 through
the spring of 2005. In 2008, with the scandal waning, Harper was
widely expected to secure his majority in Quebec. That hope was
shattered, however, when Harper scored a spectacular own goal
by deriding funding for the arts—something that played well
among some English Canadians, but which allowed the BQ to
play a powerful cultural nationalist card. In Hébert's view, events
had disguised the underlying weakness of the sovereigntist party.

The 2011 election campaign would suddenly, and dramatically,
expose that weakness. Gilles Duceppe, fighting his sixth election
as Bloc leader, initially played down the party's sovereigntist
aspirations. The BQ adopted a neutral slogan, *Parlons Québec*
(Let's talk Quebec), and Duceppe mounted a scorching attack
on Stephen Harper. On the first day of the campaign, he called
Harper a liar. What was at issue, though, was ancient history:
Harper's account of his attempt to dislodge Paul Martin's minority government in 2005 with the help of the NDP and BQ. The
Bloc's TV ads demonized Harper: one said the party's objective

was to "defend the interests of Quebec," with Duceppe looking right into the camera and saying, "Only the Bloc Québécois
can prevent a Conservative majority." Another ad asked, "Does
becoming prime minister mean you aren't accountable to anyone?" But Duceppe's bitter rhetorical blasts were not matched
with much energy on the campaign trail. He got off to a lazy start,
popping up around Montreal but barely venturing out of the city
until the second week.

While the BQ's campaign was angry, personal, and aimed at
Harper, the NDP managed to strike a sweet and humorous tone
even in its attack ads, which were aimed equally at the BQ and
the Conservatives. One French-language TV spot depicted a large
black dog barking back and forth with two smaller dogs. "Always
the same debates that lead nowhere," said a title on the screen,
as they yapped away. "It's time for that to change." The ads did
not feature Layton, by the way. They played off the BQ's negative
role in the federal parliament—as a party that did not aspire to
power—and implicitly aimed at Duceppe's strident and humour-
less persona. Another NDP ad depicted a hamster spinning in a
wheel, subtly toned BQ light blue, with whimsical music playing
in the background. "Politics isn't going anywhere in Ottawa," it
said; and again, "It's time for that to change." It was another of a
thousand variations on the slogan Dwight Eisenhower used in his
revolutionary 1952 television ads: "It's time for a change." Barack
Obama himself had dusted it off in 2008, claiming to embody
"Change we can believe in." Now it was the NDP's turn.

The irony was that the NDP had, with a few exceptions, an
almost identical voting record to the Bloc in parliament. Part of
its appeal to BQ voters was precisely that not much would change
with Quebec's representation, except that the issue of sovereignty
would no longer be even nominally at play, and its MPs could, at
least, theoretically participate in government. In 2005, the NDP had
adopted the so-called Sherbrooke Declaration, which accepted the

right of Quebec's National Assembly to draft a referendum question on sovereignty that could be approved with a bare majority of 50 per cent +1 (though it also noted that the federal government had the right to construct its own political response under an earlier Supreme Court ruling). But that was background in the 2011 election, not foreground. Layton's specific pitch to Quebecers was quite modest—certainly by the standards of leaders such as Trudeau, Mulroney, and Bouchard, who had previously swept Quebec.[8] He proposed that the federally regulated workplaces in Quebec—banks would be an example—should be subject to the provincial language laws that ensure a French workplace. In the French-language televised leaders debate, he discussed reopening the Constitution to address Quebec's demands under "winning conditions" for Canada, a deliberate echo of the phrase Lucien Bouchard had used about holding a referendum on sovereignty. This was an attempt to soften the party's federalist image with an aspirational message, but it fell well short of a bankable promise.

Whether it was a premeditated attempt to shore up his sovereigntist support or just an unlucky happenstance, Duceppe's campaign took a sharp turn when he made a command performance at a convention of the provincial Parti Québécois mid-campaign. Before such an audience, he could hardly play down his sovereigntist beliefs; instead, he played them up, way up. "We have only one task to accomplish," he told a cheering crowd of PQ delegates. "Elect the maximum number of sovereigntists in Ottawa and then we go to the next phase—electing a PQ government. A strong Bloc in Ottawa. The PQ in power in Quebec. And everything again becomes possible." This arresting reminder that Duceppe and his provincial allies were proposing to plunge the province into a third decade of turmoil in just forty years was apparently unwelcome to many voters. As BQ support continued to crumble in the aftermath of that speech, Duceppe realized that even hard-core sovereigntists had begun to desert him. His message turned yet more insistently sovereigntist as he tried to "save the furniture" in an oft-repeated phrase. He wheeled out that ultra-sovereigntist warhorse, former premier Jacques Parizeau, onto the campaign trail, and hit the hustings with PQ leader Pauline Marois. The Bloc, which had once appealed to soft nationalist voters, was now going begging even among the diehards.

So there was more going on in Quebec in 2011 than just a Jack Layton charm offensive. The supposed "charisma" of politicians, whether Obama, Blair, Trudeau, or Layton, is two parts circumstance and one part personality. But personality does count for something. Layton had the highest leadership ratings in Quebec by the end of the campaign, as he did in many parts of English Canada. In Quebec, he was ranged against the scowling Duceppe and the morose Harper, Michael Ignatieff having practically vacated the field. In contrast to his opponents, Layton had a sunny disposition, and many Quebecers took to referring him as "Jack"—a first-name familiarity not extended to his opponents. A charming, humble, now fluent Layton appeared on the crazily successful Quebec talk show *Tout le monde en parle,* early in the campaign. It didn't hurt that he was seen soon after in a television clip shot at a bar in Montreal, abruptly interrupting an interview to cheer exuberantly at a Montreal Canadiens' goal. One NDP organizer said that Layton's resonance in Quebec came earlier than the breakout in the polls, but was just as big a surprise. "We could see that something was going on."

Many commentators later described the NDP sweep in Quebec as a protest vote. Protest against a Harper government that was malattuned to the province on the environment, law and order, social programs, culture, and gun control. Protest against a Liberal party whose shenanigans had shamed and disgusted Quebecers, and whose legacy on federalism seemed hostile to the province's aspirations. And protest most of all against the Bloc Québécois that was locked into a culture of complaint in Ottawa, where the question of sovereignty was not going to be resolved in any event. Certainly there is no reason to think that Quebecers voted with detailed knowledge of the NDP's history or policies. Their affinity to the social democratic voice of the party was more to its tone than its substance, perhaps. But the NDP vote was not just an expression of protest. Neither Layton's rhetoric nor the NDP's ads had been angry. They had been hopeful. In a focus-group study done immediately after the election, Ensight Canada reported, "We heard that the Bloc no longer represented the needs of the province, especially as sovereignty was not top of mind...Others had confidence Layton will try and bridge the divide between Quebec and the rest of Canada, but cautioned that he must be careful not to alienate the rest of the country."[9]

The small, concentrated media market in Quebec, and the much greater connection to a collective culture, had once again allowed the province to turn on a dime. It had in 1958 with the Diefenbaker sweep, in 1984 with Mulroney, and in 1993 with the BQ. In an era of declining partisanship nationally, Quebec has been in the forefront of spasmodic vote-switching. One of these sweeps, the BQ's, lasted six elections and eighteen years. Mulroney's lasted two elections and nine years. Diefenbaker's Quebec sweep was a singularity. While the NDP victory in Quebec was rightly hailed even by partisan opponents as a federalist victory, there is no evidence that it marked any sudden shift in Quebecers' attachment to Canada. Through most of its history in Quebec, the NDP's fortunes have been more or less inversely proportional to sovereigntist sentiment—that is to say, when support for sovereignty went up, the NDP went down.[10] But the breakthrough in 2011 was not associated with a collapse in support for sovereignty. Rather, it was that the salience of the issue had momentarily waned: many Quebecers seem to want to move on, as was suggested by the initial burst of popularity for François Legault's provincial party when it was created later in the year.

One post-election survey in the province noted that although two-thirds of NDP supporters said they had an attachment to Canada, this was almost precisely the provincial average, which had remained unchanged since before the election. Not surprisingly, Liberal and Conservative supporters were substantially more attached to Canada than were those of the NDP, while Bloc supporters were much, much less.[11] It seems that, while the NDP attracted much of its Quebec support directly from the BQ, it also won over former Liberal and Conservative voters in substantial numbers.[12]

It is very difficult to say how sustained the NDP's success in the province will be. Clearly, the 2011 victory demonstrated that there was a large universe of potential support in Quebec for a progressive federalist party—a truly historic turn and an important first step out of the power trap in which Canadian progressives have found themselves. The NDP's numbers sagged in Quebec after Layton's death and during the weak interim leadership of Nycole Turmel. But its support did not collapse, and the NDP quickly rebounded in the province in the immediate aftermath of native son Thomas Mulcair's accession to the leadership.

Organization—or the lack thereof—was unimportant in the NDP's 2011 victory in Quebec, because voters were motivated for change. As my Carleton colleague Elly Alboim astutely noted during the campaign when many doubted it, in "wave" elections, voters find their own way to the polls;[13] it is in the hard grind of a normal election year that parties need an organization to drag their supporters out to vote. The NDP will find it harder to forge the same close links with organized labour in Quebec that it has elsewhere, because most union leaders in that province have a long association with the sovereigntist movement.

The NDP now has a Quebec leader in Thomas Mulcair, and the party's candidates, now mostly MPs, will have much greater visibility in the next election. But the NDP was able only to raise its Quebec membership rolls to just over twelve thousand in the course of the leadership campaign in 2011–12, which works out to just a little more than two hundred for each of the party's MPs now sitting, and it is reasonable to suppose that no more than half of those voted in the 2012 leadership race.[14] That suggests a level of active support for the party in Quebec significantly below the critical mass it would require to run an effective province-wide, ground-based campaign. The decimation of the Bloc seems a much clearer result of the 2011 election in Quebec than the ascendancy of the NDP, though even that might be in doubt were there a recrudescence of sovereigntist support between now and 2015, something always possible. In an era of unaligned vot-ers, Quebec is the *ne plus ultra*. The Ensight study characterized some participants in its Montreal focus group this way: "Given their dissatisfaction with the Conservatives and Liberals, the NDP became the only remaining option for many voters. That NDP strength in the province may not last, many openly acknowl-edged, since Quebecers do not exhibit loyalty in their voting patterns. We found some belief that Layton was opportunistic in targeting Quebec."

ORANGE CRUSH

Outside of Quebec, the NDP's results were decidedly more mixed. In Ontario, the party gained seven percentage points in the popu-lar vote, tying them with the Liberals. But as the Liberals tumbled twenty-seven seats in the province, the NDP picked up just five to the Conservatives' twenty-two. That's the majority right there. And what about the West? The CCF had first bloomed there, and three of the four provinces have long traditions of electing NDP governments. In 2011, NDP support in British Columbia grew by about seven percentage points, and it gained three seats. But it lost two seats in Manitoba, didn't win any in Saskatchewan, and held on only to its lonely Alberta seat, albeit by a comfortable margin.

The Conservatives took seventy seats in the West to the NDP's fifteen. In Atlantic Canada the NDP picked up a meagre two seats, for a total of six, in the course of the best election in its history.

In English Canada, Layton ran an effective, if not quite spectacularly effective campaign. Strangely, all the parties in 2011 began their campaigns with narrowly political messages. Harper urged voters to help him stop the "reckless coalition" of the Liberals, NDP, and Bloc. Ignatieff said only he could stop Harper. Layton too urged voters to think tactically. He launched his tour with a stop in Edmonton, of all places, where the party had no more than dim prospects of making gains. His message: "Here in Edmonton, only New Democrats defeat Conservatives." And he repeated that theme in such places as Saskatchewan and the lower mainland of British Columbia, trying to undermine the Liberal message. Like Ignatieff, Layton attacked the Conservatives for their malfeasance in office, but with a particular New Democrat twist. Layton told that same audience in Edmonton that while Harper had been elected to fix Ottawa and end Liberal scandals, "He had simply replaced them with scandals of his own." This was a repetition of one of the oldest gambits in the NDP playbook: the Conservatives and Liberals are all the same, but we are different.

In the first week of the campaign, Layton was subjected to endless media speculation on his health. He publicly acknowledged that he was recovering from both prostate cancer and a (possibly related) broken hip. His campaign stops were less frequent than in previous elections, reporters noted, and the venues were smaller. Cameras fixed on the cane he carried on account of his hip, which sometimes seemed to embarrass him. But the party's organizers responded: cranking up Layton's schedule and making sure he appeared almost daily before large, enthusiastic audiences. Layton began to brandish his cane, as if to defy the media's storyline. If there was any surprise in the media's narrative about his health it was that their near-obsession with the topic in the first week did not return even when he was clearly destined to become leader of the opposition—and perhaps even something more.

By mid-campaign, Layton had steadied his tour but had not yet broken through in the polls. He did an extensive interview with Peter Mansbridge on the road, which makes fascinating viewing now.[15] Asked whether the party would make a quantum leap in the election, he replied: "I think we are laying the groundwork for it. You never really know in politics when that's going to happen. You can't actually predict it. And if you do, you're getting a little too cocky." Two days after the interview aired, the NDP busted loose in the polls. But the interview is interesting from another perspective. Layton was more explicit about his political strategy than he had ever been. Mansbridge put it to Layton that it was hard to see any difference between the NDP and the Liberals, except on Afghanistan. "The difference is in the record," Layton replied, saying that the Liberals had a history of breaking campaign promises. When Mansbridge pressed him whether it was really just the Liberals' record, as opposed to their policy, that defined the two parties, Layton answered: "The major difference is that we are committing to get things done. They've made commitments and then turned around and broken those commitments time and time again. That's the major difference." It is hard to say how deeply Layton really believed this. But it goes to his understanding of the voters both parties were chasing: that they wanted a party that was not just rhetorically progressive but progressive in its bones. It was also the closest Layton ever came in this election campaign to saying explicitly that the NDP's target was Liberal voters.[16]

Substantively, it is true that the NDP's platform was not very different from the Liberals' in 2011, in part because of a campaign lurch to the left by Michael Ignatieff. Unlike the Liberals (and more like the Conservatives), the NDP built on themes it had incorporated into its identity over many years: relief on credit card debt, better pensions, tax breaks to small businesses creating jobs, reversing corporate tax cuts, and an end to "subsidies" to corporate polluters. Unlike the Liberals, the NDP didn't feel the need to explain to the public precisely who they were: everyone knew. Their policies were aimed more at the economically insecure middle class than at the outright poor, and at progressive voters worried about climate change and inequality: swing Liberal voters, in other words.

One of the NDP's great tactical achievements in the 2011 campaign, which was among the most negative in our history, was to be negative without appearing to be so. It helped that the Liberal and Conservative attack ads had great similarities—unflattering pictures of the other party's leader, rendered in contrasty monochrome, with ominous, or sometimes sarcastic, voiceovers. "Deceit, Abuse, Contempt," said one Liberal ad. "Michael Ignatieff has a problem with the truth," began a Conservative one. The difference with the NDP ad campaign was not that it stayed away from attacking its opponents, even in personal ways, but that it stuck in the shiv in a light-hearted way, derived more from Jon Stewart or Rick Mercer than Fox TV. A health care ad in the party's "not so great Canadian moments" series started with a cartoon stage and a "ta-da" fanfare, followed by Terry-Gilliam–inspired graphics telling the story of an emergency room patient relegated to a stretcher in the Tim Hortons shop in a BC hospital. A cutout image of Harper with weirdly blinking eyes gave way to actuality of Layton, over rising music, delivering a hopeful message of determination to make things better. "I won't stop. Until. The job. Is done," he finished, in what became his signature phrase of the campaign.

One of Layton's most effective moments was in a personal attack on Ignatieff. During the English-language debate, he fired off an unexpected zinger: "Why do you have the worst attendance in the House of Commons?" he asked, claiming that the Liberal leader had failed to show up to vote 70 per cent of the time.[17] A more adept politician than Ignatieff might have sloughed off the comment by saying that he preferred to be out learning what Canadians think to squabbling endlessly in the House of Commons with professional politicians like Layton and Harper. But, instead, Ignatieff seemed unnerved and defensive. The NDP capitalized on the exchange by releasing another in their "not so great Canadian moments" ad series, this one claiming Layton had a 94 per cent attendance record, compared with 30 per cent for Ignatieff. It cleverly meshed with the Conservative trope, begun long before the campaign, "Ignatieff didn't come back for you." Another NDP ad showed a Monty-Pythonish cartoon cutout of Ignatieff flipping a pancake in a frying pan while standing in the House of Commons—a visual metaphor for his having "flip-flopped" on corporate tax cuts, the ad argued. It was so cute you barely noticed that the NDP was ripping the poor man to shreds, just as the Tories had been doing for two years.

Layton's claim that the NDP was best situated to grab votes from the Conservatives, particularly in Western Canada, was not borne out by the results. In fact, on the prairies, where the philosophy of markets has, perhaps, its deepest hold, the NDP's vote grew but it lost one seat to the Conservatives and another to the Liberals.[18] In British Columbia, two of its three gains came at the expense of the Liberals. In other words, there was no net gain at all by the NDP from the Conservatives in the West. In English Canada more broadly, the NDP made its gains by tearing at the flailing Liberal party from one end as the Conservatives mauled the other. For example, according to a massive post-election online poll conducted by Ipsos Reid, the NDP took an impressive 41 per cent of the votes among immigrants who had arrived in the last ten years, and 38 per cent of visible minority immigrants—much more than either of its rivals. The NDP also succeeded, despite a conspicuous lack of effort, in another demographic where its principal opponent had been the Liberal party: young people. One post-election survey suggested that the party had surged from just 24 per cent support among 18–24 year olds prior to the campaign to 44 per cent by the end. The NDP led among young people in every province except Alberta.[19]

It is an easy leap from here to the conclusion made by many Liberals late in the campaign and again after the election that the NDP had "split the vote," particularly in Ontario. The premise for this claim is that the eight-percentage-point growth in the NDP vote was largely responsible for the nine-point Liberal decline, thereby allowing Tories to "come up through the middle," taking 73 of the province's 106 seats, and guaranteeing them a majority. Though superficially appealing, the evidence for this is not particularly strong. If vote-splitting means anything, it would be that the Conservatives won seats, not by wooing former Liberal voters, but because the growing strength of the NDP pulled down Liberal opponents. But, for the most part, in ridings where the Liberals lost seats to the Conservatives they appear to have done so because they lost votes to the Conservatives. In seats where the Liberals lost to the NDP, they did so because they lost votes to the NDP.[20] Take the example of Mississauga-Brampton South, a hotly contested riding in which the Liberal incumbent and rising Liberal star Navdeep Bains lost to the Conservative, Eve Adams. In the days after the campaign, the *Globe and Mail* casually referred to the riding as an illustration of vote-splitting.[21] It is true that the NDP increased its support by about four thousand votes over its total in 2008. However, Bains lost to the Conservative Adams by roughly five thousand votes. Moreover, the Green vote shrank by almost two thousand votes, which must account for at least some of the NDP gains. The best explanation for Bains's loss is straightforward: the Conservatives increased in strength by nine thousand votes between 2008 and 2011, and much of that increase came directly from the Liberals.

The most important single reason that the Conservatives did so well in Ontario in 2011 was that they increased their own support from 39 per cent to 44 per cent, while the total vote for progressive parties—the NDP, Liberals and the Greens—fell from 60 per cent to 55 per cent. One element in this shift was likely a reaction by "blue Liberals" to the prospect of a strong NDP, which led them to move their votes to the Conservatives late in the campaign. In Ensight's report on the focus groups it conducted in Toronto, it commented that "we heard a great deal of fear of NDP policies attributable to the province's years under Bob Rae." The bad news for progressives is that there was a genuine underlying shift to the Conservatives; the good news is that many of the blue Liberals, whose desertion might arguably compromise the future prospects for progressives, have already gone.

DIPSY DOODLE?

The achievement of Jack Layton and the NDP in the 2011 election might well be transformative. The NDP is now a truly national party, with substantial representation on both sides of Canada's linguistic divide. It has seats in every province but two. It is Canada's official opposition, and not by a small margin. It has three times the seats that the Liberals do, based on winning 4.5 million votes to the Liberals' 2.8 million. Though the Conservatives are shutting off the per-vote subsidy to political parties, the New Democrats automatically receive considerable new resources as a result of their breakthrough. With 102 MPs[22] paid full-time to do the party's work, each with staffs in Ottawa and in their ridings, and additional resources for the leader's office and parliamentary research, the NDP is now operating on a whole new level. Most important, unless they falter the media and the electorate will treat them as the obvious alternative to the Harper government. Increased visibility should allow them to raise more money. This sets up the possibility of further gains in the 2015 election if

Canadians tire of Harper and his party after nine years.

But there are just as many reasons to imagine 2011 may turn out to be the apex of the NDP's success. Jack Layton is gone, and cannot be replaced. As Brian Topp remarked during the leadership campaign, the Jack Layton who won the leadership in 2003 could not have replaced the mature Jack Layton of 2011, who had been leader for almost eight years and was fighting his third election. The Conservatives will naturally try to take down Thomas Mulcair with a barrage of TV attack ads, which played a role in the unmaking of Stéphane Dion and Michael Ignatieff. Moreover, NDPers are if anything more easily caricatured by the Conservatives than the Liberals were: as ferocious taxers and incontinent spenders, as tools of malevolent labour bosses, as the enemies of international trade, as wild-eyed radicals who would rather sit down for tea with Palestinian militants than have a beer with the president of the United States. Outside of Quebec, New Democrats are the party of the less-well-off. Ironically, insecurities about their middle class status might make it difficult for some voters to identify with the NDP as they once did with the Liberals.

Mulcair's apparent centrist leanings might make it harder for the Conservatives (and the Liberals) to pin some of the stereotypes on him that might have succeeded with a more traditional choice as leader—Peggy Nash, for example. However, unlike Layton, whose roots in the party were deep and who was trusted by the party's moderate left, Mulcair will be subject to close internal scrutiny whenever he deviates from the NDP's traditional policy lines.

The NDP also has significant regional challenges. The first will be to put down roots in Quebec, socially and organizationally. Mulroney managed to increase his hold on Quebec in 1988 after his sweep of the province in 1984, but he did so on the strength of free trade, which was popular in Quebec, and the support of Robert Bourassa's provincial Liberals. It will not be easy to meld a young, inexperienced NDP caucus from Quebec with the stalwarts from English Canada, who have always tended to be more federalist and centralist than the party's official platform. Along with greater media coverage will come greater scrutiny, and since conflict is a core news value, the party's internal tensions will now be played out on the front pages in a way that it is unaccustomed to.

In the West, the region from which the party sprung, and which contributed the majority of its seats in all but one election prior to Layton's leadership, the party appears to be in gentle decline. In 2011, its banner year nationally, the party won just fifteen seats in the region, one less than its historical average. In Saskatchewan, the sagging fortunes of the provincial party did not help; but how about Manitoba, where the provincial party would win an unprecedented fourth consecutive victory just a few months after the federal party was reduced to just two seats? Put another way, the NDP is looking a little like the Liberal party did for forty years: capable of winning seats in BC in a good year, but largely frozen out of the Prairies. In the country's fastest-growing and most economically dynamic region, the Conservatives' market philosophy is ascendant, creating an increasingly tough environment for the NDP. Mulcair is not well known in the West and may seem to some like yet another in a long line of national leaders from Quebec who didn't "get" the region.

In Ontario, where the NDP would have to make its big gains if it were ever to form a government, its 25 per cent share of the popular vote was actually lower than it got in the West, if you leave out Alberta. However, its strategic position is quite different in Ontario, which is where its future may be determined. Unlike the West, where its central task is to retain what it has and perhaps begin to reverse its decline, or Quebec, where the party needs to consolidate its gains, Ontario offers the possibility of a second breakthrough, from official opposition to government, and possibly even to majority government. And the NDP's strategic target in Ontario is inevitably going to be former Liberal voters, who overwhelmingly say that the NDP is their second choice. There were as many Liberal as NDP voters in Ontario in 2011. Just as Chrétien and Martin were once able to appeal to NDP sympathizers to cast a "strategic" vote for the Liberals to stop the Conservatives, Mulcair may be able to pull that trick in reverse. Perhaps in 2015 Liberal sympathizers in Ontario will vote for the NDP for strategic reasons.

However, the NDP's task is more daunting than it may first appear. In most of the Ontario seats that the Conservatives now hold, the runner-up was a Liberal. Indeed, many of the twenty-two seats the Conservatives gained in Ontario in 2011 were taken by razor-thin margins from the Liberals. In the Greater Toronto Area in particular, the Liberals lost Etobicoke Centre to a Conservative by less than thirty votes, and five other seats by less than a thousand. In only one seat, Bramalea-Gore-Malton, did the NDP candidate leapfrog past the Liberal incumbent to run a close second.[23] Moreover, all the seats the Conservatives picked up from the Liberals in the GTA were won by Dalton McGuinty's Liberals in the 2011 provincial election on identical boundaries, with the exception, once again, of Bramalea-Gore-Malton, which was won by the NDP. Even if the NDP is running ahead of the Liberals in the polls nationally in 2015, it may still have difficulty persuading progressive voters that it is in the best position to defeat Conservatives in the old Liberal bastion of the GTA, as well as in the fertile crescent stretching around Lake Ontario.

After Layton's death, at the outset of its 2011–2012 leadership race, the NDP had three strategic options, to oversimplify just a bit. The first was to move to the centre, leaving no oxygen for the Liberals, but distancing itself to a degree from organized labour and some of its traditional policies, such as the reflexive suspicion of free trade. The second was to re-emphasize its traditional social democratic policies, lay out the clearest possible set of alternative policies to the government on the economy and the environment, and try to capture some of the unsettled energy around movements ranging from organized labour to Occupy Wall Street. The third was to seek out some sort of collaboration with the Liberals, whether tactical, as in joint nominations for parliament in 2015, or strategic, as in a full-fledged party alliance or merger. Each of these options was canvassed in the leadership race. Brian Topp, Paul Dewar, and Peggy Nash each in different ways emphasized the NDP's traditions and distinctiveness. Nathan Cullen daringly advocated outright cooperation with the Liberal party.

In choosing Thomas Mulcair, the NDP appeared to decide on the first course. He was the most experienced politician among the candidates running, having served in Quebec's Liberal cabinet. He was the best-known in Quebec, with the widest support among its new MPs from that province, and so best positioned to hang onto the party's 2011 gains there. He had the combative personality seemingly best matched against Stephen Harper, and best able to shove aside Bob Rae, who had usurped the role of leader of the opposition during Nycole Turmel's interim leadership. And he was the candidate least tied to the party's social and political traditions on the left. For the first time since the nascent NDP picked Tommy Douglas as its first leader in 1961, the party chose someone primarily because its members thought he just might be a winner. As his convention backdrop, Mulcair had a huge sign saying *"Progressives United."* It was a promise not just to rally the NDP's existing supporters and activists, but to woo away the remainder of the Liberal party's electoral base. The danger, of course, is that as it mutates under Mulcair the NDP may begin to look inauthentic, just as the Liberals have sometimes done, and fail to sculpt a genuine alternative to Conservative policy that can be enacted in office. It might also create dissension in the NDP that could be exploited by the other parties.

But in 2012, NDPers were in the mood to pick a winner, not a true believer. This was due partly to the heady dreams inspired by Jack Layton's success in 2011. It was also a reflection of the long, strange decline of Canada's "natural governing party."

CHAPTER 5

WHY THE LIBERALS' STRANGE DECLINE

Whatever its origins,[1] the phrase "natural governing party" was popularized by the political humorist Allan Fotheringham as a sardonic tribute to the Liberals' arrogance. Much to the consternation of his aides, Michael Ignatieff picked up the phrase and used it in a serious tone for a while after he became leader—as if it hadn't occurred to him that it might not have the same appeal to others as it did to him. But then, after more than a year on the job, he proclaimed the phrase was henceforth forbidden. "We have to have the courage to tell ourselves things we don't want to listen to," he told his caucus, as if he were sharing an internal struggle. "We have to listen to people that the party has not listened to. We have to open the doors and open the windows…That is the process by which a great party earns—earns—the right to be the next government of Canada. We talk too easily within this party about being the natural party of government. If I can achieve one thing as a leader of this party, it's to get that out of our vocabulary."[2] It was what the Victorians would have called a self-restraining ordinance, and one long overdue.

Arguably, the Liberal party has been in decline since the 1950s, and there has been no "natural governing party" since.[3] Between Confederation and Diefenbaker's first victory in 1957, the Liberals won thirteen elections. Their average share of the popular vote in those winning elections was 47 per cent, or very nearly a majority of the electorate. In five out of those 13 elections, the Liberals took 50 per cent or more of the popular vote. It is certainly true that the Liberals continued to dominate Canada's public life in the half-century after Diefenbaker's defeat in 1963. However, they won those elections much less impressively. The Liberals' average popular vote in winning elections since 1963 is just 41 per cent. Their strongest performance was in the 1968 Trudeau "landslide," when they won 46 per cent of the vote, just short of the *average* for the earlier period. The Liberals have not won a single "true majority," in Peter Russell's phrase—of votes as well as seats, that is—in the last half-century.

So how is it that the Liberal party continued to dominate our politics, usually with majority governments, long after it ceased even to aspire to win a majority of our votes? The explanation is that the electoral grip of the Liberals and their main rivals, the Progressive Conservatives, had been weakened by the emergence of third parties. In every election but one prior to the 1950s, third parties took less than 10 per cent of the vote in total.[4] In the last half century, in contrast, there has been a host of smaller parties with significant impact: the New Democratic Party, Social Credit, the Créditistes, Reform, the Bloc Québécois, and latterly the Greens. Even in the midst of Trudeaumania in 1968, smaller parties won 22 per cent of the vote. When Jean Chrétien won the largest of his victories, in 1993, they took more than 36 per cent of the vote.[5] It is has been routine in recent decades for smaller parties collectively to take about a third of the vote at election time.[6] These new entries into the party system invariably had more popular roots than the Liberals, and had paradoxical effects. They chipped away at Liberal support, but they divided the electorate up into smaller chunks. And this, through the magic of first-past-the-post, allowed the Liberals to win elections with fewer votes—for a while.

SLIP SLIDIN' AWAY

For a significant chunk of the twentieth century, the cabinet table *was* the Liberal party, or, at least, its heart, soul, brain, and nervous system. The cabinets of William Lyon Mackenzie King and Louis St. Laurent represented some of the most important strands in the economic, social, regional, and linguistic fabric of the country. There was C. D. Howe, representing industry; Paul Martin (Sr.), a socially liberal francophone Ontarian from a union-dominated seat in Windsor; Jimmy Gardiner from Saskatchewan, presiding over a patronage machine to rival Tammany Hall's; Jack Pickersgill, and eventually Lester Pearson, representing the bureaucracy. In an important sense, they *were* the Liberal party— a coming-together of disparate interests at the parliamentary and governmental level. Their fights were mainly behind closed doors. The *extra*-parliamentary Liberal party had so little influence on government affairs that it did not meet in national convention even once between the leadership selection of Mackenzie King in 1919 and that of St. Laurent in 1948. If anything, St. Laurent was less interested in the extra-parliamentary party than King was. At election time, it was the regional barons in cabinet, plus a few outside it—Newfoundland's Joey Smallwood, for example—who were expected to rev up their personal organizations for the fight and, often, to raise the money to fuel it. The party's appeal to disparate communities with sometimes conflicting objectives was that it was a proven winner. By voting for the party of government, you could get some of what you wanted in policy terms, and maybe a little patronage on the side. That was the deal.

The Liberals' winning formula frayed first in the West—a

region they had dominated for half a century. In 1953, the last election before Diefenbaker's victory, the Liberals were past their peak in the region, but they remained the largest party.[7] Still, the West had been chafing at the Liberals' style of brokerage politics for a while, flirting with the Progressives in the 1920s, and increasingly opting for the CCF and Social Credit provincially. Although Diefenbaker led a major party, he came from the West and very much had the flavour of a third-party politician. Diefenbaker was no Bay Street Conservative, part of the reason the West remained loyal to him long after he lost his grip, first on power, and then, seemingly, on political reality. The Liberals did not win a single seat in the West in 1958. They won a few seats back under Pearson and managed twenty-seven seats in the Trudeaumania election, nearly two-thirds of them in British Columbia, but that would never happen again. Since then, the Liberals have been lucky to crack into double digits in the West, retaining an increasingly tenuous grip in British Columbia and in the prairie cities. In 2011, they won just four seats.[8]

It was not an option for the Liberal party, in response to the setbacks of the 1950s, to become a populist party itself—something that would have betrayed its history and compromised its considerable residual strength in the country's corporate, intellectual, and bureaucratic elites. But it did adapt to the challenge of this new competition. In fact, the 1960s were the years in which the Liberals became a modern, professionalized party that mimicked some of the policies and structures of their populist opponents.[9] Under Lester Pearson's leadership, the Liberals held the 1960 Kingston conference, a meeting of about two hundred hand-picked liberal-minded intellectuals, who proposed a new program of social reform. Their ideas were translated into party policy by the "National Rally"—a Liberal policy convention held in Ottawa the next year, and carefully stage-managed by the young Paul Hellyer, MP, and the progressive-minded nationalist

Walter Gordon, who had not yet entered parliament.[10]

The program that emerged shifted the party away from the business-oriented policies of the St. Laurent years towards a more socially conscious agenda, including improved pensions and medicare. Pearson also wedged off of Diefenbaker's effusive anglophilia and instinctive anti-Americanism to forge a new, more inclusive national identity, which would be one of the Liberal party's most distinctive contributions to Canadian life. Dief's Conservatives attacked the new maple leaf flag introduced by Pearson because of its abandonment of the British tradition— precisely its appeal to new Canadians and Quebecers, as well as to nationalists in English Canada. The centennial celebration of 1967, with Expo 67 in Montreal as its centrepiece, embedded the Liberal vision of nationality into our national consciousness, with its bilingualism, multiculturalism, cosmopolitanism, and modernity. For many Canadians, these Liberal values came to be seen as *Canadian* values.

The new Liberalism created in the Pearson era had popular appeal, but it was the product of an elite of political pros closely tied to the leader. In these same years, Walter Gordon and his acolyte Keith Davey, a former ad salesman, expanded the extra-parliamentary Liberal party into a much broader, membership-based organization. They set up a formal system of fundraising and eliminated some of the low-level patronage of the earlier era. Constituency organizations would become more active, peaking at election time, but having some continuous life and sending delegates to increasingly regular national party conventions. Party workers got manuals and workshops to professionalize their campaign techniques. Davey, known as "the Rainmaker" during his many elections as campaign director, introduced scientific polling to the Liberal party arsenal, and lashed it closely to campaign strategy, policy, and advertising. The strong, centralized national organization he built displaced the regional and special-interest barons of an earlier era, like Gardiner and Howe. Although Trudeau toyed with the trendy notion of participatory democracy in the Liberal party when he first became prime minister,[11] he was nothing if not an elitist by temperament. Trudeau was never going to be a man who took his directions from a party convention. For a time, he even cold-shouldered the political pros, thinking he could do it all on his own. The shuddering near-defeat of 1972, however, thrust him back into their embrace, and returned party management to people like Davey and his protégé Jim Coutts.

Until it foundered on internal divisions, the Liberals' professional class of political apparatchiks, perched in ministers' offices, or in lobbying, polling, and advertising firms, constituted one of the Liberal party's most substantial "natural" advantages over its rivals. One of their jobs was to stage-manage the party to fit the strategic objectives of the leaders. In his memoirs, Jean Chrétien's closest political aide, Eddie Goldenberg, explained how the Aylmer conference of 1991, which imitated some of the features of the Kingston conference, was important in steering the party away from its opposition to free trade.[12] Michael Ignatieff held a similar conference in Montreal in 2010, this time supplemented by real-time video streaming and social media input. But when he summed up at the end of the weekend, he ignored most of what he had heard and replaced it with a program clearly devised in advance.[13] A former senior executive of the party remarked to me a couple of years ago that getting party members involved in policy development was a "noble lie."

In contrast with more populist parties, including the New Democrats, where there is a never-resolved tension between the idealism of its members and the practical compromises of its leaders and managers, Liberals have occasionally grumbled, but for the most part have meekly accepted the dominance of leaders and their cadre of apparatchiks. Party members may have criticized their performance when they lost elections, but not their legitimacy. Even at their successful 2012 post-defeat convention, heralded as the start of a new era of openness and renewal, delegates opted to preserve the leader's veto over the election platform.

WHAT QUEBEC WANTS…AND DOESN'T

The Liberals' new definition of Canadian nationality, fashioned in the 1960s, was in part a response to the Quiet Revolution, by then well under way in Quebec, and one of its great virtues was its openness to francophone Quebecers, their language, and their aspirations in a wider Canadian community. But unlike in English Canada, where it filled a cultural void, in Quebec it competed with an already well-rooted and rapidly flowering Québécois nationalism. That contest framed the most familiar aspect of the Liberal party's strange decline: the apparently irretrievable loss of fortress Quebec. From Laurier's first election in 1896 until the Diefenbaker sweep in 1958, the Liberals never failed to win at least thirty-six seats, or roughly half the province. Even when the party did well in the rest of the country, Quebec MPs always made up well over a third of the party's caucus in Ottawa. In 1958, the party was reduced to twenty-five seats when the Union Nationale machine swung in behind Diefenbaker's Tories, but it recovered substantially under Pearson. Under Trudeau, it returned to absolute dominance, peaking not in the Trudeaumania election of 1968, in which it won "only" fifty-six of seventy-four, but in Trudeau's last run, in 1980, with René Lévesque in power in Quebec City, when the Liberals took all the province's seats but one.

It has been the peculiar curse of Liberal governments since then to be on the right side of Quebec public opinion in the moment, but appear later to have been on the wrong side of history. Trudeau's most dramatic interventions each enjoyed contemporaneous support in Quebec polls: the imposition of the

War Measures Act, the campaign for the "No" in the sovereignty referendum of 1980, and the patriation of the Constitution. The same was true of Jean Chrétien's *Clarity Act* in 1999. But the Liberals' opponents, including Lévesque, Brian Mulroney, and Lucien Bouchard, wove a highly credible narrative that pictured the Liberal party as a federalist bully standing athwart the road to every legitimate aspiration Quebecers sought for over a quarter of a century.[14] Since 1984, when Mulroney swept Quebec, the Liberals have won the popular vote in the province only once (in 2000) and have never again won the majority of the seats. The Liberals' reputation in Quebec congealed around their party's tortured reaction to Mulroney's Meech Lake Accord, which split the Liberal party in two—the low point coming when some Paul Martin supporters denounced Chrétien as a *vendu,* or sell-out, helping to poison the party's Quebec turf for good. When the Progressive Conservatives collapsed in Quebec, it was the charismatic sovereigntist Lucien Bouchard and his nascent Bloc Québécois that reaped the rewards in a populist upswelling.

Martin dreamed of reaching out to "soft nationalist" Quebecers once he had ousted Chrétien as leader. He dumped the outspoken federalist Stéphane Dion from cabinet, and appointed the former BQ MP Jean Lapierre as his Quebec lieutenant.[15] It was the Liberals' last best hope at returning to dominance in Quebec—and the Liberals briefly did return to first place in the opinion polls. But it was not to be. In the 2004 election, the sponsorship scandal, which was centred in Quebec and had its greatest impact there, created a heavy odour around the Liberal party brand. By mid-campaign, desperate to stave off complete collapse in the province, Martin called Dion off the bench to reprise his role as the slayer of separatists. Martin decided, in other words, to polarize the election in Quebec around the issue of separation, further solidifying the party's ultra-federalist image in the province. From the party's post-Trudeau high of thirty-six Quebec seats in

2000, the party slumped into the teens in the twenty-first century, and into single digits in the 2011 election. It would have fallen even further if it had not been for the strong personal following of candidates such as Justin Trudeau and Irwin Cotler. When the BQ finally did collapse, it was hit by an orange, not a red, wave.

HAPPY CAMPERS

So the Liberals lost the West and Quebec, had a slipping grip on minority communities, and found themselves facing parties whose populist energy they would have trouble matching. How then to explain that Jean Chrétien ended up being the second-longest-serving prime minister in half a century? Part of the explanation is surely Chrétien's gifts as a politician and statesman. Having come to office in 1963 by defeating a sitting Créditiste MP, he knew how to beat populists at their own game. Despite being six feet tall and having spent the better part of thirty years in parliament before becoming prime minister, he could still fashion himself the *p'tit gars de Shawinigan*. But it was not just Chrétien. In 1993, the Liberals had two assets that would not survive into the next century. The first was an indisputable edge in the quality of their professionalism and organization. And the second was a divided conservative movement, particularly in Ontario.

For the election of 1993, Chrétien assembled one of the best campaign teams ever in Canada. Not for nothing that the first time I stumbled across the Chrétien press corps in an Edmonton hotel bar during the early days of the campaign were they singing, to the tune of the old Barbra Streisand song: "Reporters… that cover Liberals…are the luckiest reporters in the world!" The tour ran on time, its photo-ops worked, and there was even a rose on the tray table of female reporters when they joined the campaign plane. The Chrétien team included personal loyalists like Eddie Goldenberg, Jean Pelletier, John Rae, and Jean Carle, party veterans like Gordon Ashworth and David Smith, and shiny new recruits like Peter Donolo and David MacInnis. Most striking, Chrétien had his bitter leadership rival, Paul Martin, co-author the party platform.[16] Eleven days into the campaign, the Liberals surprised their rivals by releasing the famous Red Book, probably the most detailed platform ever presented by a Canadian political party. It ran 112 pages in English and contained a chart at the back purporting to show how its spending promises could be squared with a reduced deficit. With every chance he got, Chrétien waved the Red Book in the air, and it was the centrepiece of an effective ad in which he said, "We have the people. We have the plan." When reporters had a question, they were referred to Paul Martin's aide, Terrie O'Leary, who would unload torrents of information from within a cloud of cigarette smoke, sitting at the back of the media smoking bus (there were still such things in those days).

From one perspective, the results of the 1993 election were unremarkable. They could be seen as simply the swing of the pendulum, back to the Liberals after nine years of Tory rule. The Liberals took 177 seats, a comfortable majority. As befitted a national party, they won seats in every single province and territory. However, the foundation of the victory was Ontario, where the party won a stunning ninety-eight of ninety-nine seats. The Liberals' ability to repeat this trick of winning virtually every Ontario seat in three successive elections under Chrétien is astounding. All the more so given that in 1995 Ontarians swept Mike Harris to power provincially, leading the most conservative provincial government in living memory. The key to the Liberals' success was not just that their policies were superbly attuned to Ontario—which they were—but also that, federally, there were two conservative parties locked in a power trap. In about a quarter of the seats the Liberals won Ontario in 1993, they had fewer votes than the combined total of the Progressive Conservative and Reform party candidates. Had the Liberals lost these seats to a united conservative party—and just a few others like them in other provinces—Chrétien would never have had his first majority. His government would have looked more like Pearson's than Trudeau's—demonstrating, in other words, the party's relative weakness even in victory. But conservatives did not unite, as it happened, until Chretien's very last week in office, in 2003.

The 1993 election was also remarkable for another reason: the willingness of voters to switch parties and the huge changes in the party system that resulted. The political scientist Jon Pammett estimated that more than half of those who voted in both 1988 and 1993 switched parties. This was a dramatic illustration of how far Canadians had become "de-aligned" from political parties, which would have to win the voters' allegiance anew in every election campaign. Although it was not yet fully clear in 1993, this dramatic switching was the prelude to the destruction of the Progressive Conservative party: more of its voters from 1988 moved to the Liberals or the BQ than remained loyal. The NDP lost a million and a half votes between 1988 and 1993, and its nine-person caucus would not be enough to maintain official party status.[17]

More remarkably, nearly half of Quebecers voted for a party that had not even existed in 1988, the Bloc Québécois. Perhaps two-thirds of those voters supported outright Quebec sovereignty, while the remainder were unhappy about the constitutional status quo in the wake of the failures of Meech Lake and Charlottetown.[18] The BQ took very nearly half the votes in Quebec, and because of our first-past-the-post system won fifty-four of Quebec's seventy-five seats, shutting the Liberals out of francophone Quebec with the exception of a few redoubts such as Chrétien's seat in the Mauricie. The Reform party, meanwhile, went from the single seat it had won in a by-election in 1989 to fifty-two when the dust had settled.

THE LITTLE RED BOOK

The Liberal party had long been divided between social Liberals like Paul Martin (Sr.) and business Liberals like C. D. Howe. The party's vaunted centrism was a reflection of compromise within the Liberal cabinet as much as it was among the elements in Canadian society that the party represented. This was key to its success as a brokerage party. But in the latter part of the twentieth century these two traditions in the party hardened into rival camps in the course of several leadership battles. In the convention of 1968, Trudeau won only on the fourth ballot over a now-forgotten businessman, Robert Winters.[19] Trudeau included many business Liberals in his cabinet, including Edgar Benson and Donald Macdonald. But he was unafraid to intervene in the economy, as he showed most dramatically with the National Energy Program in his last mandate, and this triggered a degree of rebelliousness among business Liberals, most of whom eventually gravitated to John Turner. There was a clear line in the party from Winters to Turner to Martin, just as there was from Trudeau to Chrétien.

The Liberal party of the 1990s and early 2000s would be defined by the battle between its leadership rivals, Chrétien and Martin. But their vicious factional struggle disguised the fact that the two men did not differ as sharply over policy as had their respective predecessors in the social and business Liberal camps. In fact, the 1993 Red Book, in which both Chrétien and Martin had a hand, is a pretty good place to start in defining the modern Liberal party. The Red Book portrays a party of progressive impulses with a clear eye to the practicalities of governing. Its major promises were a renegotiation of the North American Free Trade Agreement (NAFTA), reduction of the deficit to 3 per cent of GDP, replacing the GST, the creation of fifty thousand new childcare spaces, a large increase in immigration levels, and a national infrastructure and job-creation program. First shown to reporters in a "lock-up" meant to imitate the release of govern-

ment budgets, the Red Book would show up again in the years
that followed when Chrétien would summon up "Red Book
report cards," ticking off commitments as they were supposedly
honoured. But the true story of the Red Book—and the government it framed—is one of a party whose progressive impulses
were quietly muted in a largely collaborative project between
Chrétien and his finance minister.

Of all the big promises, the quickest to go was the pledge to
renegotiate NAFTA. The 1988 election had been fought primarily over NAFTA's predecessor, the free trade agreement with the
United States. Globalized trade was to a degree inevitable and
desirable, and Canada needed to be part of it. But the terms on
which this globalization took place were proposed worldwide
by businesses, and keenly adopted by conservative politicians
including Reagan, Thatcher, and Mulroney. Not surprisingly, the
corporations that promoted the lowering of trade barriers and
investment regulations were also the chief beneficiaries. And, not
coincidentally, working people and governments lost considerable leverage in the process. In 1988, John Turner had defied his
backers in big business and tried to capture the popular anguish,
calling the battle against Mulroney's government's free trade
agreement with the United States "the fight of my life." But neither Paul Martin nor Jean Chrétien supported Turner's crusade.
Martin had just come from big business, and Chrétien was enjoying his only hiatus from politics, acquiring some personal wealth
working in a corporate law firm. After becoming leader in 1990,
Chrétien began to soften the party's opposition to free trade, and
he got virtually no resistance from the former Turner camp, most
of whom had become Martin supporters. As prime minister, he
did make a half-hearted attempt to interest President Clinton in
renegotiating NAFTA but it wasn't going anywhere and the whole
matter was quickly dropped. And thus ended the Liberal party's
brief spasm of critical interest in the details of globalization.

But of all the promises that might have misled a voter, the most substantial was certainly the Red Book commitment to reduce the deficit to 3 per cent of GDP. At first you may think: now, wait a minute, wasn't deficit reduction the defining feature of the Chrétien government? How could a promise to cut the deficit have been misleading? Here's how. By 1993, the Canadian public was well aware that the deficit was a real problem. Interest payments on the debt had become the largest single element in the federal budget—and they were rising. The deficit was not only crowding out new initiatives; it was leading to demands for cuts to existing programs. In the 1993 election campaign, Kim Campbell, who had succeeded Mulroney as prime minister earlier that year, pledged to eliminate the deficit altogether, as did the Reform leader, Preston Manning. In the Red Book, the Liberals tried to signal that they were serious about the problem while reassuring progressives that they were not about to go on Sherman's March to the Sea. In contrast to their rivals, they pledged to cut the deficit to 3 per cent of GDP—a benchmark borrowed from the European Union. To the extent that Chrétien explained how he would get even that far, it was by invoking populist implausibilities like ending the controversial EH-101 helicopter purchase and reducing the size of ministers' offices.

Within less than a year of coming to power, however, the government decided to eliminate the deficit completely. Let me be clear: I believe that deficits matter. I subscribe to Tommy Douglas's dictum that governments that run up excessive debt deliver themselves into the hands of bankers and investors, who seldom care about the human cost of their diktats. And this, more or less, was what happened in the 1990s here in Canada. In his autobiography, Paul Martin says his epiphany came after his 1994 budget when he took a tour of the world's financial capitals—New York, London, Tokyo—and was instructed that he had to cut much, much deeper if he was going to avoid an upward spiral in interest rates.[20] The *Wall Street Journal* called Canada a "third world country" because of its rising debt. Of course, deficits can be reduced by raising taxes as well as by cutting spending. But here too the Liberals found themselves in a bind. Raising taxes would only scare away the increasingly liquid pools of capital created by globalization that Canada would need to extract itself from recession. It seemed self-evident, then, that deficit reduction would come mainly through budget cuts, including transfers to the provinces for health, education, and welfare, that would course like a shock wave through the system in the next couple of years. Unemployment insurance was slashed as well. It was a much more dramatic reduction in the social safety net than Mulroney ever attempted—or, for that matter, than Stephen Harper ever has.

Martin came very close to resigning over his demand for one additional cut—an increased clawback of old age pensions—believing it was a matter of fairness[21] that everyone, including seniors, take a hit. In his autobiography Chrétien says this made sense in theory, but that it "it didn't take into account the real lives of ordinary people."[22] Chrétien quotes a university friend, Angèle Garceau, saying that women would be furious because, "after thirty or forty years of begging their husbands for every cent, [women] can buy themselves a new hat or take a friend out for cake and coffee without answering to anybody." What is so fascinating about this dispute is that the question of social need didn't come into it. Martin's scheme had been crafted to spare low-income families. Chrétien's fanciful anecdote has a kind of homey feminism to it, but is explicitly not about need: the woman in the story is using her pension cheque to buy a hat or some cake. Nor, for Chrétien, was it about the principle of universality in social programs. "In theory," he says, Martin's proposal made sense. In the end, the resolution to the dispute between Martin and Chrétien was not ideological but *political.*

Chrétien was concerned that by goring one ox too many Martin would destroy support for the budget and, potentially, the government. But Chrétien was prime minister, and likely a better judge of the politics, too, and he won the round.

Of the six major commitments in the Red Book, only the infrastructure program ever came to be. Paul Martin eventually apologized for failing to replace the GST,[23] which he decided was indispensable to the deficit fight. Far from jacking up immigration targets, the government actually imposed what amounted to a head-tax on applications, to raise money. And the childcare pledge was never seriously pursued. Everything, it seemed, had been subordinated to the deficit fight.

So how come a Liberal party would so meekly accept such a conservative policy? Lloyd Axworthy, the Liberals' left-leaning human resources minister, was in the midst of a social policy review that was simply overtaken by the relentless demands from Martin's department of finance for cuts. There was grumbling, but not a single resignation from cabinet or the caucus. Brian Tobin, perceived to be on the left of the party, became an enthusiastic member of the so-called "Star Chamber" that brought ministers in to serve up cuts from their departments. Sergio Marchi accepted the steep head-tax on immigrants, although with some bitterness. When Sheila Copps resigned to run in a by-election, it wasn't about cuts to social programs (or NAFTA, for that matter), but about Martin's failure to "scrap the GST" as she had promised the Liberals would, in her 1993 campaign.

Part of the answer must be in the Liberal party's anomalous history and structure. Practically unique internationally among parties of the centre-left, the Liberals have never sought the formal support of organized labour. Even the Democratic party in the United States derives substantial financial and organizational support from the unions. While the Democrats have never been dominated by labour, as the British Labour party once was, they do need to consider its demands, making sure they will pay a price for moving too far to the right.

Remember too, that while there had been reforms to party financing over the years, the Liberals remained heavily dependent on business donations for their operations and campaigns. One of Chrétien's great behind-the-scenes contributions to the Liberal party was to *increase* corporate fundraising, by 12 per cent in 1992 alone, to $8 million—something made easier by the party's drift towards free trade.[24] Many of the people closest to Chrétien came from the business world, including John Rae, Gordon Ashworth, and David Smith. Only Chaviva Hošek, among his closest advisors, came from a background of social activism. So the extra-parliamentary party was mainly funded and directed at its senior levels by businesspeople. Whatever misgivings they might have felt at so suddenly changing directions from the progressive rhetoric of the campaign—and it has to be said that none of them ever spoke up—the budgets matched the norms of the social and business milieux in which they circulated.

Over time, the party's drift was unmistakable. The Liberals' fierce opposition to the "Mulroney trade deal" in 1988 had turned out to be no more than a mirage. Their role as defenders of the caring state was compromised with cuts to health care, unemployment insurance, and welfare. Climate change was the subject of reverent concern and resolute inaction. Hobbled by the sponsorship scandal, Paul Martin managed one last blast of the progressive horn in his *fin de régime* days, with the Kelowna accord and a belated attempt to fulfil the Liberals' by now hoary pledge of national childcare. But it was too late.

THE HIDDEN AGENDA

Despite the government's conservative fiscal policies—or maybe because of them—the Liberals needed to project their most liberal face at election time. The cuts to unemployment insurance produced a modest revival of the NDP and the Progressive Conservatives in the 1997 election—particularly in the Atlantic provinces. Over the course of the next half-dozen elections the Liberals would adopt a two-pronged narrative, though with decreasing effectiveness.[25] First, they argued that their future intentions were more liberal than their recent history. Second, they tried to frighten progressive voters with the prospect of the alternative: the "hidden agenda" of Preston Manning, Stockwell Day, and finally Stephen Harper.

Jean Chrétien provided the model for each of these approaches. By the time of the 1997 election, the government, wafting on the unexpected upward breeze of an improving economy, could already see the end to deficits in sight. He propounded the "fifty-fifty formula"—what he called a balanced approach to future government surpluses. The idea was that half of these surpluses would be devoted to new spending, and the other half to tax cuts and deficit reductions. It was a promise of more progressive policies to come, and it was no less central to the Liberals' campaign in 1997 than the Red Book had been in 1993. What's interesting is how this pledge played itself out in practice once Chrétien won re-election. Paul Martin had never been keen on the formula, but quickly realized it was vague enough to ignore in practice.[26] Was a tax credit to be considered spending or a tax cut, for example? The budget's "contingency reserves" were not counted in the formula, but automatically went to debt repayment if they were not needed. In fact, much more than half the surplus in Chrétien's second government was devoted to debt reduction and tax cuts notwithstanding those little charts dutifully printed in each budget purporting the opposite. And this seemed fine with Chrétien. The formula had never been about arithmetic; it was about perceptions.

That having been said, it would be wrong to conclude that the Liberals had become conservatives, pure and simple. In fact, when the government began running surpluses, there was broad agreement in cabinet that social spending should begin again. There was even agreement between Chrétien and Martin on where money should go. They converged with surprisingly little angst on emphasizing research and development, post-secondary education, early childhood development, and health care. The Canadian Foundation for Innovation was created to fund elite research in the public and non-profit sectors. Later, a national system of academic chairs was established to stock our universities with world-class researchers. The RESP system was set up to encourage middle class Canadians to save for their children's university education. In 1998, the Liberals negotiated the National Child Benefit with the provinces, which has made significant, measurable inroads on child poverty. In 1999, the government began restoring some of the cuts it had made to health and social transfers to the provinces and increased direct federal spending by about a billion-and-a-half dollars. Tax cuts, when they did come, were generally progressive—at least at the outset.

This modest tack in policy was accompanied by a fierce new rhetoric against the right, which only intensified when Stockwell Day replaced Preston Manning as the leader of what had become the Canadian Alliance. Unlike Manning, who had devoted considerable intellectual effort to translating his evangelical beliefs into secular political language,[27] Day and the media gaped at each other in mutual incomprehension. In the 2000 election, the core of the Liberal party's strategy was to create a chilling contrast between it and the Alliance, while relegating all the other parties to the status of also-rans. Chrétien remarked that the Canadian Alliance represented the "dark side of human nature." Stockwell Day was portrayed as man with a hidden agenda who secretly favoured a two-tiered system of medicare and a referendum on abortion. Day cooperated in the Liberals' mission to frame him with a spectacularly incompetent campaign in which he seemed quicker to qualify or change his program than he was to defend it. The CBC dropped a late-campaign bombshell in the form of a profile of Day in which he was said to believe that humans had walked the earth with dinosaurs. In mockery, the Liberals' designated hit man, Warren Kinsella, went on TV the next morning with a stuffed toy Barney to underline Day's flakiness.

This formula became the central feature of Liberal electioneering. Part of Paul Martin's appeal, his supporters had originally believed, was that his fiscal conservatism would attract support in the West and in rural Canada. This was[28] how they dreamed of getting to 200 seats—something his advisors thought was perfectly realistic just a year before he became Liberal leader. But when he first led the party in the 2004 election campaign, his slogan was "Choose Your Canada"—a not so subtle invocation of the "hidden agenda" theme—and his central promise was to "fix medicare for a generation" with renewed spending. This was an attempt to highlight Harper's vulnerability on the health care issue, but it wasn't enough. When it was apparent that the Liberals were in real trouble in the campaign—due to the sponsorship scandal in Quebec and a health care tax by the Liberal government in Ontario—Martin resorted yet more explicitly to the spectre of a hidden agenda, telling an audience of women in Toronto that their abortion rights were under threat. That full reversion to the Chrétien formula saved him. Just. There was a sharp shift in support from the NDP to the Liberals, particularly in Ontario, and it came so late in the campaign that it befuddled the pollsters, most of whom had thought Martin was a goner.

OK, LET'S FIGHT

As the policy differences among Liberals narrowed, however, the leadership rivalry only intensified. Martin dutifully supported Chrétien's national campaigns, but his half of the party apparatchiks were gradually downing tools. In 1997, there was no smoking bus for the media following Chrétien, and no Terrie O'Leary either. By the 2000 election, some of Martin's supporters were actually seeding stories in the media that reflected poorly on Chrétien. I know because I wrote some of them in the *Globe and Mail* where I was then working. Martin's supporters devoted their considerable energies in these years not to fighting the NDP, the Bloc, or the Canadian Alliance, but to taking over the party apparatus in pursuit of their eventual leadership campaign—a pursuit to which Chrétien's supporters reacted with perplexing passivity. The Martinites were disdainful of their internal rivals, and rightly distrustful. When Martin ultimately became prime minister, it was not just Allan Rock, John Manley, and Stéphane Dion who were pushed out of cabinet, and Sheila Copps who was driven out of politics altogether, but many less recognizable figures in the caucus and in the party organization were shunted aside. Indeed, after 1993, the Liberals never again fielded their full team of political professionals—thus squandering one substantial advantage they had held over the other parties.

In this atmosphere, no one really noticed that the party structure itself, which had been radically decentralized under John Turner, was too unwieldy to run a modern campaign. The party had inaccurate and inaccessible membership lists, and there was no single party database. When Chrétien, as one of his final acts in government, passed legislation that eliminated the corporate donations on which the party had been heavily dependent, he made no preparations for the party to adapt to the new regime. Nor did Martin, once he became prime minister, fuelled as he was by a pool of cash he had accumulated under the old rules during his one-sided leadership campaign. This foreseeable disaster would befall the hapless Stéphane Dion, who proved to be a feeble fundraiser for the party, hampered as he was by a debt for his own leadership campaign that was not paid off until 2011!

By the time Michael Ignatieff became leader, the party

organization was something of a shambles. The 2006 convention that had chosen Dion had also passed reforms aimed at streamlining the party's structure, transferring administrative responsibilities to central party headquarters with the aim of having the provincial and territorial arms focus on campaigning. But a special party committee reported two years later that the Liberals had been unable to create an integrated national membership system.[29] The provincial associations were still gobbling up a quarter of the party's public funding, even though they had not taken up the new organizational roles assigned to them. According to the report, the party wasn't even getting tax receipts out in time and, by the way, was failing to deliver services to its members in both official languages. Ouch! What the report did not mention is that even though sitting MPs had been guaranteed automatic renomination for the next election if they met minimal standards of membership in their riding associations and recruited a modest number of donors, fewer than 10 per cent of caucus had managed to do so. Many MPs had also personally failed to max-out their own $1,000 annual party contribution limit—something that earned them a reaming-out in caucus from the party's campaign chair, Senator David Smith.

In retrospect, the Liberals' behaviour between their election in 1993 and their defeat in 2006 looks like political malpractice. It wasn't that they failed to renovate their organization: it was that they barely tried. So preoccupied were they with internal battles, they were not prepared for a real national opponent. Once they found themselves in opposition, they did not have the leadership or the resources to make up for lost time. This malpractice can be put down to a single thing. It seemed at the time as if the Liberals were living in a miraculous age: one in which they did not have any serious rival for power.

HAIL TO THE CHIEFS

Ever since Pierre Trudeau's triumphal rise in just three short years from a desultory career as a journalist, civil servant, academic, labour activist, and itinerant intellectual to the height of popularity and power as prime minister, the Liberals have believed in saviours. Several modern leaders have had oddly similar creation myths built around their early careers: Trudeau coaxed from academe by Jean Marchand and Gérard Pelletier; Martin wooed from business by young Liberals Peter Donolo, Alf Apps, and Terrie O'Leary; and Ignatieff sought out at Harvard by Ian Davey (son of Keith), Alf Apps, and Dan Brock. Like Cincinnatus pulled from his plough, these men are recruited into public life for the good of the nation. Honey, get my toga, we're going to town!

The idea that there is a saviour waiting to come to their rescue persists among Liberals in the face of obvious facts, and it disguises from them the historic nature of the party's decline. The truth is that the Liberals' leadership problems very much parallel their broader decline. Prior to John Turner, only one leader in the entire history of the Liberal party—Edward Blake—had failed to win a single election. No Liberal leader had ever served fewer than seven years, and the average was around seventeen years. However, three of the Liberal party's recent leaders have failed to win an election and the *average* period as leader has been five years. Three leaders—Martin, Dion, and Ignatieff—served three years or less. The Liberals' ability to pick a winner, at least in the last half century, seems more suspect than many of them instinctively recognize. As Tom Flanagan remarked to me: "Leadership is a necessary but not sufficient condition for the revival of the Liberal Party."[30]

The question to ask is why, in the last half-century, have so many Liberal leaders failed to launch? One answer is the television age, of course, with its fickle obsession with personality. But another is that the Liberal party has continually felt the need to disavow itself. Pearson and Trudeau were untainted by association with the Liberal party of C. D. Howe and the pipeline debate. Turner represented a polar alternative to Trudeau in character and policy. Chrétien in his turn was the antidote to Turner. Martin was supposed to cut a similar contrast with Chrétien, shedding his baggage in French Quebec and the West. Dion was the squeaky clean answer to Liberals' sponsorship ills. And Ignatieff's appeal, similarly, was in significant part his distance from the Chrétien-Martin regime—at the time, he wasn't even living in the country! And, unlike Dion, who had staked his claim with the Canadian people around a complicated program of taxation and environmental legislation, Ignatieff would give the other parties no robust proclamations of policy to attack.

You can see the tactical sense in this. But, cumulatively, the effect is to give the impression of party without consistency or direction. This vulnerability was exposed after 1993, when the PCs ceased to be their rival for power, leaving the Liberals as the only brokerage party remaining in the system. All of their opponents now—the Bloc, Reform and its successors, the NDP, and, eventually, the Greens—had their roots in extra-parliamentary movements based on ideologies or ideals. Even in their most craven moments these parties were going to look like beacons of principle next to the Liberals.

Somewhat surprisingly, the 2006 leadership race to replace Paul Martin saw very little discussion of the party's organizational and fundraising woes.[31] The front-runners, Michael Ignatieff and Bob Rae, each ran on a platform of "winnability." No one questioned the Paul Martin legacy on economic policy: indeed, his famous "no-deficit rule" was treated as the anchor of Liberal probity and inoculation against Conservative accusations of "tax and spend." The surprise winner, Stéphane Dion, who rose from third place on the initial ballot, had had very little interesting to say on the economy during his campaign, but he ran on a strong, clear environmental platform, building on his success as Martin's environment minister. His supporters called themselves Dionistas, with an intended hint of insurgency and ideological commitment. One battle-hardened party backroom boy, who had supported another candidate, described the choice of Dion to me as "interesting, beautiful, naive, even…showing the least cynical, most appealing side of the Liberal party."

It is worth saying that, in a deep sense, Dion was right. The most pressing and significant issue we face as humankind is the destructive potential of climate change. Sadly, Stéphane Dion proved to be a deeply flawed vessel to carry that message. No national party leader since Diefenbaker seemed as oblivious to the need to cultivate personal allegiances in the party, or as incapable of mobilizing the skills of party apparatchiks. Dion himself has blamed his demise on the relentless Conservative attack ads—"Dion: not a leader"—to which the Liberals did not have the money to respond. There's a little truth to that, but he gave the Conservatives lots to work with.

Dion's critical failure was his inability or unwillingness to pivot from the environment to the economy during 2008. In June of that year, Dion released his Green Shift plan, which was to impose a carbon tax and use the revenues for a mix of income and corporate tax cuts and environmental programs. It was a well-conceived policy response to the threat of climate change and to Canada's responsibilities under the Kyoto protocol. But it was too complex to explain easily. Because of its spending elements, it was not fully revenue neutral.[32] It was easily caricatured by the Conservatives as a tax hike. Dion, whose English was at times difficult to understand, tended to respond to questions about his plan with professorial detail. More importantly, Dion's signature policy seemed serenely disconnected from Canadians' rising economic anxieties.

There was also an election south of the border that year—just two and a half weeks after ours, as it turned out. Barack Obama had been propelled into contention by his opposition to the Iraq war. But by the early summer, when Dion was just announcing the Green Shift, Obama had already shifted to the economy. This happened months before the failure of Lehman Brothers in mid-September launched the world into full-fledged financial crisis. Dion, however, seemed so certain of the righteousness of his Green Shift that he could not be persuaded to move onto the economy, even *after* the collapse of Lehman. It was obvious that Dion had never thought about climate change as a failure of the market model of our economy. While others began to question the rampant deregulation and denigration of the state that had created the conditions for the financial crisis, this was not a connective thread that apparently occurred to Dion. He seemed to view his Green Shift plan as a sub-program that would run as part of a fundamentally sound operating system. Astonishingly, as Stephen Harper himself offered little more than complacent conservative bromides, the Liberals were unable to offer a competing vision. While Obama and his Republican rival, John McCain, scrambled to demonstrate their concern about the financial crisis south of the border, both Harper and Dion treated it as an unwelcome distraction from the campaign they had previously decided to run.[33] No one would have expected that Canadians could absorb and reflect upon the lessons of the financial crisis in the remaining few weeks of the campaign. That the debate did not even begin is shocking, and the Liberals have some responsibility for that.

THE END OF DAYS

Fast forward three years. Just seven days until the 2011 election. The news of the NDP breakthrough in Quebec and its surge past the Liberals in the rest of the country was still sinking into the collective consciousness. Michael Ignatieff was holding one of the last of the town halls that had become his trademark, this one in Vancouver Kingsway, a riding once held by the Liberal-turned-Conservative David Emerson, and narrowly lost by the Liberals to the NDP in 2008. The event was at the Alpen Club—"The Heart of the German Community"—and waitresses in dirndl dresses handed out bar menus for spaetzle and schnitzel as hundreds of people streamed into the hall, filling the balcony as well as the main floor, and standing in the aisles. Pop songs played on the loudspeakers, including "Rise Up" by Parachute Club. It was an echo of a recent Ignatieff refrain, a call for Canadians to rise up against the abuses of the Harper government.[34] The audience was a mix of white, Asian and native, young and old, prosperous and not-quite-so: the very picture of Liberal Canada. One woman had a T-shirt with Ignatieff portrayed in high-contrast, à la Trudeau in 1968 and Obama in 2008. In the front row were the stalwarts of Liberal Vancouver, present and past, many of them new Canadians: Ujjal Dosanjh, Hedy Fry, Herb Dhaliwal.

When Ignatieff strode out onto the stage, he did so with a natural enthusiasm that startled me every time I saw it during the campaign. There was no podium: he prowled the stage, mic in hand, with the confidence of an afternoon talk show host or a TV preacher. Such a contrast from the diffident academic he had so often seemed (or that Dion had so obviously been). "Did anyone ask you whether you were a Liberal when you came in?" he asked, to cheering and applause. "Did anyone check your Facebook?" It was a crowd-pleasing jab at Stephen Harper's closed, suspicious style of campaign, in which supposed interlopers were hustled out the building, and which seemed a perfect metaphor for a government that had abused its power so often—taking down civil servants when they got in the way; proroguing parliament when the government got into trouble; and ignoring votes in parliament, rulings by the Speaker, and even court orders. The theme energized Ignatieff, and Liberal audiences loved it. The media had loved it too. At first. But by now they had grown bored, having realized that the general public just wasn't listening. At the back, several reporters were standing on the threshold of an outside door that streamed cool, moist Vancouver air into the over-warm hall, checking their smartphones, tweeting, and exchanging witticisms. This dog was nearly dead.

Ignatieff riffed through the Liberal platform. With some passion he described the "learning passport" he had proposed that would make it easier for families to get their kids through post-secondary education. He told a sentimental story about a twelve-year-old boy he had met in Toronto who was waiting for a liver transplant—an entrée into the Liberals' commitment to medicare. With feeling, he addressed the growing inequality in Canada. And he talked bitterly about Canada's "lost place of honour and respect in the world." It was a significant change in tone from Ignatieff's two years as leader: he sounded, well, as if he could have been a New Democrat. Except, that is, when he actually talked about the NDP for a few minutes in the middle of his speech. Then, abruptly, he became Mr. Fiscally Responsible, from the party that had balanced budgets and then got them into surplus. He warned about expensive promises. The NDP, he said, was proposing an "energy tax, because that essentially is what it is"—an oblique reference to the NDP's cap-and-trade greenhouse gas plan, which in principle was not that different from his party's own. "I'm not perfect," he told the crowd. "But I don't think I'm scary"—making the contrast not only with Harper but with Layton.

In these desperate days, this weird Janus-face characterized the Liberals' advertising as well. One ad said the NDP had made promises of $70 billion in spending "they can't possibly pay for." It predicted "chaos" in the economy and higher taxes if the NDP were elected. It all sounded strangely familiar…Oh yeah, just like those Conservative ads attacking the Liberals. In another ad, released soon afterward, the Liberal message lapsed into complete incoherence. Harper and Layton were portrayed as two sides of the same coin: a golden dollar spinning with a strangely pensive bas-relief of Harper replacing the Queen, and a snarling Layton replacing the loon—or was it the other way around? Harper and Layton had conspired to ditch Liberal plans for daycare and environmental protection, the ad said. What, I wondered, would an ordinary viewer make of this? Harper and Layton the same thing? It made no obvious sense. The NDP enemies of daycare and environmental protection? Ditto. Though it had a slender basis in fact,[35] the Liberals were springing this counterintuitive narrative on Canadians out of the blue. When I saw the ad, it seemed to me that viewers were more likely to believe that these accusations were an example of Liberal mendacity than of NDP apostasy. A sophisticated viewer might even be tempted to note that, despite nearly thirteen years in power, the Liberals had never made good on their promises of either daycare or control of greenhouse gas emissions. Which side of the coin was responsible for that?

The incoherence in the Liberals' message during the dying days of the 2011 campaign was not simply evidence of panic, though it was surely that as well. It was also deeply rooted in the party's history as a "centrist" party without an enduring ideological core, with a tendency to "run from the left and govern from the right." This ambivalence had been painfully evident in the Chrétien-Martin years. Under Ignatieff, the party compounded this fuzziness through a deliberate tactical decision to avoid any statement of policy prior to the campaign itself that would attract incoming fire from the Conservatives. Instead, it would rely on a seemingly inevitable "swing of the pendulum" against the unlikeable, secretive, manipulative, and undemocratic Harper. By choosing to de-emphasize policy, the party implicitly decided to put more emphasis on its leader, even as that came to seem an increasingly unpromising proposition.

When he first became leader, Ignatieff mused about holding a policy convention in the Liberal tradition of Kingston and Aylmer. But that was quickly shut down by his advisors. Senator David Smith told me that spring that there was no time for a "big think" on policy with elections looming every eighteen months. "A little think, maybe," he said. Behind the scenes, there was an argument going on over policy between those closest to Ignatieff and a small group of outsiders, most of them former Martin-supporters, clustered around the Saskatchewan MP and longtime minister Ralph Goodale. Ironically, given their close association with Martin's deficit-fighting policies of the 1990s, this group argued that the party needed to relax its commitment to balancing the budget quickly after the 2008 recession. Only then could the party make a credible commitment to, for example, shoring up the pension system—a key concern to struggling middle class Canadians, who were available to the Liberals at election time. What the Goodale group hadn't counted on, and what would likely have been a surprise to Liberals more generally, was the degree of Ignatieff's fiscal conservatism. In public, he often borrowed language from the United States about his aversion to "big government"; in private he went further, musing about the "nanny state," a term popularized by Mrs. Thatcher in Britain during the years Ignatieff lived there. When the Liberals finally had their "little think" at a Kingston-style policy conference in Montreal in the spring of 2010, Ignatieff did commit the party to a modest package of education, pension, unemployment insurance, and aboriginal programs. But he made them all subject to a pledge to get the deficit down to 1 per cent of GDP within two years of taking office. After reaching this initial target, Ignatieff pledged, a Liberal government would continue to reduce the deficit each year. In essence, he had ratified the Conservatives' consecration of deficit-elimination.

Ignatieff's first chief of staff, Ian Davey, later explained the strategy in an article in the *National Post*. Quoting the "old adage" that people vote governments out, not in, he warned that "while the opposition always faces unyielding pressure to offer detailed policies, the reality is that succumbing to this pressure only makes Liberals, instead of the Conservative government, the issue."[36] One of the consequences of this strategy was that whenever, as opposition leader, Ignatieff threatened to provoke an election—something he did repeatedly—he was never quite able to explain why. He talked about Canadians having a choice between the "blue door" and the "red door." If you don't like Harper and the Conservatives, in other words, you need to vote for me and the Liberals, not waste your vote on the NDP. There are no other options. When it came to the English debate during the campaign he barely mentioned his platform, preferring to attack Harper and argue that the other opposition parties represented obstacles to the strategic objective of defeating the Conservatives. By failing to define himself or the Liberal party, Ignatieff made it much easier for Conservative—and NDP—attack ads to do the job for him. In their post-election focus groups, Ensight Canada reported, "Canadians simply could not name a compelling reason that the Liberals had given them to vote for their party."[37]

As you stare at the wreckage of what was arguably the most successful party in the history of the democratic world, there are various explanations for its utter demagnetization in 2011. Some of them were very long-term. But one of them, surely, must have been its willful refusal to differentiate its policies from those of the Conservatives. The Conservatives' greatest strength was their reputation as competent economic managers—a reputation they owed in part to the lack of effective opposition from the Liberals.

The Liberals fell from 77 seats in 2008 to just 34, a historic low. They were in second place in just 76 more ridings, for a total of 110. This compared with the NDP, who were first or second in 224 seats nationally, and the Conservatives, who were first or second in 231.[38] The Liberal vote share fell from a previous historic low of 26 per cent in 2008 to just 19 per cent. In Quebec, the province that Laurier had cemented to the Liberal party and arguably to the country, the Liberals took seven seats and 14 per cent of the vote. In Ontario, the province that had guaranteed the party dominance in the Chrétien years, they won just 11 of the 106 seats, and were almost exactly tied with the NDP at 25 per cent of the popular vote. Among young voters, a traditional base of support, they took just 19 per cent compared with the NDP at 44 per cent and the Conservatives at 24 per cent, according to one post-election survey.[39] Their historic lead among women had disappeared. Among Catholics they were in third place; among Jews they were second. Among visible minority immigrants they trailed both the NDP and the Conservatives, according to a huge post-election online poll,[40] and among non-visible minority immigrants they did even worse, taking just 15 per cent of the vote. They had hung onto just two seats in Vancouver, one each in Regina and Winnipeg, one in Halifax, and seven each in Montreal and in the Toronto area in which they had once been indomitable. This from a party that once hoped to embody urban Canada. Whereas nearly half the caucus had been from Ontario before the election, that portion was now less than a third— slightly smaller, in fact, than the party's new Atlantic caucus. Interestingly, Liberal MPs now represented voters that were, on average, slightly poorer than Canadians in general, an artifact, at least in part, of the collapse of their "blue Liberal" support in Ontario to the Conservatives.[41]

Will the Liberals die a slow, lingering death like the old Progressive Conservatives did? Or will they hang on, persist and eventually thrive again as the NDP did after the apparently fatal blows they sustained in the 1990s? Many of us at that time thought the New Democrats were unlikely to survive federally. We were wrong. Or is it possible that the Liberals will eke out an existence at the intersection of the two great tectonic plates either side of them, as the Liberals have tried to do in Manitoba, and the Liberal Democrats in Britain? All possible. But what seems most likely is that the Liberals will be caught in the power trap. They will devote much of their energy to squabbling with the New Democrats over the affections of progressive voters. Like the PCs in the 1990s, to the extent that Liberals will succeed, it will be at the expense of those whose values they claim to represent. Might the Liberals vault back past the New Democrats and the Conservatives to form a government in 2015? According to the political number-cruncher Éric Grenier, if the Liberals did so, it would be the greatest political comeback in Canadian history.[42] But anything is possible in an animated cartoon, as Bugs Bunny once said. The greater likelihood is a war of attrition with the New Democrats, and possibly also the Greens, in which none of them wins, but progressive voters most certainly lose.

CHAPTER 6
WHY WORKING TOGETHER IS HARD

Just eight months after the 2011 election, the NDP lost the first of its retinue of new Quebec MPs. Lise St-Denis had to that point escaped the notice of the media or the public. A long-time NDP supporter in Montreal, she had let her name stand in a riding where she had never lived: Saint-Maurice–Champlain in central Quebec, long held by Jean Chrétien. Without a critic's portfolio, she had languished in the last row of the backbench, relegated there, she said poignantly, by the alphabetical accident of her last name. That gave her lots of time to contemplate the NDP, the Liberals, and her future. The matters St-Denis cited in her decision to cross to the Liberals were vague, even obscure—she preferred the Liberals' social and job-creation policies, and disliked the NDP's criticisms of Canada's involvement in the last phase of NATO's intervention in Libya. Obviously still unaccustomed to speaking in public, when she was asked whether she thought the voters back in May had voted for her or for the NDP, she responded with shocking bluntness: "They voted for Jack Layton, but Jack Layton is dead." The NDP reacted with predictable fury, denouncing St-Denis, belittling her qualities, and demanding she resign and face a by-election.[1] But they went one further, unleashing a campaign of robocalls, in which constituents were instructed by a recorded voice on the phone that if they objected to her crossing the floor they should "press one," redirecting the call to her office. Her phone lines were jammed for days, St-Denis complained.

It is very likely that the Conservatives will once more be the largest party in the best position to form a government after the 2015 election if the Liberals and the New Democrats fight instead of collaborate—failing, in other words, to put the interests of their electorate above those of their individual parties. Strange as it may seem after the May 2011 election results, some Liberals still harbour dreams of majority government. But even they, in the throes of this ecstatic vision, see it as a two-step process: replace the NDP as the second-largest party in 2015, and replace the Conservatives in the election after that. That seems like an awful long time to me—too long. For the NDP to win outright in 2015, it would need to hold its broad but shallow support in Quebec, stifle even a small revival of the BQ, win straight fights with the Conservatives in the West, and, most important of all, collapse the Liberal vote, particularly in Ontario. Put another way, Thomas Mulcair would have to outdo Jack Layton's 2011 performance, the Liberals would have to fail utterly at revival, and the Conservatives would have to waste the opportunities presented by four years of majority government to consolidate and expand their political base.

It is possible, of course, that the Liberals and New Democrats could spend the next four years banging away at each other, competing for many of the same votes, attacking each other's credibility and competence—hauling water for the Conservatives, in effect—and still form a coalition government *after* the next election. It might not do much to allay the public's cynicism about politics, but if the Conservatives were to fall to, say, 35 per cent of the vote (closer to what some people regard as their "core") in 2015, and the Liberals and NDP split 50 per cent of the vote between them, the result might be roughly 160 seats for the Conservatives and 170 seats divided between the Liberals and NDP (in the enlarged House of Commons currently planned). In a parliament like that the Liberals and NDP would be sorely tempted to join together as a majority coalition government, whatever they had said about each other—or a coalition[2]—on the campaign trail. And that government would surely produce more progressive economic, social, environmental, and foreign policy than we have from the Conservatives. It might also deepen the relationship between the two parties over time, perhaps leading to some more permanent union. But this is by no means the most direct or efficient route to a more progressive government in Canada.

Under our first-past-the-post system electoral system, running as separate parties will understate their combined strength. Remember that after the old Progressive Conservatives and the Canadian Alliance combined to form the Harper Conservatives, their total vote went *down* but the number of seats they won went dramatically *up*. The most direct and efficient way to replace the Conservatives with a more progressive government in 2015 is for the Liberals and NDP (and possibly also the Greens) to agree *before* the election to present a common platform and candidates, preferably under a single leader. Instead of ripping away at one another, NDPers accusing Liberals of being Conservative Lite, and Liberals decrying the NDP as blinkered by ideology and the unions, they would work together to draw on their individual strengths. Progressives who grew up in Winnipeg, Vancouver, and Regina and joined the NDP—a party of government in their provinces—would link together with progressives who grew up in Toronto and gravitated to the Liberals. They would find a lot in common and—who knows?—might actually learn something from one another.[3] As the pollsters Darrell Bricker and Keren Gottfried pointed out, based on Ipsos Reid's massive 2011 post-election survey: "What's especially notable…is how little the attitudes of Liberal voters differ from the attitudes of voters who supported the New Democrats. What this suggests is that the attitudinal fault lines actually place the New Democrats on the same side of the divide as the Liberals. Stated another way, New Democrats and Liberals seem to think alike."[4] But, unfortunately for them, a single progressive option may not be on the ballot for Canadians in 2015, because of a party tribalism and institutional self-regard in which the interests of the voters are barely considered. It is the parties themselves, in other words, who divide progressive voters.

The idea of deep collaboration between progressives in the Liberal and New Democratic parties is by no means a fringe idea. At one time or another, in one form or another, in recent years it has attracted the support or attention of party leaders Jack Layton and Stéphane Dion; of former leaders Jean Chrétien and Ed Broadbent; of sometime leadership hopefuls Bob Rae, Brian Topp, and Nathan Cullen; of prominent MPs such as the Liberals' Denis Coderre and the NDP's Pat Martin; of backroom strategists including Eddie Goldenberg, Robin Sears, and Jamey Heath; not to mention labour leaders Buzz Hargrove and Ken Lewenza, and even the occasional policy wonk, such as former Clerk of the Privy Council, Alex Himelfarb. It has won the support of progressive political groups working outside the party system, such as Leadnow and the Canadian arm of Avaaz.

But these various players came to similar conclusions about the need for a common progressive voice for a complex variety of often conflicting reasons. They had different visions of how and when a compact among the parties might be forged. And in many cases, they have put personal, party, or other loyalties ahead of the project of uniting progressives.

Perhaps the most unfortunate development for the prospects of party collaboration was that both the Liberals and the New Democrats found themselves looking for new leaders soon after the 2011 election—the Liberals because of Michael Ignatieff's inevitable resignation, and the New Democrats because of Jack Layton's tragic death. The dynamics of leadership contests is that they emphasize loyalty to the team. In the case of the NDP, Thomas Mulcair was chosen by party members. Although Nathan Cullen intrepidly raised the idea of joint Liberal-NDP nominations in the course of his own leadership bid, his rivals all opposed the idea, often with knee-jerk appeals to party loyalty. The Liberals' decision at the January 2012 convention to allow any party "supporter"—including non-members—to vote for their leader may attenuate the party-loyalist impulse. But in the early days after the 2011 election, it ran like an electric current through the Liberal party's post-election leadership planning.

"MR. CHRÉTIEN CAN MUSE"

In some ways, the prospects for deep collaboration between the two parties never seemed more auspicious than they did right after the 2011 election. The Bloc Québécois, whose sovereigntist ideology was a huge barrier to uniting progressives in this country, had virtually disappeared. For some time, Jack Layton had been open to working with the Liberals, most recently after the 2008 election, when he had initiated talk of a coalition. Moreover, within just a few weeks of the 2011 election the Liberals selected Bob Rae as their interim leader, himself a former NDP premier who had advocated a coming-together of progressives, both as a provincial and a federal politician.

On the morning of May 3, 2011, I got out of bed early, only a few hours after turning off the TV and shutting down my laptop as the last results trickled in. I was part of a post-election panel discussing the future of the Liberal party on CBC Radio

with Anna Maria Tremonti, and one of the other guests was
Eddie Goldenberg, arguably Jean Chrétien's closest aide over
a professional lifetime. To my amazement, he sounded almost
nonchalant about the Liberals' electoral disaster. "Parties come
and go," he said. It wasn't yet nine o'clock the next day and
Goldenberg seemed ready to consign his party to history. He was
using the shock of the election results to force consideration of a
merger into the reeling minds of Liberal activists. The logic was
almost self-evident. The Liberals were unlikely to return to power
on their own any time soon, and the party had more in common
with the NDP than it did with the Conservatives. The quickest
way back to government would be in some sort of close arrange-
ment with the NDP. There were two other Liberals on the panel,
however: the former caucus research director and academic
Brooke Jeffrey, and Liberal activist and commentator Robert Sil-
ver. They reacted to Goldenberg's words with an almost palpable
shudder, their words quivering with indignation. The Liberal
party represented an entirely different political tradition from the
NDP. The analogy with the Conservative merger was a false one.
Liberals and NDPers had *always* been rivals, whereas the Conservatives had reunited after less than a decade apart. The Liberal
party stood for a strong federal government, national unity, and
individual liberties as no other party could. Their words were
reasoned; the tone was visceral.

In speaking as he had, Goldenberg was not making an uncon-
sidered or isolated remark. In fact, there was a coordinated push
on. In subsequent days, Goldenberg's patron, none other than
Jean Chrétien himself, stepped out too: "Some would prefer
to build back the Liberal party. Others think that, as the right
managed to amalgamate, perhaps amalgamation would be a
good thing." Although Chrétien and Goldenberg had left active
politics, there was another voice in this little choir—arguably the
most formidable politician left in the much-diminished Liberal

caucus: Bob Rae. Rae had close connections to Chrétien and Goldenberg, through his brother, John Rae, who had managed many of Chrétien's political campaigns. Bob Rae started talking up a merger almost as soon as the polls had closed on election night. "It would be irresponsible not to listen to what Canadians think about this question," he repeated over the days to come—a rare invocation of the public interest in the ensuing debate.

Rae knew something about party collaboration; as leader of the Ontario NDP, in 1985 he had forged a parliamentary pact with the Liberals that ended a forty-three-year Conservative reign and put the Liberal leader David Peterson in the premier's office. In 1990, Rae defeated Peterson to become premier himself but famously lasted just one term: his first budget in 1991 was an audacious Keynesian gamble that he could power the province out of a recession—a gamble that failed. Rae brooded on his defeat, in 1995, by the hard-right conservative Mike Harris. A prominent provincial Liberal organizer later told me that he first met Rae and his wife, Arlene Perly Rae, at a dinner party in this period, and he got an earful about party collaboration being the only way to get rid of Harris. Meanwhile, Rae had also become disenchanted with the NDP, not least because of his battles as premier with public-sector unions affiliated to the party. Rae joined the federal Liberals, and then ran for the leadership of the party in 2006. Part of his appeal to the Liberals was that he might just be able to win over erstwhile NDP voters. Though he lost, Rae was elected to parliament in 2008 and supported Stéphane Dion's bid to oust the Harper minority government in coalition with the NDP.

So what Rae had to say about the possibilities of working with the NDP in the spring of 2011 was not an impulsive reaction to a disastrous election night—it was an enduring feature of his politics. But not, as he quickly learned, of most life-long Liberals'. Dominic Leblanc, an MP, a former Chrétien aide, and a possible rival to Rae for the party's leadership, caught the mood when he declared: "The Liberal party is a resilient national institution. I think it has a bright future as a progressive, centrist option in Canadian politics." He acknowledged that the Liberals had failed to offer a coherent or compelling vision in the election. "I think it would be a mistake to say that somehow we need to fold up the tent. What we need to do is start renovating from the basement up." Many Liberals—from Trudeauites to "blue Liberals"—had ideological reservations about getting into bed with the NDP.

But the language Liberal insiders used in private was more personal than ideological. Several Liberals who preferred not to be named, so they could speak frankly, told me that a merger with the NDP in the present circumstances would "feel like a takeover." As one remarked, many Liberals who had supported collaboration in the past had "never imagined joining as the junior partner." With so few MPs, the always-influential legion of Liberal party apparatchiks—organizers, fundraisers, strategists, and lobbyists—were, if anything, more significant now. At least they didn't lose their jobs on election night. But these people do not necessarily see the world from the vantage point of the party's election platforms or, indeed, the party's voters. "The notion that we see ourselves as progressives is not as true as people on the outside perceive," one staffer from the Chrétien years, now a lobbyist, told me. "If we disappear, why is a merger important to me?" He told me that Chrétien's apparent support for an amalgamation of the Liberals and the NDP had greatly undermined the former leader's stature and influence in the party.

I was surprised, too, at the number of Liberal organizers and strategists I talked to who cited personal animosities towards, for example, Brian Topp and former Layton communications director Jamey Heath. Although Topp had played a leading role in negotiating the coalition agreement for Layton in 2008, he also had a long history of strategizing for the NDP in bruising election campaigns, not only federally, and in Saskatchewan, where he had been an aide to Premier Romanow, but in other provinces where he had often been a five-star general in the party's itinerant army of election organizers. One prominent Liberal, known for his own elbows-up style of politics, told me that he regarded Topp as too ruthless to work alongside.

Heath, who had once been a close advisor to Jack Layton, wrote a book in 2007 advocating unity among progressives: but it had been entitled *Dead Centre,* and contained a splenetic attack on the "meaningless middle" represented by the Liberals in their current form.[5] Most Liberal activists, even the most progressive among them, came to regard him not as a potential ally but as a committed partisan foe.

More broadly, many Liberals see themselves as serious people— serious about government, that is—and had trouble picturing themselves in a party where the likes of MP Libby Davies and left-ist Ontario labour leader Sid Ryan got a respectful hearing. "It's not in our DNA: we don't like these people," one former party executive told me.

Very few of the Liberal insiders I spoke to made any direct reference to the interests of Liberal party voters, although a number said that Canadians would still expect a Liberal "offering" in 2015. They discussed policy mainly in instrumental terms—that is to say, that the Ignatieff platform hadn't "worked." Some ticked off policy options no longer available to them—the environment, for example, tainted by Dion's cratered campaign for the Green Shift, or the buzzwords of competitiveness and innovation, now seeming tired and empty (if not actually scary). There was a sense among many Liberals that NDP policies were wrong-headed, even though the two parties' platforms had been almost indistinguishable in 2011. When they talked about developing a new platform for the party, it sounded as if they were looking for a policy gadget that would distinguish them from the other parties and restore them to life in the next election. Very little of what they were thinking was based on an analysis of the current failures of our economic system, or the failure of the Liberal party to confront the Conservatives' economic program. One Liberal, who opposed a merger in the near-term at least, told me that "tribalism and institutionalism" lay behind much of the party's resistance to the idea. Most of those I spoke to believed that Rae's attempt to open up a discussion had been, as one put it, a "huge miscalculation," and even his supporters agreed that it had complicated his ambitions to be elected Liberal leader.

This was the background against which Rae became interim leader. Right after the election, Rae may have seemed to many outsiders as the logical choice to lead the party in the House of Commons, at least until a permanent leader could be selected. In the much-depleted caucus, he was the only experienced parliamentarian with national name recognition who could make the party's case fluently in English and French. Rae had also attracted a significant following in the Liberal party, even if, as a relative newcomer, his roots in the party had been largely grafted on by supporters who had been around much longer. Yet, despite his affable public persona, Rae can be cold in person, even to close colleagues. And he can be a difficult colleague, sometimes stepping out of line on issues he feels strongly about, because of either personal conviction or political calculation. Moreover, he was also clearly a candidate—arguably at the time the frontrunner—to become the permanent leader of the party. Traditionally, interim leaders had been thought of as caretakers who did not themselves have leadership ambitions. There were plenty of Liberals, even some former Rae supporters, who were far from ready to be rushed into handing Rae any easy path via the interim leadership to the permanent leadership for the 2015 election. Finally, Rae had antagonized many of Michael Ignatieff's supporters, first during the 2006 leadership race, again at the time of Ignatieff's highly irregular seizure of the leadership in late 2008, and in the course of keeping his own leadership ambitions alive. Rae's eventual selection as the party's interim leader was by no means smooth, and one effect of the politicking around it was to squelch discussion of any future relationship with the NDP.

There were a couple of potential rivals to Rae for the interim leadership, including Justin Trudeau and Ralph Goodale. However, Trudeau quickly took himself out of the race, whether as he said at the time for family reasons, or because he wanted to keep alive the possibility of running for the permanent job sometime in the future. For his part, Goodale faced an insurmountable wall of opposition due to his inability to speak French. But there was another obstacle to Rae's taking the interim leadership. The president of the Liberal party was Alfred Apps, a Toronto lawyer who had helped recruit Ignatieff from Harvard to run for parliament in 2006, hoping he would eventually become prime minister.[6] Thus Apps was no friend of Bob Rae. He also believed that the extra-parliamentary party should take the lead in party renewal. Like Apps, the rest of the national board had been selected at the 2009 party biennial meeting that confirmed Ignatieff's leadership, and, not surprisingly, was generally suspicious of Rae. One possibly jaundiced Rae supporter told me that opinion on the board ranged from a belief that Rae shouldn't be handed the leadership on a platter to "No goddamn way I will let that pinko become leader." In any event, the national board commandeered the process of selecting the interim leader with a set of rules that can only be described as extraordinary. Candidates for the interim leadership, the board ruled, would be required to "execute in writing a solemn undertaking" not to seek the permanent leadership of the party. More important for our purposes here, the candidates would have to make a similar pledge not to *engage in any discussions or negotiations that would require any fundamental or change to the nature or structure of the party absent the prior approval of a resolution by delegates at a convention of the Party held in accordance with the Constitution duly authorizing such discussions or negotiations."* It took some days of agonizing before Rae decided to accept what amounted to a bill of attainder and remain in the race. Although Rae faced a nominal opponent in Marc Garneau, he won the interim leadership easily at a caucus meeting on Parliament Hill in late May. As he emerged from the meeting, he declared, "We have a great history as a party and I believe we have a great future." He also said, "I have no hesitation in saying that the Liberal party is here to stay. We're here to fight for the things that Canadians believe in."

It would be a mistake to suggest that Rae's "solemn undertaking" to the party's national board is what killed the talk of merger. In the near term, no sizeable element of the caucus or the extra-parliamentary party had rallied to the idea. Rae probably could not have won over enough MPs to become interim leader as its champion. And he would have severely damaged his prospects of becoming permanent leader, which remained his ambition. Certainly many of his supporters in the party were happy to say in confidence that they believed he would make himself indispensable as interim leader, and some sort of fix would be found to get around his promise not to run for the permanent job.

Rae emerged from the interim-leader fight with relative success. The casualty was the idea of a merger. In the months that followed, Rae was poacher turned gamekeeper. When Jack Layton died in August there was a brief flurry of merger talk in the media once again, given that both parties were now without permanent leaders. At the Liberals' summer caucus, one prominent Liberal MP, Denis Coderre, an experienced Quebec organizer who was sometimes discussed as a possible leadership candidate himself, publicly raised the issue. "I think that it would be a valid discussion to continue what Chrétien, Broadbent, and Romanow did in the past," he said. "[Although] I'm not saying we should do it right away. You don't pull a flower to make it grow faster." Coderre may have been thinking about his own riding of Bourassa in the east end of Montreal, where he had often taken 50 per cent of the vote in the past against BQ challengers, but had been reduced to just 41 per cent against the surging New Democrats in 2011. Rae quickly dismissed Coderre's remarks: "A debate will happen, but if somebody says to me, 'Is it a debate about something real?' my answer is, no. I'm not running a political seminar here. I'm running a political party that's looking at real issues in front of it." Rae was also surprisingly brusque in dismissing similar comments Jean Chrétien made immediately after attending Layton's funeral. "Mr. Chrétien can muse," Rae said. "It's not on our agenda."

WHAT? WE WORRY?

If anything, Rae's candidacy for the permanent job seemed more viable after a "virtual" meeting of the national party in mid-June of 2011 decided to delay the selection of the permanent leader until the spring of 2013. That gave him time to establish himself as the leader—something he did seemingly unfettered by the "interim" label. That the NDP was hobbled for a time with its own quite ineffectual interim leader, Nycole Turmel, allowed Rae to achieve something close to what the Liberal party had in fact lost in 2011, the role of official opposition in parliament. As the party crept up on the NDP in many polls through the autumn of 2011, the impetus for a deep rethink of the Liberal party seemed to fade.

One Liberal strategist, David Herle, Paul Martin's former pollster and campaign manager who had been closely associated with the Martin/Chrétien fiscal policies, did offer a startling, if largely overlooked, analysis of the Liberals' failure in the twenty-first century. He noted the growing inequality in Canadian society, which had arisen, in his view, in part from the economic policies of previous decades. In a country polarized between richer and

poorer there would be less room for the Liberal party's politics of
the centre. The Liberals' "unwillingness to veer from conservative
economic orthodoxy meant they could not propose any measures
that would have a meaningful impact on the circumstances of
people clinging to their middle-class lifestyles," he wrote. "Once
the middle has shrunk sufficiently that there are really only two
groups in society—economic winners and economic losers—
there will only be a need for two parties, one to represent each
group." Although he was calling for a fundamental reconsidera-
tion of the Liberals' economic program, he was not advocating
collaboration with the NDP: rather, he was warning that it might
continue its rise and displace the Liberal party. But Herle was, in
any event, an outlier. It was much more common for prominent
Liberals to argue vaguely for the continued need for a "centrist
alternative," often implying not much more than splitting the
difference between the Conservatives and the NDP. Where there
was some definition put on the term, as, for example, by former
MP and leadership candidate Martha Hall Findlay, it was little
more than a demand for a more consistent application of the formula of the Chrétien years: in short, leaning right on economic
issues, and left on social issues.[7]

In January of 2012, the Liberals held their first biennial meeting since the election. The convention, held in the midst of a
brutal Ottawa January, was surprising for the number of delegates it attracted as well as their youth and enthusiasm. Indeed,
in the previous months the Liberal party had defied predictions
of complete collapse, showing some spring in its step—and not
just in the opinion polls. The party had just enjoyed its best
fundraising fourth quarter since 2006—$2.8 million, compared
with the NDP's $1.6 million, which was *its* worst in years.[8] And,
somewhat surprisingly, it had added fifteen thousand members
since the election. The convention was in many ways a victory
for Rae, consolidating his position as party leader—albeit still

on an interim basis. There was a turnover in many of the party's executive members from those who had been elected in 2009 at the convention that ratified Ignatieff's leadership, many of whom had been suspicious, if not outright hostile, towards Rae. Equally important, the convention adopted a controversial new rule for selecting a leader permanently in 2013, which would allow self-declared "supporters" of the party, who were not actual members, to vote. Rae had advocated the resolution from the floor, and he had good reason for high-fiving the people around him when it passed. Given his history with the NDP, he was much likelier to hold onto the party leadership if the electoral base was broadened beyond the Liberal party's core of long-time members.

But the Liberal biennial of January 2012 was as important for what it ignored as for what it actually accomplished. There was, first of all, simply no discussion of any kind of whether the Liberal party should consider collaboration with other parties. None. It was not even an issue worth raising and then dispensing with. More shockingly, there was no serious contemplation of the economic or environmental issues we face, their scale, or the past failures of the Liberal party in addressing them. The policy resolutions discussed by the convention were small-bore, anodyne, and incremental. They were as serenely undisturbed by the aftermath of the 2008 financial crisis as they were by the 2008 and 2011 elections. They would have fit just fine in a don't-rock-the-boat convention in the mid-term of a Liberal majority government. There was, in short, no evidence at the convention that the Liberal party had in a serious way come to terms with its recent history.

SEEK OR DESTROY?

For good reason, the New Democrats had spent a lot more time than the Liberals *before* 2011 in considering their place in the Canadian party system, and how and whether that might be changed. Their astonishing performance on election night diverted the course of a debate that was already well underway in the NDP. Had Jack Layton lived, the party would likely have continued to press its advantage as the official opposition, but remain open to opportunities for collaboration with the Liberals. Layton would have been in a position to hold his strategic cards close to his vest. Layton's approach to the Liberals was laid out in a book about the abortive coalition attempt in late 2008, written by none other than Brian Topp—still the best, though a highly partisan, account of the episode.[9] In contrast to Rae, whose interest in cooperation was born of his desire to oust right-wingers like Harper and Harris, Layton always saw cooperation in partisan terms. As Topp described Layton's strategy, it had two tracks: make common cause with the Liberals when it advanced the NDP's interests, but otherwise seek to displace them as the national alternative to Harper and the Conservatives. This was seek *or* destroy, depending on the circumstances. Layton's view was rooted in party competition, not, like Rae's, in an attempt to supersede it.

It was Layton who first recognized an opportunity after the 2008 election, in which the Liberals suffered their lowest popular vote ever to that date: 26 per cent.[10] Given the Liberals' bewildered state, Layton thought the Liberals might consider a coalition that would turn the tables on the minority Conservatives. The NDP's elder statesmen—Ed Broadbent, Allan Blakeney, and Roy Romanow—supported Layton. They believed that even as the junior coalition partner NDP ministers would be able to implement party policies—and receive the political credit. It would give Layton and the other NDP ministers the credibility that comes from sitting in cabinet. But Layton's initial feelers were rebuffed. Dion, who had shocked many in the party with his insistence on staying on as leader until a new one was to be chosen in 2009, had neither the political capital nor the inclination for such boldness.

Then everything changed. At the end of November, Harper's

finance minister, Jim Flaherty, delivered his fiscal update, which promised to eliminate the annual $1.95-per-vote subsidy to political parties.[11] The money from this subsidy was vital to all the parties—except the Conservatives, who had a large base of small donors. Elimination of the subsidy would damage the NDP, but it would devastate the Liberals. Equally important, the subsidies were critical to the Bloc Québécois, for whom they were sufficient to finance its entire operation. Flaherty's proposal was aimed at sending the Liberal party, as well as the BQ, into a death-spiral. This was a fight for survival. It was the opposition's good fortune that in the same fiscal update Flaherty shrugged at the prospect of a recession that was scrambling finance ministers elsewhere in the world to battle stations. Harper had already signalled that the government might have to run a small deficit due to falling revenues, but Flaherty's statement had no new measures to help Canadians cope with the economic downturn. This obtuseness created a magnificent opening. Joined by partisan self-interest to preserve their public subsidies, the opposition parties now also had a plausible public reason for forming a coalition and taking down the government. The Liberal party might be able to sidestep the bullet Harper was aiming straight through its heart and vault back to power. And for Stéphane Dion, a successful coalition would allow a degree of personal redemption, even if he were to be prime minister only through its first phase.[12]

It is critical to understand that, while this audacious attempt at combination was lubricated by the many similarities between the opposition parties on public policy, it was triggered by a moment of mutual self-interest. Antagonism to Harper and his government certainly helped, but it is not as if either the NDP or the Liberals woke up one morning and thought, dammit, we just have to do this to keep faith with our voters and for the good of the country.

Nonetheless, during their negotiations the Liberals and NDP

agreed on an agenda for the coalition government, with reasonable ease. What is striking about the document they drafted is that it read like a throne speech that could be delivered by either a Liberal or an NDP government, even without a coalition. It charted a Keynesian approach to the recession. It called for a stimulus package focusing on infrastructure, housing, and key manufacturing industries. At the same time, it called for a return to a budget surplus over four years, reflecting the fiscal conservatism of two of the negotiators, both from Saskatchewan: Ralph Goodale, the former Liberal finance minister, and Allan Blakeney, the former NDP premier of the province. It called for training and income support for the unemployed, and an improvement to childcare and the national child benefit "as finances permit"—classic weasel words inserted, presumably, out of concern for the deficit. And it advocated a North American cap-and-trade system to curb greenhouse gas emissions. It was, in other words, neither a Liberal nor an NDP document as such; but it was certainly a *progressive* document, contrasting sharply with the policies of the Harper Conservatives. Neither party had to swallow itself whole to sign; neither party needed to be ashamed of what it had compromised.

Although the fury of the Conservatives' response to the proposed coalition was predictable, their willingness to, plain and simple, lie—and their ability to get away with it—was not. Stephen Harper repeated over and over that the Bloc Québécois would be a member of the coalition. Untrue: the BQ pledged to support the coalition in confidence votes for a period of about a year and a half. The BQ would sit on the opposition benches as they had always done. Harper even claimed that there were no Canadian flags in the room when the coalition accords were signed—a palpable untruth, exposed by even a cursory glance at the video. These attacks were very effective with many Canadians.[13] But it wasn't just Harper's bold tactics (which eventually included an unprecedented prorogation of parliament) that brought the coalition down. There was another critical element: the spectacular incompetence of the Liberals, including Dion.

Just days before a non-confidence motion was likely to occur in the House of Commons, likely precipitating the fall of the Conservative government, Stephen Harper announced he would speak to the country about what was rapidly turning into a constitutional crisis. The networks invited Dion to submit a pre-recorded reply that would be aired immediately afterwards. The day of the broadcast, December 3, found Dion preoccupied, not with the most important public statement of his life, just hours away, but with drafting a letter to the Governor General, Michaëlle Jean, in professorial tones, instructing her on what he believed to be her constitutional duty if the Harper government were to fall as expected. It was only late in the afternoon that Dion turned his full attention to that evening's address. As a result, the taping began late. The cameraman, Mick Gzowski (son of Peter), had at his disposal only a minicam of the sort you might use to shoot pictures of your kids at the beach. Liberal staffers showed up at the parliamentary press gallery with the minicam record-ing—which was not compatible with the format broadcasters use—and had both the French and English versions on the same recording, even though they were to be broadcast simultane-ously. To make things worse, they arrived ten minutes after the 6:30 p.m. deadline. They rushed back to Liberal headquarters to retrieve the cables needed to play back directly from their mini-cam. They arrived once again at the press gallery after Harper was off the air, only to be told that the feed-point was at the CBC and they needed an escort to get there. At 7:15, the CBC finally got the recording, but needed to dub it onto separate English and French versions before it could be broadcast. CTV returned to regular programming. Such was the state of the Liberals' once-vaunted political professionalism.

It was after 7:30 when Dion finally hit the air. "…job losses and deficits for the next few years," Dion began confusingly, his opening salutation and the beginning of this sentence somehow having been cut off. "The Canadian government has a duty to act, and help Canadians weather this storm," he continued. But few viewers were likely listening to his words. Weirdly, the camera was focussed not on Dion himself, in the foreground, but on a bookshelf behind him. It looked like he might be broadcasting from the home office in his basement rec room. While Dion's eyes and nose were fuzzy, you could read the crisply rendered title of one of the books behind him: "Hot Air."[14] The air—hot or otherwise—was out of the balloon. The opposition's historic gambit to claim power from a politically isolated minority government was finished. In a matter of days, Dion was gone as Liberal leader and the notion of a coalition was dead—lingering on only as a spectral bogey-man conjured up by Stephen Harper to excite the devoted and terrify the timid and the ignorant.

The coalition fell apart not for reasons of policy, ideology, or party identity. It certainly did not come undone because its program to fight the recession was contrary to the views or the interests of most Canadians. The coalition died for more narrowly political reasons, most of them short-term. First, while most Canadians hadn't voted for Harper, even fewer had voted for Dion. All the university bigheads, try as they might to explain that a coalition was perfectly consistent with parliamentary tradition, were not going to convince Canadians that the biggest loser in the election should end up in 24 Sussex. Second, the Conservatives identified and exploited a genuine weakness in the coalition plan, which was its dependency on the separatist Bloc Québécois. You did not have to be a rabid Harperite to wonder whether this was wise. The BQ was not a party to the coalition agreement itself, but it was a signatory to the policy agenda, and, in a stunning communications misstep, the Liberals arranged for the two documents to be signed in the same room, one after the other, indelibly imprinting Gilles Duceppe's presence in the public mind. Third, the ferocity of the Harper counter-attack, which eventually included a stunning and unprecedented prorogation of parliament—left the coalition partners with at least two months to swing in the wind without an opportunity to bring the government down with a vote of non-confidence.

The coalition had been, to use a phrase from evolutionary biology, a "hopeful monster": a genetic mutation that might have turned out to be adaptive. But it was, in fact, stillborn. It did demonstrate the principle that the parties could work together to establish a common platform that would speak to both their electorates, and it had the potential to dislodge the Conservatives. The possibility the coalition represented might return, but it would only do so if once again there was a moment of exquisite equipoise in which both parties saw it to be in their institutional self-interest.

SHALL WE DANCE?

Brian Topp saw the failure of the coalition in 2008 as a historic opportunity missed, but also as a contribution to the NDP's subsequent historic breakthrough at the polls. Shortly after the 2011 election, Topp wrote that Layton's support for the coalition, while not particularly popular in English-speaking Canada, was part of his growing appeal in Quebec: "It showed an open-mindedness and a willingness to work with others to get things done. Those events transformed Layton into a senior national figure in the eyes of francophone Quebecers, and a source of hope that change is possible. It got them to thinking about playing a positive role rather than a defensive one in federal governance. In other words, the 2008 coalition helped shake Quebecers loose from their prior boycott of federal politics." Not coincidentally, the NDP's election slogan in Quebec had been *"Travaillons ensemble."*[15]

So when Jack Layton woke up on the morning of May 3, 2011,

as leader of Her Majesty's Loyal Opposition, he was conscious that his willingness to collaborate with the Liberals had been part of his appeal. Yet, he also watched as the Liberal party tumbled precipitously into a discussion of merger in the first few hours after their electoral drubbing, and saw how many Liberals gagged reflexively at the very thought. Layton, in serene control of his own party, was able to manage the issue much more delicately. Seeing that the Liberals were not ready to deal, he took the issue off the table. In an interview, Layton said that he was "not having any conversations" about a merger, and that the NDP now represented the "true alternative" to the Conservatives. Asked about talk that former party leaders such as Ed Broadbent and Jean Chrétien had been chatting about collaboration, he replied, "We have too much work to do to stop Mr. Harper from doing certain things that he would like to do." On background, some of his advisors acknowledged that he was picking his words carefully: he certainly never ruled anything out. But the news stories sharpened his position beyond what he had actually said, as perhaps he intended. The *Globe and Mail*'s website, for example, headlined that Layton was "not interested" in a merger. At the party's triumphal post-election party convention in Vancouver a few weeks after the election, it was a time to celebrate, not supplicate. One NDP strategist remarked to me, "We're not going to waste tons of time worrying about [whether the Liberals want to cooperate]. We'll wait and see…Job number one for the Liberals now is to break us."

At the convention, NDP delegates debated a resolution that would have prohibited any discussions of a merger with the Liberal party. "It's about rejecting everything the Liberal party has stood for…and everything about the Liberal party that was rejected by Canadians," said one delegate who supported the resolution, from the floor. Clearly, many in the party implacably opposed playing footsie with the Liberal party. Some pointed out that, while they had often advocated policies similar to the NDP's during elections, the Liberals had a history of cutting sharply right once in office. Other delegates felt the ideological chasm was too wide ever to be bridged.

Indeed, the images of contempt that many Liberals had built of NDPers were reflected back in full measure. The most recent Liberal prime ministers, Jean Chrétien and Paul Martin, were regarded by many New Democrats as shape-shifters who represented the corporate world in government but presented themselves to voters as progressives at election time. Their strategists, such as Eddie Goldenberg and David Herle, were seen as cynics who coveted the NDP's votes but spurned the party's ideas. Some individual Liberal MPs, for example Scott Brison, who had once been a Progressive Conservative and who mixed politics with a Bay Street career, were cited as the kind of Liberal no NDPer could ever consort with. Even the hapless Stéphane Dion, who attended the NDP's Vancouver convention as an observer, was singled out by one delegate from the mic as an implacable foe of social democratic ideals—to which he reacted characteristically with a nervous smile. You might imagine that Bob Rae, as a former NDP premier, would catch a break from his erstwhile party compatriots: just the reverse. Speaking of Rae, one former senior advisor to an NDP prairie premier remarked to me that "a traitor is a traitor is a traitor."

But there were also many disparate groups within the NDP who saw it all differently. There were those, like Layton and Topp, who took the strategic view that the NDP leader should be able to evaluate whatever opportunities might present themselves. There were also provincial New Democrats from the prairies whose own voter support overlapped that of the federal Liberals, as did their ideology and policies.

And the openness to collaboration within the NDP was by no means limited to "centrist" New Democrats. Some leftist intellectuals, like economists Jim Stanford and James Laxer, had long been more concerned about the advance of progressive politics than about narrow party advantage. A decade earlier, they had been proponents of the New Politics Initiative (NPI), which had hoped to reinvigorate the seemingly moribund NDP by broadening it through closer links to anti-globalization, environmental, feminist, and other political activists. Though the NPI eventually disbanded, Stanford later wrote of the 2008 coalition attempt that "the idea of progressive electoral coalitions fits naturally within the NPI's view of politics."[16] These ideas were shared by elements of the union movement, centred around the Canadian Auto Workers, where Stanford works. CAW leaders Buzz Hargrove and, later, Ken Lewenza, had advocated a tactical approach to supporting Liberal as well as NDP candidates in provincial and federal elections, and had called for cooperation and even merger of the two parties.[17]

In the end, the resolution to prohibit talks with the Liberals was easily defeated at the NDP's Vancouver convention, without Layton's even having to go to a mic to oppose it. Yet that would by no means be the final word. The issue would be revisited in the aftermath of Layton's sudden and unanticipated death. And, this time, it would be considered through the strangely refractive prism of a leadership race.

DIPPERS DECIDE

On its face, you might have expected the NDP leadership race to show more openness to collaboration with the Liberals than it ultimately did. Thomas Mulcair, always among the front-runners, was himself a former provincial Liberal cabinet minister. Breaking from NDP party tradition, but cleaving to the dominant sentiments of his home province of Quebec, he was sympathetic to free trade agreements. He also called on the NDP to "modernize" its language and approach, reflecting, perhaps, the less class-based nature of the party's support in Quebec.[18] He seemed the candidate most suited to replacing the Liberal party by occupying its existing political space, or at least that of its centre-left elements. For different reasons, you might have anticipated three other front-runners remaining open to collaboration. Brian Topp, of course, had been an architect of the 2008 coalition deal. Peggy Nash had spent most of her career as a staffer at the CAW alongside Ken Lewenza, Jim Stanford, and other advocates of a progressive alliance who supported her for the leadership. Paul Dewar had established himself in parliament as a non-ideological moderate in his foreign affairs critic post, and as a pragmatist, befitting his family's roots in municipal politics. Yet all these candidates rejected talk of merger or other close collaboration—at least until after the 2015 election. And they had good tactical reasons for doing so.

In the midst of a leadership race, the voters—party members, that is—are at their most tribal. However, Thomas Mulcair—who was always seen either as the front-runner or the one to beat in the 2011–12 leadership race—was a relatively new recruit to the tribe. And this had a formative effect on all the campaigns. As a newcomer, Mulcair could not afford to look like he was a fifth columnist, come to convert the NDP into an extension of the Liberal party. More than any of the other candidates, he needed to establish his NDP bona fides. He not only ruled out merger or cooperation with the Liberals before an election, but even a coalition afterwards.[19] It was a way of stamping his party ticket in capital letters: N D P.

In order to expose Mulcair's weakness as a newbie, the other leading contenders emphasized their own deep roots in the party. One of the core dynamics of the campaign was a contest among all the other candidates to see which one would survive onto the final ballot, facing Mulcair. Whoever succeeded might benefit from an anybody-but-Mulcair sentiment. During much of the seven-month race, Brian Topp was regarded as the likeliest to win this secondary contest. Topp was a former aide to the Saskatchewan moderate Roy Romanow, an advisor to Jack Layton as he steered the federal party into the mainstream, and widely regarded as the force behind the attempt to remove the word "socialist" from the party's constitution at the party's convention less than a year before. But in the course of the campaign, he transmogrified into the avatar of the party's social democratic tradition. Of course in defining himself this way, he could not simultaneously be a stalking horse for collaboration with the Liberals. Speaking at a leadership debate, Topp, the lifelong political organizer, explained his opposition to working with the Liberals in terms of strategy: "I say we should listen to the counter-party [i.e., the Liberals]…what they believe would happen under a proposal like that is that half their party would vote Conservative." The Liberals, in other words, couldn't bring their existing strength to a joint project, even if they tried.

Topp had great strengths as a candidate: his vast political experience, his sharp eye to progressive policy that could be retailed to voters, and an appealing personal demeanour. But he had weaknesses as well. He had never run for or held elective office, and it became apparent early in the race that he had a lot to learn about being behind the podium instead of behind the curtain. Although his performance improved greatly over the campaign, his uncertain start raised the question of how he would lead the NDP's newly swollen caucus from outside the House of Commons. He was also seen correctly by some on the left as a relative moderate, and by others as insufficiently populist.

This created an opening for two other candidates, both MPs, Peggy Nash and Paul Dewar—who also sought the mantle of protector of the NDP flame. They appealed directly to long-time New Democrats and movement activists who saw collaboration with the Liberals as a form of ideological capitulation. "We need to stay true to our values as New Democrats, true to our principles," Nash told me. "That's how we won so many seats—a record number of seats—in the last election." They also spoke to NDPers who took a more tactical view, seeing the 2015 election as an opportunity to raid the Liberals' remaining strength. In an interview with me, Dewar said: "We've come to a place we've always dreamed of and we're going to say all of a sudden 'OK, tools down, and let's open the door to a party we've always had problems with in terms of what they say and what they do'?"

You may be wondering what had happened to the impulse to cooperation so visible in the bid for the coalition in 2008, and kept alive by the delegates to the NDP's 2011 convention under Layton's watchful eye. At the outset of the leadership campaign, the tempestuous and frequently foul-mouthed Winnipeg MP Pat Martin flirted with the idea of running for the leadership to promote a party merger, but thought better of it. Probably for the better. Martin's political flamethrower style juxtaposed oddly with the notion of working well with others.

In the end, the only candidate to enter the race and support a form of collaboration was Nathan Cullen, the MP from Skeena-Bulkley Valley in northern BC. As Cullen liked to tell the crowds, he alone among the leadership candidates had defeated a Conservative to get into parliament.[20] An affable, humorous speaker with decent French, he quickly became a media favourite. Cullen's strategy from the start was to carve himself a role as the representative of a new style of politics. The most distinctive element of his pitch was a proposal for Liberals, New Democrats, and Greens in Conservative-held seats to have the option of holding a run-off among the nominated candidates from each party, with the winner getting a straight shot at the Conservatives. He called this a "one-time offer," aimed at getting a progressive coalition government in 2015. Cullen said he was opposed to an outright merger of the parties. There were many technical objections to this idea.[21] But the real issues were political: Did the parties have the will to adopt such a scheme? If the local associations decided to support a single candidate, would party activists and voters follow their lead? Was cooperation with the Liberals likely to undermine the historical goal of displacing them altogether?

The other candidates were withering in their contempt for his proposal, and although it won him significant media attention, Cullen seemed taken aback by the backlash among many party activists. He complained to me in an interview that it was "disingenuous" for candidates who had supported party collaboration of various kinds in the past to start "chest-thumping" about his proposal. He criticized those who ruled out joint nominations but not an eventual coalition. "It's somewhat hypocritical," he said, "to say that these guys [Liberals] are without merit before an election but they're perfectly fine after. I don't think that washes. It isn't morally or intellectually credible." Nonetheless, for a period, he struggled to avoid being pigeon-holed as a single-issue candidate whose single issue was a turn-off for many potential voters.

In the late fall and early winter of 2011, Cullen's candidacy had hit the doldrums. A flash in the media pan, he had not yet caught fire among the party activists. The NDP's leadership selection process was based on a system of one-member, one-vote. Party members could vote ahead of time using a preferential ballot, numbering their choices among the candidates. Or they could show up at the Toronto "convention" and make their choices in real time as the ballots progressed,[22] but their votes did not count any more heavily if they voted in person. This structure meant that early in the campaign, there was a premium on candidates selling party memberships. But Cullen's joint nomination proposal turned off many of the party's diehard foot-soldiers on whom all the campaigns relied for this purpose. Perhaps for that reason, Cullen tried toning down the joint nomination idea for a while, but that left his campaign spinning in circles, no matter how much the media had taken to his gentle jokes and winning smile.

Enter Jamey Heath, the former Layton aide who had written about creating a single progressive option for Canadians. Heath had been shopping around for a candidate who would promote his ideas. In the course of negotiating Heath's takeover of the campaign, the two men agreed that Cullen would double-down on the joint nomination idea, rather than running away from it.

It may be that by the beginning of 2012, the euphoria of the 2011 NDP surge was beginning to wear off, and the reality of a full-term Harper Conservative majority was starting to sink in. It may be that the support of outside progressive organizations, such as Avaaz and Leadnow, validated Cullen's campaign. And it may be that his consistently strong performances in debates made the difference, with pundits commenting that his upbeat personality was the closest among the candidates to "Jack's." As the voting approached, Cullen's campaign became a top fundraiser, even exceeding the front-runners, Topp and Mulcair, in the number of donors if not the monetary amount of donations. Heath claimed that in the final days, the campaign turned away donors because the campaign could not spend all the money in the time that remained. Leadnow, which supports a single progressive option, invited visitors to their website to "click-through" to the NDP site to sign up and vote, presumably for Cullen. More than 5,000 did so, though only the NDP knows how many of those actually joined up.

Despite Cullen's late surge, it was clear in the latter stages of the campaign that Mulcair was well ahead of all the other candidates, based on his potential to hold onto the party's gains in Quebec, plus his combativeness and parliamentary experience. Behind the scenes, Topp's campaign approached Peggy Nash's with a proposal for a joint press conference to encourage mutual support. In old-fashioned delegated conventions, candidates who fell off the early ballots could march across the floor to another candidate, "throwing" their support, as Gerard Kennedy had done, for example, in helping to waft Stéphane Dion to victory in 2006. However, in the NDP's process, most party members would be casting their preferential ballots ahead of time, meaning that the result would be "baked in the cake" before the so-called convention even started. If Topp and Nash were going to gang up against Mulcair, they'd have to signal this to their supporters ahead of time. But Nash's campaign seems to have rebuffed the idea.

Meanwhile, the media were gripped by a ferocious attack on Mulcair by Ed Broadbent, the party's elder statesman and a Topp supporter, in which he questioned both Mulcair's temperament and his fealty to the party's traditions. New Democrats were deeply divided over the appropriateness and the effectiveness of Broadbent's comments, though it seems likely that they contributed to Topp's final push, which put him second to Mulcair in all four rounds of voting.

Barely noticed by the media in the foofaraw over Broadbent was the way in which the growing strength of Cullen's campaign had subtly coloured the rhetoric of some other candidates. Peggy Nash, while continuing to reject Cullen's joint nomination proposal, began to emphasize her history as someone who worked well with others, hinting that this meant sharing resources with the Liberals in some unspecified way. In his nomination speech in Toronto on the final day of the campaign, Mulcair spoke against a backdrop emblazoned with the words *"Progressives United."* Only so much can be made of all this. Obviously, candidates who thought they were ahead needed to appeal to supporters of other candidates for their second preferences. Mulcair, Nash, and the others all wanted to woo Cullen's supporters in case he was eliminated in an early round. But the rhetorical shifts by Mulcair and Nash did suggest that Cullen's ideas were no longer being greeted with reflexive horror by New Democrats.

Cullen's scheme and his candidacy played the role of surrogate for those in the NDP who supported any kind of interparty collaboration. Many observers had predicted that his proposal would put a cap on his popularity. In the end, he managed to last until the third ballot, taking a quarter of the vote—much more than most commentators expected. Among the minority of NDPers who voted in real-time during the convention, rather than in advance, he actually won, according to one analysis.[23] Interestingly, there was a substantial fall-off in the total votes between the third and fourth ballots, when Cullen was eliminated, amounting to about 23% of his third-ballot support. This may suggest that some of his supporters were adamant that they would only vote for a candidate supporting cooperation with the Liberals, and so they didn't bother to choose between the finalists, Topp and Mulcair, as they could have done.

Some pundits described the NDP's 2012 leadership race as a struggle for the soul of the party. And they were egged on in this view by the rhetoric of some of the candidates and their supporters, including Ed Broadbent. The fact was that there was no true champion of the party's left in the 2012 leadership—the role played in previous conventions by James Laxer, Rosemary Brown, and Svend Robinson, for example. Peggy Nash came closest, but her consensual style was utterly different from her predecessors'. The results of the leadership race suggested a much more moderate party than its opponents or the media sometimes convey. Of the final three candidates, Mulcair and Cullen were widely regarded as being on the centrist side of the party, and, while Brian Topp made fulsome appeals to party tradition, his career had been made as a party centrist. The party's traditional left-right divide was greatly scrambled, with Laxer endorsing Mulcair, the anti-globalization author and activist Naomi Klein backing Cullen, and the most prominent left-wing MP, Libby Davies, supporting Topp. Equally striking, the support of organized labour was widely distributed among the candidates, with Nash, Topp, and Mulcair each winning substantial endorsements.

There is no doubt that the choice of Mulcair was ultimately strategic, in that it was a choice made out of hope of future electoral success rather than because of a passionate personal following. Mulcair was not only the sole candidate who had sat in a cabinet, he had also talked about "modernizing" the party, loosening its ties with labour, and making its peace with international trade. It is striking, then, that to win Mulcair had to take substantial second-preference support from candidates such as Nash, Dewar, and the twenty-nine-year-old Manitoba MP Niki Ashton, who had emphasized traditional social democratic values. The choice of Mulcair also indicated a sea-change in the party's approach to Quebec, triggered by the 2011 results. In the past, the party had no problem considering or even electing candidates such as Ed Broadbent, Dave Barrett, or Audrey McLaughlin, who spoke extremely limited French. This time the only completely unilingual candidate at the outset—Nova Scotia MP and former provincial leader Robert Chisholm—was quickly forced from the race for that very reason, and Paul Dewar's struggles in his second language were a major impediment to his candidacy. Implicitly, then, in the course of the selection process, the party put more emphasis on retaining its strength in Quebec than, for example, reviving itself in its old prairie or Western heartland.

Still, if in some ways Mulcair's election seemed to set the party up for a shot at government, presumably by eating the Liberals' lunch, the leadership race also suggested the limitations of the orange wave. Topp, Nash, and Dewar were each able to mobilize existing organizational networks from provincial parties, labour, and progressive activists to promote their candidacies. Cullen had the assistance of outside groups promoting party membership behind his joint nomination scheme. And Mulcair had the support of the majority of the party's new MPs in Quebec. And yet the party managed to attract only 44,000 new members over the course of the campaign, for a total of 128,000. The Liberals had managed to recruit nearly a third as many over a similar period without a leadership race. Most worrisome, the party grew in Quebec from about 1,700 to just over 12,000, an impressive percentage increase, but well under the Mulcair campaign's goal of 20,000. The supposedly moribund BQ had managed to get more *voters* in its decidedly low-key race to choose Daniel Paillé as leader a few months before than the NDP had *members* in the province. In part because it has a single membership for both the provincial and federal parties, the NDP ended the leadership race heavily overweighted in British Columbia, Saskatchewan, and Manitoba in relation to its federal caucus, or, indeed, to its voter base. And of those eligible to vote for the leader in 2012, only half bothered to do so.

LOVE'S LABOUR'S LOST

Jack Layton's funeral was ingeniously designed, by him and those closest to him, as political theatre that would celebrate what the party had become under his leadership. There was little to feed the stereotypes of the party as a feral pack of socialists with bad hair-cuts; tough-talking, brawny-armed and overweight union bosses; and downtown do-gooders wearing Birkenstocks. The pallbearers at Layton's carefully staged funeral included two current NDP premiers (Greg Selinger and Darrell Dexter), two former premiers (Gary Doer and Roy Romanow), and two former provincial ministers (Joy MacPhail from BC and Marilyn Churley from Ontario). In contrast there were just two labour activists (Winnie Ng and Ken Neumann), matching the number of policy intellectuals (Charles Taylor and Tim Flannery). This was a way of drawing attention to the fact that the NDP has a long tradition of government at the provincial level, often over extended periods. Since Tommy Douglas was first elected premier of Saskatchewan in 1944, the New Democrats have been in government in that province for forty-six years. Since Ed Schreyer was first elected premier of Manitoba in 1969, the party has held office there for nearly thirty years. These governments have a history of progressive policy, introducing medicare, public auto insurance, home-based health care, broad-based childcare, environmental legislation, and imaginative and generous approaches to their large native populations. At the same time, they have a respectable record of wrestling with budgets—generally with more success than their conservative rivals.

To the public, Layton's achievement had been to put a cheerful, moderate face on the NDP, allowing voters to grow comfortable with the idea of NDPers in government. Internally, Layton's achievement had been to bring his party along in this process without a bitter faceoff with labour and the party's left, as Tony Blair had done in transforming the British Labour party. Layton used his own background and credibility as a social activist to draw in Libby Davies, who symbolized the value he placed on the party's activist wing. When Davies went too far, commenting that all of Israel had been in a state of occupation since 1948, Layton rebuked her but kept her on as deputy leader, along with Mulcair. Layton valued the party's left, even if it often did not get its way. Meanwhile, for better or for worse, labour's weight within the NDP was waning. First, because of falling union membership in the country, and, second, because the new party financing laws prohibited union contributions. In fact, after Layton died, and the party embarked on its one-member, one-vote process to replace him, the national executive made an explicit decision not to create a carve-out for labour, ending the unions' structural role in the party they had helped to found a half-century earlier. Yet when Layton had been baited by the Harper government soon after he became opposition leader, with arbitrary legislation aimed at workers at Canada Post and Air Canada, he had had no trouble sticking up for them. The interests of working people, including union members, were as essential an element in

Layton's NDP as they are more generally in progressive politics.

It is inevitable that the NDP's opponents, in both the Conservative and the Liberal parties, will try to put a wedge between Mulcair, with his shallow roots in the party, and these foundational elements of the NDP. But it would be a mistake for Mulcair, in response to a charge that the party is "beholden" to labour, to turn his back on a movement that provides sinew and bone to nearly every progressive party in the world, including the American Democrats. If they were wise, Liberals would covet this support (as did Paul Martin during his brief regime), not disparage it. In an attempt to distinguish themselves from the NDP, they may be further restricting their already limited social base if they attack Mulcair on this front. And they will complicate future attempts to collaborate or coalesce in government.

The other fissure that the NDP's opponents will surely exploit is on national unity and the place of Quebec in Canada. NDPers chose Mulcair more than for any other reason because he had a prospect of holding Quebec for the party. While the party's success in knocking the knees from under the BQ in 2011 was not the result of a specific set of constitutional policies, it was framed by a sense that the party was less rigidly federalist than the other national parties. The party's Sherbrooke Declaration, engineered under Layton's leadership, accepted the Quebec government's right to script a referendum question and acknowledged the significance of a vote of 50 per cent +1, while remaining somewhat vague on how the federal government should respond to such a vote. It was an implicit rejection of the approach adopted by Jean Chrétien and Stéphane Dion in the *Clarity Act*, which bespoke a kind of tough love in which sovereignty won't come easy. The Sherbrooke Declaration also advocated "asymmetrical federalism," meaning that Quebec would enjoy powers and responsibilities other provinces would not have. These views are not just difficult for a lot of Liberals to swallow; many English Canadians, many NDP supporters outside Quebec and, if push came to shove, probably some NDP MPs from outside the province, might have trouble accepting the implications of these principles. In the last election, while they created a backdrop of acceptability for the NDP in Quebec, they got no notice in English Canada (where the possibility of an NDP win seemed remote until the final days).

Mulcair will find it increasingly difficult to negotiate these shoals. To temporize on these policies would be to undermine his principal advantage in Quebec. But some Liberals closely tied to the Trudeau-Chrétien-Dion tradition will see these same principles not only as a political weakness to be exploited, but even as a menace to Canada itself. Dion himself said as much in an almost hysterical discussion with NDP MP Peter Julian on CBC television, and in a newspaper op-ed. Drawing such sharp lines among federalists in Quebec is unwise. The NDP victory in the province was a great *federalist* victory, though it could yet prove evanescent. The Liberal approach to Quebec over the last half-century has held the country together, albeit barely at times, but it has not succeeded culturally as well as it has juridically. These issues will divide progressives in the NDP, just as they divided Liberals over Meech Lake (and, for that matter, the *Clarity Act*) not so long ago. Although some Liberals will be inclined to see these differences over federalism as a reason not to collaborate or merge with the NDP, you could equally well argue the opposite: that these differences are better managed within a party, respectfully, accepting that sincere federalists have different approaches and views, than between parties where constitutional positions are inflamed with partisan vitriol. A number of Liberals have pointed out that their party's future is parlous if it does not find a way to reconnect with Quebecers,[24] and insinuating there is some disloyalty in sharing the views of most of the province, including federalists, is not really the way to start a recovery.

Quebec is sometimes described as the most socially progressive

province in Canada, which is true only to a point. But as one leading New Democrat remarked to me, the new crop of NDP MPs
elected in 2011 are in many ways socially similar to the Béquistes
they supplanted. Many of them are social and labour activists.
They reflect the social democratic sensibilities that are widely
shared in Quebec. Quebec's universal low-cost childcare program
is as much embedded in the popular political culture now as is
medicare in the rest of the country: at its essence it is untouch-
able. Until recently, Quebec has kept university tuitions low as
they have skyrocketed in the rest of the country, and even a modest attempt to change the system rocked the Charest government
in the spring of 2012. Quebecers are socially liberal, overwhelmingly supporting same-sex marriage, for example. They opposed
participation in the American ballistic missile defence system,
and later in the Afghanistan war. As Stephen Harper discovered
to his cost in the 2008 election, they feel strongly about their
(government-subsidized) cultural institutions. Not without some
grumbling, they have been willing to bear higher tax rates than
other Canadians to pay for it all. But Quebecers have also been
heterodox on crucial issues from the perspective of many English
Canadian progressives. Free trade with the United States, and,
later, with Mexico, was strongly supported across the political spectrum in Quebec. Quebecers have also been much more
willing to consider tinkering with the mechanics of medicare,
including a greater degree of private and for-profit care. Perhaps
most important of all, Quebecers do not see the federal government as the great guarantor of social programs. After all, it is the
federal government that has often mandated programs which
the provinces must deliver, only to cut funding once they are
well established. For Quebecers, the best guarantee for a strong
network of social programs is not the government in Ottawa, but
their own political culture.

The sentiments of the NDP's Quebec wing will inevitably create tensions with its traditional base in English Canada. Some, including many Liberals, hope those tensions will be so powerful as to rip the party apart. Only two parties have ever successfully straddled the French-English divide, the Liberals and the Progressive Conservatives (under Macdonald and Mulroney), and in each case their failure to manage the relationship led to their undoing. But to the degree that the New Democrats succeed, at least in the near term, the party is likely to become less ideologically rigid without being any less progressive. That should make it not only more appealing to voters, but potentially a more congenial partner for Liberals.

BUT COULD IT HAPPEN?

As his first act after becoming interim Liberal leader, Bob Rae was forced to foreswear the right even to engage in discussions with the NDP over future collaboration. In his last few days before being elected NDP leader, Thomas Mulcair told a reporter that his view of collaboration of any kind with the Liberals, formal or informal, before or after an election, was, "N.O. ...The no is categorical, absolute, irrefutable, and non-negotiable. It's no. End of story. Full stop." These positions are adopted to placate constituencies within their respective parties, and to a degree to buttress strategic positions for competition between them. But they traduce the interests of the voters that both parties purport to represent.

"My own sense is that that's the way it is for now," Bob Rae told me in an interview just days before Mulcair's election. "And whether that changes depends on a lot of factors that I think in some sense lie outside the parties. ...I think it depends a lot on the public mood...I don't sense a huge demand from the public for a merger. In fact, I think people are quite aware of the fact that there's a big difference between the structure and attitudes of the Liberal party and the New Democratic party. I think that's just a reality right now. Whether that changes over a period of time, is hard to see. But I think there are some core elements to each party which make a strong point of how different they are from each other." That perception may have informed Rae's decision a few weeks later not to run for the permanent leadership of the Liberal party.

Rae's reference to the public mood is important, because so far the voice of the non-partisan progressive public has not fully registered in this debate. I spoke to Nathan Cullen a few weeks after the NDP leadership selection, and it was obvious that he was still struggling to reconcile his views with those of the victor, Thomas Mulcair.

"There is a hunger out there [for progressive cooperation]," he told me. "Absolutely. How do I tap into it and what does it look like? Because I also want to be careful that it doesn't look like I am trying to continue the race by another means...But it was interesting from a number of the campaigns seeing the language starting to shift when they recognized that an idea that had been very unpopular within the partisan core of the party had obvious take-up to a larger group of progressive Canadians who were also willing to join the party to join the conversation." Mulcair appointed Cullen as the NDP's house leader, which suggested that he was willing for the caucus to try taking a less partisan attitude towards the Liberals in parliament, at least.

To suggest that progressives would be better off with a single choice at election time is not to claim that a party alliance or even a merged party would have an untroubled path to victory. There is no guarantee that a Liberal-Democratic party, or Progressive Alliance, which ideally would also encompass the Greens, would be able to corral all the votes won by the individual parties in the past. In particular, because the Liberal party has straddled the centre of Canadian politics, and has sometimes veered across to the right, there are many traditional supporters who would not be comfortable with a more clearly progressive party. Some "blue

Liberals" would certainly be shed to the Conservatives, though it seems than many of them already deserted the party in 2011, particularly in southern Ontario. But a merged party would likely get more seats than its predecessors combined, even if it lost, say, a third of the 2011 Liberal support to the Conservatives.

The old PCs and Reform/Alliance fought three bitter elections as much against each other as against the Liberals before they exhausted themselves and merged. I am afraid this will repeat itself now among progressives. Liberals will not easily wrest themselves from dreams of former glory. New Democrats will wonder whether one more election might not finish the job of reducing the Liberals to pulp. I believe that progressive voters will have a single viable party sooner or later. That could happen by one of the existing progressive parties' vanquishing the others—as the NDP seems very nearly to have done to the BQ. That would take at a minimum one more election. But in the 1990s, it is worth remembering, the conventional wisdom was that it would take "one more election" for the future of the right to be settled, and in the end it took three.

For all the talk that the Liberals and New Democrats represent different traditions in Canadian politics, which they undoubtedly do, there is among the opponents of collaboration a willful disregard of their symbiotic relationship historically. To the extent that the NDP has had an influence on federal politics, it has primarily been through getting the Liberal party to adopt its ideas, either as an electoral strategy or as a matter of practical politics during periods of minority government. Without dismissing the real political differences between the Liberals and NDP, the fact is that for most progressive voters the differences are not fundamental. Cultural and personal differences among the parties' activists are the real obstacles to a merger or another form of deep cooperation. True, unlike the Progressive Conservatives and Reform in the 1990s, Liberals and New Democrats have never inhabited the same party. Unlike the PCs and Reform, there are no old bonds of friendship to be restored, no sadder-but-wiser reconciliation to be achieved. At a personal level, Liberals and NDPers have never forged the deep emotional connections that come with fighting an election campaign together. Instead, they have spent their political lives building up images of contempt for one another: Liberals as power-seekers without principle, every ready to steal NDP ideas in the campaign and then abandon them in government; New Democrats either as dreamy idealists or as craven populists who see no reason to square their promises with the real world. These people have come to dislike each other, and frankly don't think it would be much fun working shoulder-to-shoulder in a campaign.

For the two parties to overcome these antagonisms would require leadership—from inside the parties, but also from outsiders: intellectuals, think-tanks, journalists, organizers, independent progressive organizations, and fundraisers who could generate the ideas and stage the conferences. There is, in fact, plenty of time to do this before the 2015 election; but it is unlikely to happen unless the Liberals and New Democrats simultaneously see it as in their institutional interest, or the pressure from outside the ranks of long-time party activists becomes impossible to ignore. There could still be another opening before 2015. If there is not, the most likely outcome is another Conservative government—extending the rule of Harper and his successors into a second decade.

CHAPTER 7

WHY CHANGE IS NOW POSSIBLE

If progressives could set aside their partisan differences, they might see that we have come to a moment, a little like that grey English winter of 1978–79, when unsettling economic forces create a political opportunity. Not an opportunity to take refuge in an empty centrism, much less chase the Conservatives to the right. Nor an opportunity to go back to the seeming certainties of an earlier era. But an opportunity to bring a progressive lens to a new set of problems that conservatives are not well positioned to address.

The Great Unwinding that began with Lehman Brothers in the autumn of 2008, spun through the foundations of Wall Street and the City of London, pitched the world economy into an era of recession, and whipped through the Eurozone and onward, should give us pause to reflect and wonder whether we've really had it right all these long years. Joseph Stiglitz, the American economist and Nobel prize-winner, remarked that the collapse of Lehman Brothers may be to market fundamentalism what the fall of the Berlin Wall was to communism.[1] For many people—even the Harper Conservatives, remarkably enough—the deregulation of banks doesn't seem like such a great idea any more. Our globalized market economies have produced levels of inequality not seen in our lifetime—something that has got the notice, not just of Occupy Wall Street and its many offshoots, but even of the OECD, the Conference Board, and David Frum![2]

Perhaps Canadians will be willing to rethink what passed for so long as common sense in the mouths of conservative politicians, business journalists, and bank economists. There may be a democratic moment when we as citizens reappropriate what is ours: the right to make the big decisions about the way our society is ordered, and the way we live with one another. But that is by no means preordained. Crises, such as the Winter of Discontent and the Great Unwinding, create opportunities for new ways of thinking—and acting—but they do not guarantee any particular result. There are stirrings across North America that the better-off need to start carrying a load more commensurate with their rewards, but very little, it has to be said, has been done about it. Across the Atlantic, those disembodied souls, "the markets," at least temporarily replaced two elected governments, in Greece and Italy, with what amount to bank-appointed trustees, and the European Union is contemplating a further dilution of its democracy, also at their behest.

Back in the Winter of Discontent, it was inflation, stagnation, labour unrest, and governments with a fiscal model that had been broken by a sputtering end to predictable growth that raised up new politicians—Thatcher, Reagan and their imitators—who claimed they knew a different way. Their prescription was radical and transformative: inflation was the target, not unemployment; regulations "fettered" the markets; taxes squelched investment; social programs infantilized populations and stole their initiative; unions feathered the beds of their members at the expense

of society. Jeffrey Sachs has argued that Ronald Reagan misdi-
agnosed the America's economic problems, which stemmed not
from "big government" but from the oil price shock of the 1970s,
the dismantling of currency stability, and the costs of the war in
Vietnam.[3] But it would be naive to suppose that the Reaganauts
simply made an intellectual error. The policies they advocated
largely had their intended effect. Sure, some of the mechanisms
they advocated, like the Laffer Curve, didn't quite work out the
way they promised. But, in their heyday, the Reagan/Thatcher
policies made a lot of people enormously rich—more or less the
same people who argued for them, as it happened.

There was a huge growth in the size and international reach
of corporate America. Globalization allowed Walmart to source
its goods abroad, and in doing so bring downward pressure on
wages at home. More important yet was the process of *financial-
ization*, whereby the real economy of goods and services became
secondary to the financial instruments used to trade in it. Between
the 1970s and 2006, the finance industry's share of the US GDP
roughly doubled.[4] The proponents of these policies argued that
markets were natural and that regulation introduced "distor-
tions." Economic decisions became the preserve of experts drawn
from a highly mathematized strain of neoclassical economics.
What used to be the fundamental questions about the distribution of work and wealth in our society became abstruse technical
issues opaque often even to the politicians who theoretically
made the decisions. Forgotten in all this were some obvious facts.

First, that markets don't exist without regulation. There is a bit
of the miraculous about markets, as Adam Smith pointed out in
his famous phrase: "It is not from the benevolence of the butcher,
the brewer or the baker, that we expect our dinner, but from their
regard to their own interest." But as Smith himself recognized,
markets exist only within a framework of rules emanating from
government. Banks should understand this better than any, since

when we deposit our paycheques we put our faith not only in the well-compensated wisdom of their corporate executives, but in the web of government regulation that will steer them away from impetuous harm, and, as we have seen when that fails, on the implicit guarantee by governments that they will not allow the banks to collapse and refuse to return our money. Similarly, regulation must exist to prevent monopoly, collusion, price-fixing, and insider trading, to pick a few examples. That markets exist only within a regulated space is a fact that no thoughtful person—conservative, liberal, or social democrat—will deny. The issue is the nature and the extent of the regulation. But this is a truth that has often been forgotten.

Second, that markets inevitably produce "negative externalities"—costs imposed on people who are not parties to their transactions. The most colossal negative externality in the annals of humankind is the production of greenhouse gases leading to climate change. Neither producers nor consumers pay for even its contemporaneous effects, much less for the disaster it may visit on our children and grandchildren—nor will they, unless required to by governments and international agreements. Another good example is the systemic risk that the financial industry has posed and which taxpayers have had to backstop. The truth is that businesses will almost never internalize the full costs of doing business unless governments require them to do so. At the same time, businesses benefit from "positive externalities," like good roads and an education system, for which they pay a diminishing share of the tax burden.

Third, that taxes have distributional effects. This is so obvious it shouldn't need restating. If you lower taxes on capital gains, on corporations, and on high incomes, the wealthy will benefit. *That's the aim of the policy.* And the rest will suffer, either through paying a larger share of the cost of government, or through the reduction of services on which they depend more than the wealthy. Conservatives once argued that the benefits of tax breaks to the wealthy would "trickle down" through greater investment: we have now had a thirty-year experiment and the thesis has failed. For three decades it has been commonplace for policy makers to argue that we should ignore the obvious and immediate direct distributional effects of lowering taxes on the wealthy in favour of the unproven, indirect effects.[5] The burden of proof has gotten more than a little out of whack here.

Fourth, that globalization has had many unadvertised, unintended, or undesirable effects. Globalization has opened Canadians up to the world and made us more cosmopolitan, and, in doing so, has made us more confident in our own identity. It has allowed us to rediscover ourselves as an immigrant nation. It has made a few of us rich, and a few more very well off. But even its advocates are now recognizing its costs. It is, to begin with, a huge contributor to global warming. It has had mixed effects in developing countries, bringing new wealth and lifting many out of poverty, while crushing others under the wheels of a rapid industrialization without the strictures of labour and environmental laws we used to take for granted in the developed world. At home, it is now clear, it has contributed to the hollowing out of our middle class, not the least because in Canada's case it has tended to push us back into our traditional role as diggers and cutters, and encouraged the deindustrialization of our economy. Enough time has passed since the epic election of 1988 to set aside the stark ideological arguments of that era and examine the actual experience of globalization, good and bad.

Fifth, that the state can contribute directly to the well-being of individuals. Conservative politicians have long disparaged the capabilities of government, mocking "bureaucrats" and praising "entrepreneurs." More importantly, they have actively worked to hobble the state, embracing trade agreements and the diktats of the markets as limitations on its powers, and using deficit reduction as the mechanism to weaken its touch on our lives. These attitudes have been absorbed into the collective consciousness. Many Canadians still want government to make things better, but have lost the faith that it can. In some recess of our minds we remember when governments were expected to do something about problems, but we've forgotten exactly how that worked. Somehow we've forgotten that the greatest social programs of them all—universal free public education and health care—make our lives better every day of the year. And the teachers and nurses who populate them are no more bureaucrats than bond-traders are entrepreneurs. Given the current suspicion of government's ability to do so many things, it may be wise for progressives to look to measures like the National Child Benefit, which has done a great deal to alleviate child poverty and does not require a large bureaucracy.[6] But some great public purposes, like lifting our native peoples from the disgraceful conditions in which many of them live, will require policies with a grander sense of possibility, as we saw nobly, if too briefly, in the Kelowna accord.

And sixth, that one of the most important objects of economic policy should be the creation of good-paying, productive jobs. In the last thirty years, monetary policy has displaced fiscal policy as the main tool for managing the economy, and it has been a tool utilized largely to a single end: maintaining low inflation. Of course, we do not want a return to the double-digit inflation of the 1970s. That works against many vulnerable people on fixed incomes and it puts enormous pressures on labour relations. But it is an ideological, not a practical impulse, that says that governments should limit their participation in the economy to maintaining price stability. Secure, rewarding employment is crucial to human dignity, social stability, and the good life we aspire to in Canada.

Most progressive people who support the Liberal, New Democratic, and, for that matter, the Green, parties can see themselves in this. There are, to be sure, some Liberals who would resist the drift of these arguments—but they are more numerous in the apparatchik class of political staffers, lobbyists, and communications and advertising consultants whose tumultuous politics have so thoroughly contributed to the Liberal party's demise than they are among Liberal voters. I am not arguing that the classic differences between the Liberals and New Democrats—between more individualist and more collectivist approaches, for example, or between federalist and decentralist perspectives—are unimportant. I am suggesting that the Great Unwinding has created a moment that calls for leadership and that progressives have more that unites than divides them. The conservative consensus of the last three decades created an air of inevitability: relentless markets demanding this and that—tax cuts, spending cuts, deregulation, privatizations. Political and social choices seemed to evaporate. But the markets have been humbled now, or at least should have been. Their claims on our choices should no longer be regarded as absolute. And now, more than any time in the last few decades, is the time to take a stand.

At the same time, progressives need to show they are realistic about government. The Liberals have often been disturbingly sanguine about jettisoning their progressive campaign rhetoric once they found themselves at the cabinet table. New Democrats, at least at the federal level, have not always shown enough interest in the practicalities of governing and the difficult trade-offs they entail. It is a sign of the party's growing maturity that in its most recent leadership race there were serious discussions of budgets and deficits, taxation and trade, as well as of programs and spending.

But the problems we face are big, and need to be directly acknowledged. In fact, there's a very specific place from which to begin the discussion of Canada's future choices, and it is to be found at 57.02° N, 111.65° W.

IT'S GETTING HOT IN HERE

Courtesy of the miracle of Google Earth, it is possible to see the Alberta tar sands from outer space. Zoom out so that Alaska is in the upper left corner of your screen and Hudson Bay on the upper right, with the Western provinces arrayed below, and you can still see the gash in the landscape just north of Fort McMurray. Thanks to the tar sands (or the oil sands, as its proponents prefer) Canada now has the third-largest proven reserves of oil in the world, after Venezuela and Saudi Arabia. Production is growing very quickly: the government of Alberta says it will jump from 1.3 million barrels a day to 3 million barrels in 2018.[7] Current projections would see production triple from current levels by 2030, raising Canada's share of the world market for oil from roughly 2.5 per cent in 2005 to around 6 per cent.[8] And it is dirty. Greenhouse gas emissions from producing and upgrading the thick, gooey bitumen into marketable oil are generally reckoned to be about three to four times those of conventional oil. Over its life cycle, emissions from tar sands oil are about 17 per cent higher.[9] The "intensity" of emissions—that is to say, the rate of emissions per barrel of production—has fallen somewhat recently, but that is likely to reverse itself as the industry must tap less and less accessible reserves.

What most Canadians don't fully realize is that the tar sands *are* our climate change problem. At the moment, they produce about 5 per cent of our total emissions, but emissions are likely to triple over the next twenty years. If Canada were to reduce its overall emissions 80 per cent by 2050—a widely used benchmark[10]—the tar sands, on current projections, would produce *all* of Canada's emissions. This is obviously impossible. In fact, the tar sands alone explain the fact that the Harper government has no chance of meeting even its own modest goal of reducing emissions 17 per cent below 2005 levels by 2020. Though any projection needs to be treated with caution in a period of such economic volatility, the respected Pembina Institute estimates that, on current policies, Canada's emissions are set, not to fall, but to rise 7 per cent during that period. None of this is to say that making our cars run better or phasing out coal-fired plants aren't useful and necessary things to do. But it is like cutting out that morning latte to get back within your household budget when the real problem is that you spend every night down at the casino playing the slots.

Right now, both the federal and the Alberta governments have a policy of exploiting the tar sands as quickly as possible, which is why the province charges much lower royalties than it could, and why both governments enthusiastically backed the Keystone XL pipeline, which would ship synthetic crude oil and diluted bitumen to refineries in Illinois, Oklahoma, and Texas for further processing. But if we don't dig it up in such a hurry the oil won't go away, and, given the state of the world's reserves, it isn't likely to lose its value, either. A slower rate of development would allow cleaner production technologies to come on stream, and would allow Alberta to develop its own capacity to refine its product and add value with industrial jobs. It would ease the upward pressure on our dollar that has been costing us industrial jobs elsewhere in the country, and it would allow Alberta a sustainable pace of growth. But, under Harper, Canada's environmental and economic policies have been fixed around ripping as much money out of the northern Alberta ground as quickly as possible, whatever the costs to other Canadians, present or future.

As a result, the Harper government's climate change policy has necessarily been to stall as long as it can, doing next to nothing here at home and obstructing action internationally. To say that Stephen Harper was at one time a climate change denier is to give him too much credit. He has never advanced an argument; at most he has tried to sow confusion by casting doubt on the credibility of the science, referring to climate change as a "controversial hypothesis" (2002) and saying that the "jury is out" (2004). As late as 2006, Harper was mocking the idea that climate change has had measurable effects, commenting that the Liberals would "have trouble explaining why it was that [Prince Edward] Island didn't actually sink into the Gulf of St. Lawrence after all." It was not until 2007 that Harper acknowledged the reality of human-made climate change. Having to that extent bent to the weight of scientific evidence and popular opinion, the Harper government then engaged in a campaign of dilatory tactics. For a time, it lashed its policy to that of Barack Obama, who had promised a cap-and-trade system to ratchet down the emission of greenhouse gases. The promise to integrate Canada's plans with those of a progressive president, hugely popular in Canada, bought Harper's government time. Even better, as it turned out, Obama failed to get his proposal past Congress, leaving Canada, as much as the United States,[11] without a policy.

The Harper government did introduce stricter regulations on car emissions and on coal-fired plants, which were designed to sound impressive but to do little, at least in the near term. By the time of the Copenhagen conference on climate change in late 2009, the Harper government had moved towards a policy of open obstruction of international efforts, famously winning a series of "fossil" awards from environmental activists, and making a small but significant contribution to the conference's failure. At the 2011 conference in Durban, Canada continued its efforts to complicate an international agreement, and formally withdrew from the Kyoto agreement a few days later. The environment minister, Peter Kent, had picked up the phrase "ethical oil," coined by Sun TV comedian/commentator Ezra Levant, to promote the tar sands.[12] The notion is that Canadian oil is a more ethical choice for Americans than oil from the Gulf and South America. It is a rhetorical shell game—an attempt to distract the attention of Americans from the environmental costliness of tar sands oil. But to the extent Levant's argument deserves any weight at all, it is from the perspective of American, not Canadian policy.[13] We export more than two-thirds of our oil production to the United States, in part because we lack the infrastructure to refine and deliver it to our own consumers. As a result, Canadians actually import about half the oil they consume themselves. Where from? Mostly from those unethical countries Kent and Levant have been warning us about. Meanwhile, according to one widely cited index of performance in reducing greenhouse gas emissions, Canada ranked fifty-first out of fifty-eight countries rated, and among the top ten emitting nations, Canada was seventh, ahead of Russia, China, and Iran, but behind the UK, Germany, India, South Korea, Japan, and the United States.[14] Ethical?

Progressives have lost a moral language with which to describe these policies, which put the fleeting acquisition of riches by some of us today ahead of the well-being of our children and our grandchildren. It takes whatever uncertainties there may be about the effects of climate change—and inevitably with such complex systems there are some—as an excuse to value our own comforts and prosperity over the very lives of others. The dry terminology of Kant's categorical imperative to which many secular progressives subscribe provides only an echo of the lively moral language available to an earlier generation, including Tommy Douglas and Stanley Knowles, whose progressive values were grounded in their religious faith. They could speak of wickedness, the sinfulness of doing unto others what we would never wish be done unto us. The lives we are blighting are not less worthy because they belong to a generation only now coming to adulthood.

Sad to say, the Conservatives don't bear all of the blame. In 1997, just a couple of weeks after Jean Chrétien won his second election, he committed Canada to reducing its greenhouse gas emissions by 6 per cent below 1990 levels as a prelude to the ratification of the Kyoto accord. In his memoirs, Jean Chrétien gives an impassioned explanation for the urgency of action on climate change, while dismissing the many objections of businesspeople and provincial politicians.[15] He says that it was important "to establish an obtainable target and then to figure out how to meet it step by step, year by year. The fact is if you have no set destination in mind, you'll never get anywhere."[16] A noble sentiment, but one he devoted precious little political capital to achieving.[17] For his part, Paul Martin used Chrétien's lack of an implementation plan as an excuse to stay out of the way of his allies in cabinet from resource-based Western provinces, Ralph Goodale and Anne McLellan, who did their best to slow or obstruct action. The result was that, as Chrétien himself admitted, Canada still had no effective plan for implementing the Kyoto accord when we eventually ratified the agreement in 2002, five years after the initial commitment.[18] Martin was born again on the issue after becoming prime minister, and eventually appointed Stéphane Dion as his environment minister. Dion, who turned out to be an impassioned champion of Kyoto, went on to chair the generally successful 2005 climate change conference in Montreal in the dying days of the Martin regime.

In his memoirs, Martin speaks of that conference as a great triumph for his government and for the fight against climate change. Like Chrétien, he speaks passionately on the urgency of the issue and his commitment to the fight—rooted in a life-long interest in the environment, as indeed Chrétien says of his own views. Martin blames Canada's failures on Chrétien and Harper. Chrétien blames his "successors" (note the plural) for succumbing to the anti-Kyoto forces, "whether for political or ideological reasons." What is not in dispute is that, after nearly thirteen years in office, the Liberals had failed. Utterly. This was not just a political failure, but a moral one. No one involved questioned the science or doubted the need for action. They just didn't do what was within their powers to do.

Stéphane Dion, to his moral and intellectual credit, recognized climate change as the overarching challenge of our age. Some of his political errors could be put down to the depth of this conviction. Unfortunately, the Liberal party learned the wrong lessons from his ignominious defeat. Although the environment could be seen as the archetypal cause of the "radical centre," the Liberal party would do everything it could to distance itself from Dion's policy after his hasty removal as leader. Michael Ignatieff, who had toyed with the idea of a carbon tax during his first run for the leadership in 2006, would as leader profess enthusiasm for the tar sands. Even tactically this was dumb, because it undercut the party's environmental appeal in central Canada, especially in Quebec, without the remotest possibility of winning seats in Alberta.

For its part, the NDP has hardly clothed itself in glory. There is no doubt about the sincerity of many New Democrats on climate change. But the party has tended to use the issue tactically. When Dion made common cause with Green party leader Elizabeth May in 2008, New Democrats could have chosen to emphasize the shared goal of getting our greenhouse gas emissions into reverse gear. But New Democrats saw the Greens as a political threat, and they saw Dion as a vulnerable foe. Instead of emphasizing what they had in common, Jack Layton's party attacked a supposed flaw in the architecture of Dion's carbon tax scheme: to the extent that it would succeed in reducing emissions, revenues would also fall, undermining the finances for social programs.[19] The moral challenge for progressives is to rally Canadians to the cause—not to dissipate our energies quarrelling about the policy architecture.

Canada is among the worst per capita emitters of greenhouse gases in the world, and, unlike comparable offenders Australia and the United States, we are headed in the wrong direction. The Harper government has lowered the goalposts, replacing the Kyoto commitment with much more limited targets of reducing greenhouse gasses to 17 per cent below 2005 levels by 2020 and

60 per cent below those levels by 2050. However, not surprisingly, since it has made few efforts to reach those goals, we are slipping still further. In 2009, the National Roundtable on the Environment and the Economy published a report on how to reach the Harper government's goals. The roundtable is a consultative body established by the Mulroney government to bring together business, labour, government, and academic experts. Its chair was a University of Calgary professor, Bob Page, who was an executive at the energy company TransAlta. Its president was David McLaughlin, a former Mulroney staffer. These are not wide-eyed radicals or tree-huggers. The Roundtable's conclusions were quite straightforward: to meet the government's targets *at the least economic cost* it recommended putting a price on carbon through an economy-wide cap-and-trade system, along with tighter regulation and more targeted investment in technology. It noted that there would be a cost to any delay, because the price of carbon would have to be ratcheted up even higher to meet the Harper government's targets. Although it acknowledged that implementing the Harper government's own policy would have an economic impact, it still forecast Canada's GDP would double by 2050. The Roundtable's scheme would at least be a beginning. It is one approach. There are others. But only governments can do this job. (No surprise that the Harper government abolished the Roundtable in its 2012 budget.)

The science tells us that the next couple of decades are crucial because the current levels of greenhouse gas emissions will have permanent, irreversible effects. We have already passed the point where we can recover the climate equilibrium that existed just a few decades ago. What we are trying to do now is to limit the damage to levels that will not threaten the lives of hundreds of millions, even billions, and potentially even destroy our civilization. To address the "fierce urgency of now," to quote Martin Luther King, later channelled by Barack Obama, we need to raise the price of carbon. There is just no way around this. A higher price for carbon would reduce the use of fossil fuels and increase the competitiveness of greener technologies, moving them more quickly from R&D to the marketplace, and potentially putting us into a virtuous circle.

IT'S THE STUPID ECONOMY, STUPID

A carbon tax would, among other things, slow the development of the tar sands and allow the intensity of emissions to fall as green technologies come on stream. The federal government might also encourage Alberta to increase its royalties on the tar sands: if Alberta declined, Ottawa could impose a targeted increase in corporate income tax. This does not mean taking the stuffing out of the Alberta economy, by the way. One study, by the respected environmental economist Mark Jaccard, suggested that an effective set of climate change policies would reduce the growth in the Alberta economy by 2020 from 57 per cent to a range of 38–46 per cent.[20] With the usual caveats about the uncertainty of economic projections, particularly in the current period of volatility, this suggests, if anything, a more manageable level of growth for the Alberta economy. It would allow time for the development of more refining capacity here in Canada, to reduce the need of shipping bitumen and jobs to the United States or China. Indeed, royalty and tax revenues accumulated at both the provincial and federal levels could be used, in part, to diversify the economy, and to move it away from mere resource extraction towards more value-added industry, which would also create jobs. This kind of policy would reassert a measure of control over not only our environment, but our economic development.

Going back at least as far as John A. Macdonald's National Policy, which built a national railway and imposed an "unnatural," "distorting," east-west pattern of trade, Canadians have always sought some compromise between shaping market forces and being shaped by them. Choosing the pace of development in the oil industry, extracting a fair value not only for the private sector but also for the public sector which owns the resources, using the wealth that is generated to diversify the economy and add value to the natural resource, balancing economic development and the environment—these are principles that could be traced back as much to Peter Lougheed as to Pierre Trudeau. Even the greatest enthusiast for the free market policies of the last three decades would have to acknowledge that things have not unfolded exactly as foreseen. When Brian Mulroney announced that Canada was "open for business"—meaning that it was open to foreign invest-ment—the promise was that this would create jobs. There has been a huge influx of foreign investment, which in principle is not necessarily a bad thing. It certainly has been a very good thing for the banks, and has created some very good jobs on Bay Street. But it has not been the employment bonanza that was promised.

Part of the theory behind free trade is the idea of "comparative advantage"—that is, that in an unfettered market each country will produce what it can produce at a lower opportunity cost than its competitors. The cascade of foreign investment into our resource sectors in recent years has made it clear what the markets think we are comparatively good at, and that's resource extraction. Unfortunately, most resource industries are capital-intensive, and the expensive equipment required is often bought from transnational companies like Caterpillar, which builds its machines and creates jobs abroad. Moreover, mining by its nature tends to have falling productivity as producers scoop the most accessible minerals first. Meanwhile, the influx of foreign investment, along with the demand for our raw commodities, has helped drive up our dollar, making it harder for manufactur-ing to survive, much less thrive. All this has tended to reinforce Canada's role as what Harold Innis famously described as "hewers of wood and drawers of water." The phrase is so shopworn in Canadian parlance now that its biblical origin is often forgotten: "Now therefore, you are cursed, and you shall never cease being slaves, both hewers of wood and drawers of water for the house of my God" (Joshua 9:23). To say that we are accursed slaves is maybe a little strong, but nor are we working for the house of God. We have lost that measure of control over our economy that puts it in perspective, balances the interests of many regions and sectors, and acknowledges that, while growth has many virtues, it is only one among many values we prize.

The lack of an industrial policy means that we do very little in this country to leverage our natural resources to develop value-added industries. As Joseph Stiglitz has pointed out, in the 1960s South Korea's comparative advantage was in rice, not computer chips and cars.[21] What happened was that the government invested in technology and education, and changed South Korea's comparative advantage. All of my professional life I have heard wailing about the low level of research and development in Canada relative to other developed nations, as if this were an inexplicable aberration, to which the only response was to plead ineffectually with industry to do more. By now we should have realized that the low level of R&D, like the falling number of good middle class jobs, is a feature of the economy we have chosen by lying back and taking what the markets give us. No one is suggesting that the government should attempt to bring our dependence on natural resources to a shuddering stop: only that we start leveraging that wealth to guide our economy towards what we want, with more brains and more brawn at work. This is not an anti-growth agenda, but one that guides growth for the benefit of the environment and the benefit of our neighbours and children who want fulfilling, sustainable, and remunerative jobs.

ONE PER CENT ARE MORE EQUAL THAN OTHERS

No feature of the market-dominated economy has captured the imagination recently more than the preposterous distribution of wealth captured in the notion of the *1 per cent*, which has been popularized by the Occupy movement. Canada's richest 1 per cent reaped about a third of the total growth in income during the economic spurt of 1997–2007.[22] In the boom years of the 1950s and 1960s, the top 1 per cent captured just 8 per cent of total growth. According to Armine Yalnizyan, who has done the most comprehensive study of the issue here in Canada, the recent cascade of wealth to the top 1 per cent "eclipses anything seen before in Canadian history." In fact, it completely reverses the trend of the previous half-century, during which income became *more* evenly distributed. Yalnizyan puts this radical reversal down to two factors: the explosion in compensation for a narrow class of business executives, and the declining rates of taxation for the wealthy. The rapid rise of inequality has now captured the attention not only of political progressives but also of conservative institutions like the IMF, OECD, and, here in Canada, the business-funded Conference Board. In a report in 2011, the Conference Board noted that, in Canada, only the wealthiest one-fifth of the population has benefited from the growth in the economy in recent decades.[23] In fact, it would probably be better policy, if not better politics, to think about the top 20 per cent than the top 1 per cent. A Conference Board study remarked that high inequality "can diminish economic growth if it means that the country is not fully using the skills and capabilities of all its citizens or if it undermines social cohesion, leading to increased social tensions." It also remarked that it "raises a moral question about fairness and social justice."

There is an argument about why salaries and compensation at the high end have grown so spectacularly in recent decades. Some claim that in a globalized world there is an intensified market for certain scarce marketable skills. Others say that it is a function of deregulation, a decline in unionization, and the capture of corporations by their own managerial elite. But there isn't much to argue about on the tax side. For several decades now, we've been cutting rates of taxation for the wealthy. The uber-rich—the top 0.01 per cent of tax-filers—saw their effective rate of taxation fall by a quarter between 1992 and 2004.[24] This was before the election of the Harper Conservatives, of course, and their determined campaign to lower corporate income taxes. A report by the accounting firm KPMG in 2010 listed Canada has having the second-most "competitive" corporate tax rates, behind only Mexico, among the countries studied, and well ahead of any other member of the G7.[25] Remarkably, during the thirty years of corporate tax cuts, business investment in Canada has *declined* by 1 per cent of GDP, while after-tax business cash-flow has *increased* by between 3 and 4 per cent of GDP.[26] So the evidence is that corporate tax cuts have done, well, absolutely nothing—except bolster corporate profits, of course.

In conservative practice, this is how it all fits together. You cut taxes on corporations and the wealthy. This reduces government revenues. Then you announce that the budget is tilting dangerously out of balance. With less tax revenue, there's no alternative but to cut spending. Spending cuts produce a smaller government. A smaller government means fewer services to the less-well-off. In this cycle, then, the tax cuts increase inequality both directly, by reducing the tax burden of the wealthy, and indirectly, by ratcheting down the capability of government to help those with fewer means.

Embedded in this seemingly ineluctable cycle is the priority that conservatives put on balancing the budget. As I've said before, Keynesian progressives used to think it was a good thing that deficits automatically went up during a recession. This happened both because of lower tax revenues (not from lower rates but from reduced economic activity) and greater demands on government programs such as unemployment insurance and welfare. By replacing some of the economic activity lost in the private sector, governments helped stimulate the economy, smooth out the downturn, and assist a return to growth. And this was of particular help to ordinary people, because the single most substantial effect of an economic slowdown is an increase in unemployment. Corporate profits—particularly bank profits—can be amazingly resilient, as we have seen in the last couple of years, even when the economy seems to be bumping along the bottom.

So you might think that when the Harper government announced in the middle of the post-meltdown downturn that it would cut the budget deficit to zero by 2015, progressive parties would howl in outrage. They would try to expose the Harper deficit reduction scheme for what it was: an abandonment of the unemployed. But that is not at all what happened. I want you to take a look at the language in the NDP's 2011 platform. This quotation is not taken out of context: it is the party's deficit policy *in its entirety.*

BALANCING THE FEDERAL BUDGET

- We will maintain Canada's commitment to balance the federal budget within the next 4 years, as per the Department of Finance projections.

Not a word of protest; just the opposite—an unqualified adoption of the Conservatives' balanced-budget policy. To be fair, the NDP's broader fiscal policy was different in important ways. The NDP promised to spend on childcare, housing, and health, for example. And it promised to fund these programs by rescinding the Harper corporate income tax cuts, though even that pledge in the platform was oddly phrased, to sound as if it would be happy sitting in the middle of a Conservative brochure:

> • We will keep Canada's corporate tax rate
> competitive by ensuring that our combined
> federal/provincial Corporate Income Tax rate is
> always below the United States' federal corporate
> tax rate.

Michael Ignatieff, who had declared himself "passionate" about corporate tax cuts, said he nonetheless wanted to slow their pace, and he, like Layton, embraced the Conservatives' timetable to a balanced budget. Progressives are never going to address the inequities in our society if they do not have the courage to confront conservative economic policies squarely, or even, it seems, honestly. Ignatieff may have believed what he said deep in his bones. But it is difficult to imagine that Jack Layton and Brian Topp and the others who drafted the NDP platform were actually saying what they truly thought about the Conservative rush to balance the budget come hell or high water. The positions the NDP and the Liberals adopted, along with much of the phraseology, was defensive—an attempt to inoculate themselves against accusations that they were rapacious taxers and spenders. But, in doing so, they crimped their ability to convey a convincing alternative set of economic policies.

In saying this, I do recognize that the federal NDP has a problem. It has not always seemed as if it really believed that resources are limited and that budgeting requires tough choices—even for progressives. But in Manitoba and Saskatchewan, the provinces with the longest history of NDP governments, the party has a pretty good record of fiscal prudence—arguably better than their conservative opponents'. Tommy Douglas's dictum that debt equals subservience to bankers is taken seriously. Progressives need to make it clear, though, that their approach to fiscal policy is different from that of the Conservatives. Their aim should be to balance the budget over the course of several years. That means a commitment to bringing down debt as a proportion of the GDP in good years. It also means a willingness to run deficits and accumulate debt during periods of high unemployment. Austerity in such circumstances, as we have seen in Britain, and even worse in Spain, leads down a spiral of slower growth, falling revenues, and demands for yet further austerity.[27] The role of the government in such circumstances is to replace some of the lost private-sector activity, not compound the problem. Unemployment represents a permanent loss of productivity, both at the aggregate and the individual level. Unlike oil, which if left in the ground for a while can be dug up later, you can never get back a year lost to unemployment. It is a dead loss to the economy and to the worker involved. While a few of those who can't find jobs, particularly the young, may be able to seize the time to improve their skills, for most of the unemployed this is an impossibility. In fact, their skills and their employability actually degrade while they are jobless.

The second element of a progressive fiscal policy is a serious discussion of taxes.[28] No one likes paying taxes, and the reluctance to pay them will be all the greater if it seems that the government does not spend with great care. Profligate behaviour—whether it is the sponsorship scandal or a defence minister's using air force choppers as taxis—erode public confidence. Ultimately, it makes the case for keeping the money in your own pocket. But conservative politicians have used this to foster an allergy to taxes that is simply unsustainable in a progressive and compassionate society. To his credit, during the NDP leadership campaign, Brian Topp raised the issue of taxes as a foundational element of his platform. He proposed a new federal tax bracket of 35 per cent on incomes over $250,000, and that both capital gains and stock options be taxed like any other income rather than at discounted rates as at present.[29] He also proposed that the Harper corporate tax cuts be phased out. This is a plausible plan—and, of course, there could be others—to refinance government. It would attenuate rather than exacerbate the income inequality in Canada. It would not be a licence to "tax and spend," but it would redefine the fiscal space within which government can work. Interestingly, Jeffrey Sachs has shown that high spending levels are not what the governments that have tumbled into fiscal crisis since the financial meltdown have in common. Rather, they are the countries with the lowest tax revenues as a proportion of the economy: Greece, Ireland, Portugal, the United Kingdom, and the United States.[30]

Tax increases would have to be imposed gradually, and there would have to be sensitivity to adverse or unexpected economic effects. And they would not allow the government suddenly to reverse decades of corrosion of the public sector. Topp claimed his tax plan would generate $18 billion a year, which would boost government revenues by less than 8 per cent. That's significant, but not transformative. Tax rates probably need to rise on upper middle class folks like me, who earn more than $100,000 a year. Part of the reason that we need a new regime is that our ageing population is going to make it difficult even to sustain our existing, substantially depleted, social safety net. In the 1990s, the Liberals worked with the provinces to put the Canada Pension Plan on a sustainable footing for many decades to come. But the same pressures of a greying population are bearing down on our health care system. The 2011 election gave us an example of the conspiracy of all the parties—left and right—to avoid talking about a question because it seems just too damned difficult. The Conservatives, who are always sensitive to charges they want to dismantle medicare, rushed to promise a continuation of the 6 per cent annual increases in funding for health care to the provinces that began under Paul Martin. The Liberals and NDP matched that promise, guaranteeing that there would be no meaningful election-time debate on the issue that poll after poll suggests most concerns Canadians. Unsurprisingly, the Conservatives' promise had a time limit, which they somehow neglected to mention during the campaign, and the finance minister soon announced unilaterally that future health funding would be tied to economic growth. The opposition—and the provinces—were right to protest this bait and switch. But no one in their right mind—with the exception, apparently, of Canadian voters—thinks that sticking to the status quo in health care, plus 6 per cent a year, will address the challenges of medical inflation and an ageing population. At some point, even progressives may have to accept that there are hard choices to be made.

BABY, IT'S COLD OUTSIDE

Despite the jarring impact of the 2008 financial meltdown, many Canadians may think we've done rather well in comparison with our neighbours and trading partners. We had a recession, the deepest in decades, but not as bad as south of the border. Unemployment rose, but not as high as in the US, and it started coming down sooner. Our banks had their windows rattled but they never popped. The pay and bonuses on Bay Street do seem a bit absurd, but nothing like those on Wall Street. The banks came out of the recession with eye-popping profits, but we (somewhat erroneously) have the impression that we didn't pour taxpayers' money into them the way we saw south of the border.[31] The money we spent on bailing out General Motors and Chrysler has mostly come back, with interest, and it is even conceivable that we might turn a profit. Inequality in Canada is worse than the OECD average, but it is not as bad as in the US, which holds the record. Inequality has been getting worse in Canada since the mid-1980s, but not at as steep a rate as in the UK. Poverty, too, is a bit worse than the OECD average, but at least it hasn't been rising in the last twenty-five years as it has in most developed countries. Sure, our median income has grown by just 0.8 per cent per annum over this period—half the growth of the GDP per capita—but at least it has grown.[32]

However, part of the reason it hasn't been quite so bad here is that our conservative politicians have been somewhat less conservative than those elsewhere. Mulroney's PCs harboured a substantial Red Tory wing, and a Quebec caucus that was more socially liberal than you would ever have seen in, say, the Reagan Republicans of the 1980s. The Liberals of the 1990s had their shoulders into the fight against the deficit, but their hearts were never completely there. Our social programs weren't quite so savagely gutted; our taxes weren't chopped quite so low. Privatization was extensive, but deregulation was a little more cautious. The anti-government ideology of the Thatcherites and Reaganauts was never expressed quite as luridly at the federal level as it was at the provincial, by leaders such as Bill Bennett and Mike Harris. Until now, that is. A quarter-century after Thatcher and Reagan, Stephen Harper came to power. Harper has cleverly disguised his radicalism under a veneer of incrementalism. But make no mistake: at the very moment that the market ideology had begun to crack around the world, it has found its political apotheosis here at home. Canada is headed deeper into the tunnel at the very moment we should be looking to exit.

CHAPTER 8

WHY WE SHOULD HAVE HOPE

On a cold April day, Kevin Lamoureux was working a modest townhouse complex across from a dreary industrial estate in north Winnipeg. A pale, compact man, with a toque pulled over his ears to protect against the biting wind, Lamoureux ran from door to door, as much out of nervous energy as the need to get the job done. He was flanked, as nearly always, by a cadre of Filipino-Canadian loyalists, some of whom came from outside the riding. He was campaigning for re-election as a Liberal in Winnipeg North, a seat he had taken from the NDP in a by-election win just a few months before. The folks around here had known struggle, and it was no wonder that many had voted NDP most of their lives. But as one woman in her eighties told me, "Kevin" was different. Gwen Gray wore a pendant around her neck with a picture of her recently deceased husband on one side and of her late lamented cat on the other. She had met Lamoureux at an exercise class at St. Barnabas Anglican Church and she had been impressed that he didn't just shake hands and head on his way.

"He exercised right along with us," she told me. "I like the way he talks to people. He doesn't belittle people." Gray was making an exception to her general habits in this election. "I'm not normally a Liberal, no," she told me. "I am for *him*."

Lamoureux had spent eighteen years as a provincial MLA before running for parliament. During that time he had been an often-truculent colleague in the tiny Manitoba Liberal party, seldom troubling to hide his view that the party would be better off with him as leader. But he had become an institution in the heavily immigrant provincial riding he represented. His stock-in-trade was helping people navigate the paperwork of the immigration process, and he was tireless in pursuing the cases of new Canadians, inside his own riding, and increasingly also beyond. Hence the halo of Filipinos seemingly everywhere he went. Every Saturday morning, he sat at the same table in the same McDonald's restaurant, so that constituents could come and see him with their problems. It was an investment that he drew on when he ran in the federal constituency, which was much larger than his provincial one. The political wiseheads in Ottawa had not given Lamoureux a chance: before the votes had even been counted they had ticked the box for the NDP, which had won the seat by a margin of nine thousand votes in 2008. But Lamoureux's machine turned out more than three times as many Liberal voters than in the previous election, and the NDP candidate, Kevin Chief, saw his party's vote cut by more than half. Some commentators thought that Chief had been hurt by his obviously native name and his close association with aboriginal causes, but most put it down to Lamoureux's superior ground game.

Kevin Chief could have licked his wounds and gone back to his job at the University of Winnipeg. Chief ran a program there for inner-city aboriginal kids, trying to get them to stay in school and maybe even go to university—the kind of innovative social outreach for which the university had developed a reputation since former Liberal cabinet minister Lloyd Axworthy had become president in 2004. But Chief decided to have another go. Less than a year after his federal by-election defeat, he was the NDP candidate for the provincial seat of Point Douglas, one of the poorest districts in Canada. "When I looked at my riding, I realized the big challenge wasn't going to be getting people to vote for me," he told the *Winnipeg Free Press*. "It was getting them to vote at all."[1] Sobered by his defeat in the federal by-election, Chief dumped many of the impersonal methods of modern campaigning. Instead, he created a social network: not a virtual one, but something real. Chief, who is himself an accomplished square dancer, staged an evening event with the popular Metis musician J. J. Lavallee. And when folks showed up there was a surprise appearance on drums by that unlikely hometown hero, the soft-spoken entrepreneur Mark Chipman, who had just brought the Jets hockey franchise to Winnipeg, and was friendly with Chief from working together for aboriginal youth. The goal of the gathering was not just to warm up potential voters; it was to attract volunteers. The objective was to get 350 of them, rather than the few dozen on which a provincial campaign would normally rely. The idea was to replace the broad but superficial contact most campaigns have with voters with deeper connections. In a seat where many people drift back and forth between the city and their home reserves, it wasn't easy tracking voters down: that required truly committed campaign workers. Chief's campaign headquarters became a social centre for the community. It obviously helped to have a dynamic young candidate. And it worked. Turnout went up 25 per cent in Point Douglas in an election where in most of the province it fell. When Chief stood in the legislature for his maiden speech, a few weeks after the election in October of 2011, there were sixty campaign workers in the gallery cheering him on.

Both Lamoureux and, eventually, Chief ran campaigns that were embedded in their communities. Their electioneering was part of building a larger relationship involving themselves, their parties, and the people they represent. American research on getting out the vote has suggested strongly that the *only* effective technique is personal contact, which can come in the form of friends or neighbours knocking on your door, or a call from a phone bank staffed by local volunteers.[2] TV ads, leaflets, and robocalls from prominent people may help persuade people to shift their allegiances from one party to another. Negative advertising almost certainly helps discourage many people from voting at all. But it is personal contact that works best for prying supporters away from their routines to go out and vote.

So here's the thing. The turnout in Canadian elections has fallen dramatically in the last half-century, particularly since the watershed election of 1993. Although this trend has been visible in many Western democracies, the problem in Canada is worse than almost anywhere else, probably exceeded only in the United Kingdom.[3] Many explanations have been offered, but two are most generally cited. First, the increasingly impersonal methods parties use to campaign—that is, through advertising and media, for example.[4] Second, the erosion of traditional social networks such as family and neighbourhood, particularly affecting the young and the poor. In his celebrated book *Bowling Alone*,[5] the American political scientist Robert Putnam argued that the decline in the US of everything from bowling leagues to parent-teacher associations—representing social isolation as much as individualism—was linked to a general retreat from the public square. Canadian scholars have seen a similar process at work here. If either of these explanations for low voter turnout is correct, we should expect a party like the Liberals, with a high degree of political professionalization in advertising and media management but relatively shallow social roots, to be most deeply affected—and, certainly, turnout has been a problem for the party. "Movement" parties, based on strong beliefs and overlapping with other social networks such as churches or unions, should be able to resist the trend better. That might mean that the Conservatives and the NDP are better positioned to get out their vote—although, clearly, in Quebec New Democrats would need to sink roots fast if they are to preserve their current purchase.

Nowadays in Canada, we expect about 60 per cent of eligible voters to cast a ballot. *Maclean's* columnist Aaron Wherry did a calculation of party support in the 2011 election as a *percentage of eligible voters* rather than the conventional calculation as a percentage of those who turned up to vote. The results: Conservatives 24.3 per cent, NDP 18.8 per cent, Liberals 11.6 per cent. Shocking, when you think about it, that the Conservatives formed a majority government with the support of less than a quarter of eligible voters. No prime minister in Canadian history has ever taken more than 43 per cent of the eligible voters;[6] however, of the ten weakest government mandates in Canadian history, using this metric, seven have occurred in the last thirty-three years—a result of both the proliferation of parties and the declining turnout. And in Canada the declining turnout is a result mainly of young people's choosing not to vote. Boomers have not been as diligent voters as their parents, whose sense of civic duty was shaped by the experience of the Second World War. But only about 40 per cent of those under twenty-five years of age can now be expected to cast a vote, while those over forty-five years old vote at a rate of 65–70 per cent or more. According to the most thorough study of the issue, one-third of Canadians under thirty have "largely checked out of electoral politics."[7]

Canadians rightly lament the fact that turnout at election time has been falling for the last half-century;[8] or, rather, *many* Canadians do. I say "many," because the conservative approach to government has likely contributed to the falling turnout, and it is primarily the Conservative party that has benefited. Conservatives (big- and small-c) have persuaded many of us that government can't make much of a difference in our lives, and of course they have made sure that, increasingly, it doesn't. That, naturally, makes the act of voting less significant. The Conservatives benefit from lower overall turnout because their supporters tend to be older, more prosperous, and more concentrated in smaller communities—demographics that continue to show up on election day. The young and the less-well-off, who aren't turning up in such great numbers, tend to support progressive parties when they do. You may have noticed how Stephen Harper seems to perform better on election day than the polls predict, and this is probably because many of the young people who tell pollsters they plan to vote Liberal, NDP, and Green don't actually vote in the end.

Whether you count low voter turnout as a conservative achievement depends on whether you think it is a deliberate strategic aim. In the United States, there has been a clear pattern of what is called "voter suppression" by Republicans, making it harder to register to vote, for example, and challenging voters' identification on voting day, which mostly discourages young people and minorities. In Canada, the Conservatives were implicated in a number of episodes of voter suppression in the 2011, which ranged from disrupting a polling booth at Guelph University to a more widespread wave of misleading calls to Liberal supporters in what was dubbed the robocall controversy. But as I write it is unclear whether these were examples of malign exuberance or a systematic campaign. More seriously, the Liberals have claimed that the attack ads run against both Stéphane Dion and Michael Ignatieff were attempts at voter suppression.[9] There would be more poignancy to these complaints had the Liberals not repeatedly used similar tactics against Preston Manning, Stockwell Day, and Stephen Harper over the years. The difference, really, was the scale of the campaigns, fuelled by the Conservatives' fundraising machine, which began long before any election had been called.

The Liberals almost surely would have responded to the Conservatives' attacks in similar quantity and kind if they had had the money. But they didn't, in part because, unlike the Conservatives, they have a much more limited bank of small donors on which to draw. Nor at election time do they have large networks of loyal supporters who will knock on doors in good years or in bad. Kevin Lamoureux won the 2010 by-election because he had a community network his party did not have, and he held on against the tide as the Liberals' lone Manitoba MP in 2011 for the same reason. Whether consciously or not, part of the motivation for Ignatieff's essentially passive strategy of waiting for the Conservatives to fall may have been that his party did not have the muscle to reach beyond its shrinking pool of habitual voters. It certainly was not a strategy designed to excite new interest in politics among the disengaged. One unrecognized feature of the Conservatives' attack on the unions, the attempt to drive a wedge between the NDP and organized labour, is that it is calculated to weaken the party's links to a significant network of social support.

The good news for progressives is that the political future in Canada will almost certainly lie with the party that is most effective at recruiting from the 40 per cent of Canadians who don't show up to vote at present. The Conservatives' dirty little secret is that if more Canadians turned out to vote, they would have a very hard time winning. If young people had voted in the same numbers as their elders, Stephen Harper wouldn't have got his majority in 2011,[10] and would have had weaker minorities in 2006 and 2008. Younger people are in many ways more individualistic that their elders, and less likely to commit permanently to any party or ideology. However, for most of them, their individualism is not of the radical "survivalist" kind, to use pollster Michael Adams's term—less so, anyway, than their American counterparts'.[11] The so-called Millennials—born after the mid-1970s—tend to be tolerant, cosmopolitan, and undogmatic. On moral issues, which they are more likely to see as lifestyle choices, their philosophy is live and let live. They are skeptical of authority and institutions generally, whether they be church, business, or government, but they do not share the conservatives' ideological hostility to government. As a rule, they don't follow the news, and especially the political news, closely. But here's an astonishing fact: young Canadians are just as likely as older folks to participate in political activities *other than voting*—signing petitions or going to political meetings, for example.[12] They also have similar levels of community participation—volunteering, for example. In other words, they have a particular problem with voting, which, paradoxically, means that at least part of the solution is in the hands of the progressive parties.

BOOMERS AND ZOOMERS

I am a child of the baby boom. My father had been de-mobbed in 1946 and started a family a few years later. I was six years old when John Kennedy was elected in 1960, and even at that age I was aware that something new was afoot. Kennedy's idealism may have been as much rhetorical as real, but it started to change the cultural climate and usher in a new era of possibility. In 1963, Martin Luther King's dream rang out from the steps of the Lincoln Memorial as more than a quarter-million people crowded around the reflecting pool of the Washington Mall. In 1964, a new president, this one from the segregationist South, steered the *Civil Rights Act* through Congress, prohibiting discrimination on the basis of race and nullifying state laws that required it. This was the practical end to legally sanctioned segregation, and arguably the most important milestone in the emancipation of American blacks since the Civil War. The man who piloted that historic reform, and had also launched the War on Poverty, Lyndon Johnson, was soon to find himself the victim of a popular political uprising. A wave of anger against the Vietnam War, led mainly by young people, many of whom were subject to the draft, was channelled into the quixotic anti-war presidential campaign of Eugene McCarthy, and chased Johnson out of the race for the 1968 Democratic presidential nomination. Meanwhile, in Europe, France's hero of the Second World War and saviour of the republic in the late 1950s, Charles de Gaulle, was nearly driven from office in 1968 by protests led by students and workers, and he resigned the next year. Germany, Italy, and many other European countries were shaken by similar protests.

In Canada, events may not have been as dramatic, but the era of possibility was clearly evident in Quebec's so-called Quiet Revolution, and subsequently in the separatist movement it spawned. In partial reaction to those events, Pierre Trudeau emerged, seemingly out of the blue, to become prime minister in 1968. Trudeau was our Kennedy. Although he was pushing fifty, he embodied a much younger spirit. He seemed at least a genera-tion younger than Pearson and Diefenbaker, and, for that matter, Robert Stanfield and Tommy Douglas, his election opponents. Unlike Kennedy, he was unmarried, and so his swinging Sixties romantic life could be played out in public. "There is no room for the state in the bedrooms of the nation," he had declared as justice minister, as he decriminalized homosexual sex, liberalized the abortion law, and eased divorce. Trudeau's staunch federal-ism was fundamental to his political persona, and to his electoral success, of course. But Trudeau represented generational change. The Andy Warhol-inspired posters, and the "Kiss Me, Pierre" bumper stickers, were not just ephemera; they were a claim to more than just routine political change. And to a significant extent the change Trudeau embodied represented the impulses of the nation's youth.

The government seemed to notice us in those days. In 1970, when I was sixteen, the federal voting age was reduced to eighteen from twenty-one. There were some neat government programs.

The Company of Young Canadians, modelled loosely on the US Peace Corps, stirred things up, supporting young social and political activists. My sister worked as a volunteer in one of the tougher sections of North Winnipeg on a CYS poverty project. I got a government bursary for a summer course of immersion French at the Université de Montréal, where I drank some beer, goggle-eyed at the beauty of the Quebec girls, picked up some French, and made my first acquaintance with the distinctiveness of Quebec life. There was Katimavik, and summer jobs in the provincial government. It was an interesting time to be young.

Now here is an important fact: Canada's median age in 1968, when Trudeau won his first victory, was about twenty-six. Or, put another way, although most baby boomers still could not vote, we were now nearing half the population. Our cultural enthusiasms, whether the Beatles and the Rolling Stones, mini-skirts and long hair, rejection of traditional religion, or sex liberated from the possibility of procreation, were reproduced endlessly by the media, imitated by our elders, and came to dominate social life. More traditional cultural strains may have remained hardy, but they were seemingly invisible to the media. And as the years passed, and the baby boomers grew older, our preoccupations remained dominant. The "don't trust anyone over thirty" slogan of the Sixties gave way to a show called *Thirtysomething* in the Eighties, showing boomers grappling with having children or having left it too late. Nowadays, there's a magazine called *Zoomer* on the newsstands, which bills itself as catering to "boomers with zip." On the magazine's website, the day I write this passage, are stories about Bob Dylan's seventieth birthday, William and Kate, chronic prostatitis, and seniors' housing. Cool.

As the boomers have aged, so have the preoccupations of the political system. There was a massive enlargement of post-secondary education at about the time I went to university, buildings sprouting everywhere. Most of my profs were in their late twenties or early thirties—recently hired to meet demand. Then, as we boomers started to buy homes, housing and mortgages became a government preoccupation. (Boy, has that gone out of style!) Tax incentives were invented to get us saving for our retirement—or perhaps to reward us for what we were starting to do anyway. Then, as we began getting concerned about our children's education, along came the Registered Education Savings Plans. And of course, lately, we have started hearing a lot about pensions. Canada's current median age now, by the way, is forty-one, expected to peak at forty-seven in 2056. In other words, boomers like me are still the dominant demographic in Canada—only now on the other side of the median.

WHOSE COUNTRY IS THIS ANYWAY?

What we know about young people today is that they are much less likely to vote out of a sense of obligation than the boomers or the war generation were, and much more likely to see political participation in instrumental terms: How can this make a difference to me?[13] These days, I am a university professor, and so I am around young people a lot. Like many of my colleagues in the journalism school at Carleton, I devoted much of my career to covering politics, and initially found it surprising how little my students knew about the political system: I was even a bit shocked at how little they cared. There is a time-honoured tradition among any professoriate of decrying the shocking ignorance of its student body. (Subtext: "I was much better than this lot.") But there's actually very little data to suggest that incoming students nowadays are less capable that we were, though both their mix of abilities and their interests are different.[14] So, I tried to think about why my generation of journalists, many of whom saw the political-investigative reporters Bob Woodward and Carl Bernstein as their models, had been succeeded by the people I meet in my classroom. Well, then, let's look at the experience of one of my twenty-one-year-old students. Born in 1991, her earliest political memories would likely be of the latter Chrétien years, when governments were literally taking more out of Canadians' pockets in taxes than they were spending on services. Her parents probably thought this was generally a good thing, as governments got their deficits and debt under control. Not much of a sense of possibility there, though. In fact, she probably spent at least some of her grade school years in a "portable." She would have found herself in larger classes than earlier generations. As she approached university, she faced a dispiriting competition for a place at her preferred institution—especially a problem in professional faculties at a time when mom and dad were telling her that education is key to a successful career. When she got to university, she found that her classes were often too large for her to have any personal contact with her profs, many of whom were harried and underpaid sessional hires. Not what she might have expected, given the size of her tuition bill. She might be lucky enough to have some classes in a spanking new lecture hall paid for by the post-2008 infrastructure program, but spends much of her time in cranky old run-down buildings. At the end of it all, she faces the prospect of a highly competitive and uncertain job market.

And what about the broader issues she cares about? Well, she hopes to live well into the second half of the twenty-first century, so global warming isn't just an abstraction: it will fundamentally alter her life. For as long as she can remember, politicians have been talking about climate change, but nothing much has ever been done, and the current government barely even makes a pretense of caring. There's a good chance she is more aware of, or at least concerned by, the challenges of the developing world than my generation was. But our foreign policy has been focused on fighting a war in Afghanistan and sabre-rattling in the Middle East, which makes her uneasy. Her Internet and cellphone charges are a monthly burden, causing tension with her parents if they are

paying, or difficult choices if they are not. Not something politicians ever talk about, really. You hear them talk about pensions
quite a bit, and to the extent she thinks about it at all, pensions
seem like a good thing. But someone was saying, it's people her
age who will end up paying for her parents' generation, and there
may not be much left when retirement rolls around for her.

What about education? That's a top priority, right? All the
parties and politicians talk about it. The Liberals made a big
deal of their "Learning Passport." But take a closer look. That
proposal was for the government to deposit $1,000 a year for
each high school student into an account for help pay for university education. While this might have made a contribution
to post-secondary education, its real aim was to help struggling
boomers. There is no principle in economics to suggest that a
$1,000 contribution to an education savings fund would result in
an incremental $1,000 available to a given student for her educa-
tion. In a sense, the money would become part of the family's
overall budget and distributed according to priority among its
many needs, of which the student's education would be only one.
Moreover, from a student's perspective, the money they and their
parents have at their disposal when the student enters university
is a given. What they worry about is tuition fees, rent, keeping
their grades up to qualify for scholarship money, and, of course,
accumulating student loans. Then, ultimately, it is about finding
a job. Psychologically, the Liberals' plan was targeted, not at the
student, but at the parents. It was not aimed at saying to students:
"We know who you are, we know how you live, we know how
you feel, and we are concerned about what concerns you." It was
aimed at saying exactly that to the parents. That's why the Liberals branded their education policy as part of what they called the
Family Pack. The NDP's platform was also designed to appeal
to mom and dad: "Give your family a break," was the phrase.
The platform did promise to lower tuition fees, but the NDP's

job-creation plans were not really targeted at the young. While the NDP platform had sections specifically for seniors, families, "kids," aboriginals, women, family farmers, immigrants, the disabled, and the provinces, there was no section devoted either to youth or to students. In 2011, many young people, particularly in Quebec, clearly did feel a pulse of possibility in the NDP campaign, but it was not because the NDP worked at it. If my student had gone and looked at the NDP platform, she would have had to work surprisingly hard to find herself lurking in its pages.

Oddly, academics studying low voter turnout have devoted a great deal of attention to the changing nature of society, culture, media, and advertising, but very little attention to the *content* of our politics. To some degree, for young people and the poor, tuning out electoral politics may be a rational response to the world in which they live. In a conservative age, governments have fewer duties and crimped aspirations, so there is less reason to care. And to the degree that politics still address the concerns of voters, they are typically those of the older and more prosperous. This is both an opportunity and a challenge for progressives.

There was one encouraging development in the 2011 election—the so-called vote mobs, in which politically engaged students tried to raise the consciousness of their peers with surprise gatherings organized through text messages, Twitter, and Facebook. John Baird's reaction to the phenomenon may have been telling: "I'm not sure what a flash mob is but it sounds a bit disconcerting...I don't know about 'flash' or 'mobs' but I don't like the context of either word."[15] There's no evidence that the vote mobs had much impact by way of increasing turnout among young voters, but they were a welcome attempt at a cultural change: *This is something we do for ourselves, not because we are told to do it by teachers, journalists, political parties, mom and dad, or Elections Canada.*

HERE'S HOPING

If I tell you that Canadian progressives need to look at Barack Obama's 2008 election campaign to figure out how to get more people to the polls, you are going to tell me that he was a once-in-a-generation politician and that, besides, 2012 didn't really stack up to his first run for president. And I am going to say, I hear you, but consider this: what Barack Obama did in 2008 by increasing turnout among young people in the primaries, and then more strikingly among blacks and Hispanics in the general election, was really the continuation of a trend. While turnout in Canada continued to bump along a 60 per cent trend line during the first decade of the twenty-first century, it was rising in American presidential elections, on both the Republican and Democratic sides of the political divide. And it was doing so because the candidates got better at getting marginalized groups out to the polls.

In the 2000 election, George W. Bush became president because of the strange workings of two peculiarly American institutions: the electoral college and the Supreme Court of the United States. Al Gore actually won the popular vote, with a shade under 51 million votes, compared to 50.5 million for Bush. In the four years that followed, however, Bush was determined to avoid having such a close shave again. Under the direction of Karl Rove, his organization became extremely aggressive in pursuing the votes of white evangelicals—a demographic group with historically low turnout. One of his tactics was to engage social conservatives in parallel referendum campaigns on same-sex marriage and abortion held on the same election day. He hoped that would motivate them to come out to vote, and that they would mark an X for Bush while they were there. The Democrats, meanwhile, tried to counter those efforts by increasing voter registration, often working with unions or community groups.

George W. Bush's Democratic opponent in 2004 was John Kerry, best remembered now as a lacklustre speaker with a mixed record in opposing the war in Iraq, who was unable to dislodge a sitting war president. It is a startling and little-remembered fact that Kerry won more votes than any previous Democratic candidate for the presidency. Ever. Fifty-nine million of them. Kerry bested Gore's total by eight million votes, and indeed took 12 million more than Bill Clinton had in winning the election of 1996. So why did Kerry lose? Because Bush was able to increase his vote total even more—by about 11.5 million. The two parties, together, managed to expand the presidential electorate by roughly 20 per cent between 2000 and 2004 alone!

Four years later, in the 2008 presidential election, the Republican loser, John McCain attracted 60 million votes, almost as many as Bush did when he won re-election in 2004 and nine million more than Bush in 2000. Barack Obama took an amazing 69.5 million votes. That's seven million more than Bush in 2004, ten million more than Kerry in 2004, and nearly nineteen million more than Al Gore in 2000, when he "beat" George W. Bush. It is worth our while to stop for a few moments and contemplate the significance of the expansion of the presidential electorate by roughly 30 per cent over less than a decade. In particular, it is worth looking at the strategy and organization of Barack Obama's campaign, which built on the already substantial achievements of the Democratic party in registering eligible voters and getting them to the polls.

In her exceptional debut address on the national political stage at the Republican convention of 2008, Sarah Palin, then governor of Alaska and a former mayor of her home town of Wasilla, fired off this memorable zinger at Obama: "I guess a small-town mayor is sort of like a 'community organizer,' except you have actual responsibilities." It was a deft attempt at undermining Obama's thin credentials for the presidency, while promoting her own—though we all remember how that turned out. Obama had indeed spent several years as a community organizer, working on

Chicago's South Side, trying to mobilize people whose lives had been devastated by the collapse of the city's industrial job-base as well as a history of racism and practical segregation. During that time he established a personal network that included the area's many churches, social agencies, NGOs, and volunteer organizations. Though his accomplishments were modest, that network turned out to be of great value when he returned to the city. Having graduated from Harvard Law, he now agreed to head up a voter registration drive in the black and Hispanic communities, called Project Vote. It was the spring of 1992, and in the November elections Bill Clinton would be challenging the incumbent president, George Herbert Walker Bush, and the Democrat Carol Moseley Braun would be attempting to become only the second black senator in Washington since Reconstruction. Employing the techniques he had learned as a community organizer, Obama set up a system of registrars, mainly volunteers from community groups. He designed an advertising campaign aimed to touch on the seemingly faded theme of black power. The point was to inspire hope that change could be achieved through the ballot box. In the end, Project Vote registered nearly 150,000 people to vote, Moseley won her senate seat, and Clinton took the state for the Democrats, something that had not happened since the LBJ landslide in 1964.[16] Though Moseley was a spectacular flame-out as senator, American blacks enjoyed one of their greatest-ever spurts of economic progress under Clinton. Ironically, that Clinton legacy was initially an obstacle for Obama when he challenged Hillary Clinton for the nomination in 2008.

In his nomination campaign, Obama originally focused on the so-called "caucus states." In the United States, the candidates for president are chosen according to rules governed largely by state law, with two basic models, primaries and caucuses. In a primary, party supporters go to the polls to choose their favoured candidate, often in the same place they would go to vote in a general election. Caucuses are more like town hall meetings, held in church basements and community centres, where there are speeches, often followed by several rounds of voting. Caucuses take much more time for voters, a much larger measure of commitment than primaries, and turnouts are much lower as a consequence. Because of that, candidates in caucus states generally target party diehards who can be depended upon to come out to vote rain or shine. However, Obama's organizers thought that with intensively local organization they could generate more energy and enthusiasm than Clinton with her initially better-financed and nationally focused media campaign.[17] The mantra of the Obama approach, as described by one senior organizer, was: "A staff is not an organization. A staff is there to support a local organization." In other words, the national campaign was fashioned to support local efforts and not the reverse. Local campaign workers played a significant role in directing the message and distribution of resources. Ultimately, Obama won the Iowa caucus—the first contest of the campaign—but more significant was the way he did it. The turnout for the Iowa Democratic caucus was 239,000 voters—close to twice the previous record of 124,000.

As Obama was transformed by Iowa into a national candidate, his organization had to look ahead to other caucuses and primaries. Although it stuck to the Iowa model in caucuses, it also relied heavily on grassroots volunteer-based organization even in primary states such as South Carolina, where the previous tradition had been for Democrats to campaign by paying pastors and political heavyweights to talk up their candidate and organize for them.[18] In states where the Obama organization did not yet commit either money or organizers, it provided online tools to enable activists on the ground to begin organizing on their own. Sometimes this loose organizational style led to embarrassment, as when a poster of Che Guevera was spotted on the wall of an Obama-campaign office. But it also meant that when paid staffers did show up to organize a state in the primaries, or, later, in the general election, they found an existing network already on the ground.

Much has been made of the Obama campaign's inventive use of the social networking tools and the Internet, particularly for fundraising. To get into an Obama rally, you needed a ticket—free on the Internet, of course. This would yield an email address and other information which would allow the campaign to follow up afterwards. The My.BarackObama.com website was ground-breaking, allowing supporters to form social networks and enabling them to engage their friends through a Facebook-like interface. The website had tools that would allow a volunteer in Oregon, say, to make calls to potential voters in Texas or New Hampshire. You could create your own fundraising page with a graphic of a thermometer to mark your progress to whatever goal you chose to set—$500 or $1,000—and invite your friends to support you (and Obama). The principle was similar to charity walk-a-thons and fundraisers like "Movember"—that we are more likely to give money in response to a touch by a buddy than because we've seen a TV ad or got a piece of direct mail. Naturally, anyone who contributed added their own email address to the Obama organization's expanding list. Once the campaign had a track on a supporter, it graduated its requests: that is, it started modestly, looking for a small donation, or a small bit of volunteer work, and then progressed individually according to the response. There was also massive effort to maintain regular communication about issues and even campaign strategy with people who signed on. There were contests for dinner with Obama and his family, which you entered by accomplishing specific tasks.[19]

The significant point about the Obama organization's use of the Internet, which is often lost, is that the goal was always to convert the virtual network it created into real human networks. Supporters who lived near one another were connected, and assisted in organizing small fundraisers, door-knocking campaigns, and phone banks. In many cases, these semi-spontaneous grassroots groups combined with existing networks created by unions and community groups. (Something similar happened in more dramatic fashion in Egypt during the Arab Spring, which began on the Internet but persisted and grew even when the Internet was cut off.)

Obama was a once-in-a-generation phenomenon in 2008, of course, and there is no doubt that this is what allowed the infrastructure his organization created to blossom into such a mighty political force. The organization was undergirded by his opposition to the war in Iraq, and lifted by his uniquely inspirational voice, the message of which turned in part on his belief in the positive potential of government married to a progressive patriotism. One of the striking elements of Barack Obama's campaign to mobilize large numbers of previous non-voters was his insistence on the power of governments to make a difference in troubled economic times. The theme of "change" in his campaign is, of course, pretty much the oldest political slogan in the book. But Obama didn't stop at saying it was "time for a change"; he talked about "change that matters." The most famous of his slogans—Yes We Can—captured not only the novelty of his individual candidacy, but a belief that governments could effect positive, meaningful change. Unlike Michael Ignatieff—who continually spoke of his allergy to "big government" and his reluctance to countenance "big, expensive government programs"—Obama explicitly undertook the work of reversing the conservative anti-government ideology. Although his presidency has been a disappointment to many progressives, it did attempt to create a national system of health insurance, which would be the most significant extension of the social safety net since LBJ.

YES, WE CAN

For progressives, young people pose something of a puzzle. Their life experience has taught them not to expect much from government. Their individualism means that they are resistant to social democratic appeals for solidarity, whether it is to occupational group, class, or, for that matter, generation. Nor are they likely to be excited by "centrism," which tries to bridge the differences between models of economic and social organization of which they are only dimly aware. They are less likely than older voters ever to have been members of a union, but they are also less likely to be regular church-goers. They are the very definition of post-partisan voters, unlikely to make firm and enduring attachments to any party. And yet many of their predispositions suggest that they are more likely to be recruited by progressive than conservative parties. They have a deep belief in the autonomy and the worth of the individual, which leads them to what look like traditionally liberal views on rights and social democratic views on equality. Their reservations about government are practical, not ideological. They are likely to respond to appeals that speak to both their self-interest and their idealism. If progressives can tap the large and growing reservoir of infrequent or non-voters, as American Democrats have more frequently been able to do, it could transform their prospects.

The potential for something like this has actually been opened up by Stephen Harper's style of leadership and organization. Ideologically, the modern Conservative party is more the child of Reform, a populist movement party, than of the Progressive Conservatives, whose brokerage politics more closely resembled those of the Liberals. However, over the last decade, Harper has created a highly centralized party structure and organization, which has significantly eroded the party's populist tradition. Harper's highly disciplined, highly tactical style dictates, for example, that whatever his personal views—and, more importantly, whatever the views of his party—the Conservatives must not be seen to be aiming to change the abortion laws. This causes chafing and frustration among many of the party's most zealous supporters, and may eventually reduce their enthusiasm in organizing at the constituency level. Under Harper, the Conservatives have shifted their organizational model towards less-personal campaigning techniques. First, that entails a superb fundraising apparatus, run via direct mail and centralized phone banks. Second, it means a heavy reliance on a so-called "permanent election campaign," run through media advertising. This has proven to be a potent combination. This is what campaign professionals, who like using military jargon, call the "air war," and it is very effective at suppressing the support of opponents through negative ads. But these techniques are less well suited to the "ground war" of local party organization, which becomes more important in a struggle to turn out voters, as we have witnessed in the United States in the first decade of this century.

What would progressives need to become better at getting out their potential support? Of course they need to channel the anger of many voters towards the Harper government—as Kerry and Obama did against the Republicans over the war in Iraq, for example. But sometimes it seems that that is all the Liberals and NDP try to do. Among the politically disengaged there is already an amorphous sense that little good comes from politics, and this vocabulary of anger may to a degree reinforce that. They need to be inspired by big positive themes and practical policies associated with them that will touch their lives directly. The themes are not difficult to discern: a Fairer Economy and a Greener World. Nor are the policies that flow from these difficult to imagine, though progressives need to resist the temptation to suggest that they can do everything at once.

For a politics like this to work, there has to be a return to basics—connecting with communities, social groups, students, progressive churches, and, yes, unions, which can link progressive electoral politics to broader social networks. This is not news to New Democrats, of course, but it is an area in which the Liberal party has never been as strong as its rivals. Progressives also need to match the Conservatives technologically, in creating and maintaining sophisticated databases of donors, supporters, and sympathizers as well as effective fundraising machines. I say "match," rather than mimic, because it would be a mistake for progressives to imitate the highly centralized and hierarchical structure of the modern Conservative party. The approach should be much more like the 2008 Obama campaign, which had a highly efficient central staff structure, but one that was designed to support local initiative and organization.

The influx of NDP MPs in their twenties, and even in their teens, in the party's sweep of Quebec was widely mocked—not the least by a parliamentary press gallery, itself like the population as a whole getting a little long in the tooth. I remember experiencing, as a young man, the epiphany that the average NHL star was younger than I was. How much harder to accept that you have to cover and may one day even be governed by these impudent pups. Some of them will stumble, sure enough, but others will no doubt emerge as leaders, allowing young people to see themselves in the political world. In her campaign for the NDP leadership, twenty-nine-year-old Niki Ashton marked herself out as a potential cabinet minister, and perhaps a prime minister, someday. If the Liberal renewal means anything, it also will generate generational change, with the potential to appeal to the young.

PROGRESS, WHAT PROGRESS?

When it comes to technology, we take progress for granted. It's not just that each iPad is better than the last, but that iPads exist, when they didn't just a few years ago, and in a few years there will be some new thing that will change our lives again. Of course, the progress in technology is based largely on the progress in science. Today, our kids are routinely taught about subatomic particles unimaginable to Sir Isaac Newton, and have reason to hope that gene therapies will spare them from diseases afflicting their parents and grandparents. Progress in the economy, in the sense of growth, is so embedded in our social arrangements that even a small and temporary setback produces a political crisis. And yet, thirty years of conservative ideology have led most of us to forget even the possibility of social progress—the idea that the next generation may not only be able to cope with new challenges, but actually achieve a better, healthier, happier state of affairs for more people.

Recently, scholars taking a longer view have rediscovered the reality of progress in human affairs. Steven Pinker, in his magisterial book *The Better Angels of Our Nature*, has chronicled the spectacular fall in violence through human history, persisting even through the twentieth century despite horrific episodes of savagery in Nazi Germany, the Soviet Union, China, and Cambodia. Pinker is an unabashed liberal, but a parallel story has been elaborated by the one-time neoconservative Francis Fukuyama, in his *The Origins of Political Order*—the story of humankind's progression towards more sophisticated political systems, which place the autonomy and well-being of the individual at their heart. These writers do not take the nineteenth-century Whiggish view that progress is inevitable in human affairs. But they do show that it is possible, and, indeed, that along certain dimensions it is historical fact.

For the last thirty years, however, progressive politics has shrivelled in its ambition. The most successful progressive politicians have aimed, at best, to take some of the rough edges off the market ideology championed by Margaret Thatcher and Ronald Reagan. I am not saying that Bill Clinton, Tony Blair, and Jean Chrétien were no different from their conservative opponents—only that they represented an attenuated form of progressive politics. Their aim was not really social progress, it was to create an acceptable face for an often harsh market system. We know that centrism has often been a successful electoral strategy, as the Liberals demonstrated so consistently in the twentieth century, from Mackenzie King to Jean Chrétien. We have seen it in Blair and in Clinton—the latter famous for his strategy of "triangulation." It has also been successful for conservative politicians, including Dwight Eisenhower, Harold Macmillan, Bill Davis, Robert Bourassa, Arnold Schwarzenegger, George Herbert Walker Bush, Brian Mulroney, and Paul Martin. For many Liberals, of course, centrism has always been beguiling: the idea that they are neither left nor right but take the best from both; the idea that when voters start to desert the Conservatives, they won't want to move too far. Centrism is, by general agreement of newspaper columnists, business-funded think tanks, and university economists, the way to go for the Liberals and the NDP, whether they decide to proceed on their own or together. Let me go further, and say that, on the surface, centrism may even seem like a good fit with the loosey-goosey ideological perspective of the politically disaffected young.

However, I believe centrism fails us today, both intellectually and tactically. It avoids a clear analysis of our current economic troubles—the volatility and the inequality—and the recognition that they are rooted in the economic system created over the last thirty years through deliberate acts of public policy. It shirks the responsibility to confront climate change: the overarching moral challenge of our generation. Tactically, while centrism might seem like it would fit with the attitudes of the young, it has no inspirational element to rouse them into action politically. It is a damp squib. For the Liberals, clinging to the notion of centrism spares the party the need for genuine self-examination. It avoids the necessity to consider whether it was a mistake to embrace the conservative consensus so completely in the 1990s, and whether a failure to generate a serious critique of that consensus has debilitated the party since.

A moment's reflection tells us that very few of the towering political figures of our era have been centrists. They have been conviction politicians: Thatcher, Reagan, George W. Bush, Mike Harris, and, most recently here in Canada, Stephen Harper. These people had objectives beyond that of simply getting elected; they wanted to transform society, and in important ways they did. They not only brought fundamentally new directions to government policy, but they were willing to lead and change public opinion rather than simply follow it.

A ludicrous narrative has grown up among some populist conservatives and newspaper columnists, that Stephen Harper has become a kind of Chrétien of the Conservatives—essentially a pragmatic politician, motivated mainly by power, who makes whatever compromises he thinks necessary to attract the centrist voter. This Harper is concerned about holding office, not about changing Canada. The roots of this idea lie in the way in which Harper has narrowed and focused the Conservative party's public agenda, and has allowed himself considerable tactical flexibility, notably by toning down the party's moral agenda. This misconception may be abetted by the degree of fiscal conservatism of the last Liberal government. But it also confuses Harper's incrementalism with pragmatism, or even with centrism. Even in his minority government years, faced by a Liberal-NDP-BQ majority across the aisle, Harper was able to cut corporate taxes, curb regulatory agencies, defang many government watchdogs, and ignore climate change. No sooner was the majority in place than the government shut down the Canadian Wheat Board and began a direct assault on collective bargaining and the union movement. In Canada, where crime is falling, we are building new prisons.

Why can't a progressive party do something similar? Why can it not pursue *progressive* principles the way conservatives pursue theirs? Not, of course, ignoring the facts of our economy or climate change, but rising to the challenges they present. There is no reason why not. But to do so with any effect means winning the next election, and that requires working together.

CHAPTER 9

WHY?

In this book, I have tried to explain why I think we have come to an important moment in our politics. The doctrine of market fundamentalism has acquired new force in Canada through the Harper Conservatives, who dominate our politics for two reasons. First, they represent an economic and social doctrine that has been relentlessly promoted for thirty years now, but only feebly opposed. Their ideas have so completely penetrated the collective consciousness that it seems unremarkable that they make deficit reduction a priority at a time of high unemployment and slow growth, something that would have left us slack-jawed in amazement not so long ago. Second, they have the good fortune of a divided opposition, caught in a power trap the parties don't yet have the will to escape.

Students of public opinion see two large clusters of beliefs among the electorate: a smaller group of usually less than 40 per cent who strongly hold conservative views, and a larger, somewhat more amorphous, but clearly distinguishable group that holds more progressive views. But this latter, larger group is the object of desire of not one, but four parties: New Democrats, Liberals, Bloquistes, and Greens. In their struggle for power, the opposition parties may target the Conservatives' policies, but they seek mainly to win supporters from one another. Why? *Because these voters are so similar.* Party activists prize the distinctions they see among their various traditions even as they try to persuade voters that the differences are not, after all, so very great. But it is the interests of citizens that ultimately matter, and they lie, not in sustaining the differences among progressive parties, but in securing a progressive victory that will lead to a change in government and in policy.

Today, we face two enormous challenges that the conservative ideology is unprepared to address. Our economy, with sputtering growth, high unemployment, rising inequality, and serial financial crises, is the product of the economic system that conservatives have created. Thirty years ago, conservatives could argue plausibly, if not entirely correctly, that high taxes, wasteful government, regulation, restraints on trade, and uncompromising unions were the underlying causes of "stagflation." It is hardly credible that the economic problems we face now—from the Great Recession to the Great Unwinding, from Lehman Brothers to the Eurozone—are the consequences of the policies of the 1970s rather than those of the last three decades. We need policies that deal with the problems of today, not the phantasms of yesteryear. And looming largest among today's problems is climate change. As I have discussed, climate change is what market economists call a "negative externality"—a problem that the normal operations of the marketplace will never address. Governments must force reductions in greenhouse gases, because the marketplace never will.

For the record, I do not believe that a merger of the New Democratic and Liberal parties or an electoral alliance between them are the only ways we can ever get progressive government here in Canada. I think it is possible that one of the two parties will grow sufficiently to extinguish the other, though which is best positioned to do that is not entirely clear, and the perception will shift according to the polls. But, if that happens, it will almost certainly take a number of elections—not just one or two. As a progressive, I want more, and I want it faster than that. It is also possible, of course, that the Conservatives will wane somewhat by 2015, and that the New Democrats, Liberals, and Greens will be able to form a coalition, along the lines of the agreement negotiated between Dion and Layton in 2008. It is unclear whether Canadians would see this outcome as legitimate if the Conservatives had more seats than any of the individual coalition parties. But my real concern is that if your strategic goal is a progressive coalition, then fighting an election with multiple parties is tactically absurd. Under our first-past-the-post electoral system, you simply need a lot more votes to get where you want to be.

I haven't spoken much in this book about the Bloc Québécois or the Greens—the two other parties that have attracted substantial numbers of progressive voters in the Harper era. The experience of the abortive coalition attempt in 2008 has convinced me that the formal participation of the BQ in any collaborative political project, even in a supporting role, is unacceptable to most Canadians. Without defending Harper's dishonest portrayal of the BQ's role in the coalition proposed by Stéphane Dion, I think it is legitimate to say that a party dedicated to the breakup of the country should not have a formal role in its governance. Progressives will need to win the votes of BQ supporters, as the NDP proved capable of doing in 2011, and not depend on an alliance with the party itself.

As for the Greens, there is no doubt that they represent one of the most important impulses, if not *the* most important, in progressive thinking today. If we had a proportional representation system, as they do in New Zealand, where I spent some time during the writing of this book, the Greens would be a significant party. It is taken for granted in New Zealand that if the Labour party returns to power the Greens will be its main coalition partner. And the Greens have achieved this status with levels of support not very different from those of the party led by Elizabeth May here in Canada. But the punishing arithmetic of first-past-the-post forced May to set aside the Greens' national ambitions to concentrate on winning a single seat, and perhaps a few more in elections to come. I would hope that if the Liberals and New Democrats were to merge, the Greens would join in a new progressive party. If they did not, I think that their national significance would likely continue to decline.

And so, in my final words, I would like to address the three groups of people who would be most important for the success of a united progressive party: Liberal and New Democrat partisans and currently frustrated and unattached progressives.

TO THE LIBERALS

Your party represents one of the great political achievements of the democratic world. This is not just because you were so successful in winning elections throughout the twentieth century. It is also because of what Liberals have done with their time in office. While John A. Macdonald may have laid the foundations, it was the party of Laurier that truly built us into a country. You brought French Canada to the heart of power and showed Quebecers that there is a vital path not just to survive, but to thrive, within a united Canada. As a Westerner, I cannot forget that it was Clifford Sifton who opened up the West to settlement: by the Ukrainians and Mennonites and Jews who transformed our country. Canadians tend to think of Confederation in 1867 as our moment of independence, but the Liberal party led the process by which we wrested control of our domestic affairs, and then of our international affairs, from the Palace of Westminster. It was a Liberal government that gave us our own citizenship in 1946— much more recently than most Canadians realize. In the 1960s, it was your party that gave us much more than a new flag, bilingualism, and multiculturalism: you gave us a new way of thinking of ourselves as a nation, and not just as a relic of the Old Country or an appendage of the United States. In 1982, under Trudeau, you gave us true, legal independence through the patriation of the Constitution, and erected the *Charter of Rights*, one of the greatest prizes of our citizenship and a sturdy new bond in our sense of being Canadian.

The Liberal party took on mighty projects to strengthen our economic union: the St. Lawrence Seaway, the Trans-Canada Highway, and the Pacific Gateway. Though Conservatives might blame Liberals for the runaway deficits of the 1970s and 1980s, it was the Liberal party that set the country on a more manageable fiscal path in the 1990s. And the Liberal party's economic achievements have been matched over a century by progressive social legislation. It was a Liberal government that established unemployment insurance as a matter of federal jurisdiction. It was a Liberal government that introduced a system, first of hospitalization and, later, of national medicare. Even as it struggled to contain the deficit in the 1990s, a Liberal government negotiated the National Child Benefit with the provinces—a program that has significantly improved the life-chances of poor children, through nutrition and education. Paul Martin negotiated the Kelowna accord, which, had the Conservatives not abandoned it, would have created the most significant decade of social and economic progress for aboriginal people in the history of our country.

I know that for most of you, when you think back to how you became a Liberal, two things come to mind. Not a lust for power, as the Liberals' detractors would have it, but a desire to make a difference. Being a Liberal meant being at the table when decisions were made, and playing a role in what Canada would become. You could have chosen to join Mulroney's PCs or Harper's Conservatives with that same purpose. But you did not. Why? Because you believe that Canada is not just about making money. It is about making a country in which businesspeople and working people, francophones and anglophones, new Canadians, old-stock Canadians, and aboriginal Canadians, young and old, all feel they have a stake, and all can look to the broader community to watch their backs. For a long time, you felt that that was exactly what the Liberal party enabled you to do.

The last decade has changed a lot, though. It isn't easy to see how the Liberal party can return to where it once was in just one election—perhaps not even in a decade. It is not impossible, but very difficult to see that path. Even so, it is hard, very hard, to swallow what I am suggesting: a merger with the New Democrats in a new party that will be unapologetically progressive.

Some of you—not many, I think—feel you'd rather be a Harper Conservative than a member of a progressive party, as difficult as that choice might be. There's not much I can say to you. We have come to a point where there are stark choices to be made on the economy and the environment. This polarization was not of our making; it was created by a creeping radicalization of conservative policy. But it is no longer possible to straddle the centre as it moves further and further to the right. I think that you'll agree with me on this much: that it is not intellectually honest for Liberals to appeal to Canadians at election time as a progressive party with the full intention of governing along much more conservative lines. I'll be sorry to see you go, but you represent a much larger element in the Liberal party's machine than you do in its base of voters.

Many more of you worry that the New Democrats are wide-eyed idealists, oblivious to the difficult choices of budget-making, or indeed to the realities of making a market economy run. I want to remind you of two things. First, that you will be part of this new progressive party and bring the experiences you have of government—one of the reasons your presence will be prized. Second, take a look at the history of NDP governments in Manitoba, Saskatchewan, British Columbia, and Nova Scotia, where budgets have been balanced and economies have grown. Third, when it comes to international trade, have the grace to recognize that the Liberal party has been on both sides of that great issue in the last thirty years. Remember, too, that it is no longer an abstract issue of ideology: we have come to the point where we can see both the benefits and the costs of freer trade and make judgments on each. Take a closer look at what the NDP is actually saying about trade these days, particularly since Thomas Mulcair became leader. You might find that its position is not as far from your own as you thought.

For some of you, the stumbling block is national unity. So many members of the NDP's Quebec caucus, including even its interim leader after Jack Layton died, Nycole Turmel, have such recent ties to the sovereigntist movement. But isn't that how we are going to win the fight for Canada in Quebec? By persuading Quebecers to work with us, not against us? When we discuss a merger, there's a tendency to draw a false portrait of a monolithic Liberal party and contrast it with a similar caricature of the NDP. Although Pierre Trudeau's influence over the party's constitutional tradition has been strong, it has always had to contend with a less centralist vision. Meech Lake fired Trudeau's ire and attracted Jean Chrétien's opposition, but it had the support of both Paul Martin on the party's right and Sheila Copps on the left. Similarly, the NDP has contending streams, and will continue to wrestle with these issues, as indeed will Canada.

Unfairly, perhaps, many francophone Quebecers have closed their ears to the Liberal party. They ignore the Liberals' historic role in integrating Quebec into Canada and ignore the party's evolution since Trudeau towards a more collaborative federalism, which was evident even when Lucien Bouchard was premier. You will find that New Democrats are not all that different in this regard. A new party is a chance to turn a page with Quebecers, begin the dialogue anew, and find a better place in Canada for Quebec than the BQ could ever offer. Working with New Democrats in Quebec, rather than against them, offers a chance to consolidate a great victory for Canada that occurred there in 2011.

Of course, for many of you, the issue is not just what New Democrats stand for; it is who they are. Many of them are union activists, who come from a tradition of confrontation and rough language that is foreign to the Liberal tradition of compromise. I want you to stop and look at parties in other countries that you root for when they have elections. You'll notice that almost all of them, including the Democrats south of the border, think nothing of having organized labour in their midst. Unions play a fundamental part of progressive politics everywhere in the world, and they bring resources, community connections, and institutional strength that the Liberal party lacks.

Finally, there are the individual personalities that you loathe. The MPs who made reckless accusations during the sponsorship scandal, or the ones who have said ill-considered things about the Middle East. If you work high in the party, there are no doubt strategists on the other side with whom you've done battle, whose motives—and perhaps even whose ethics—you suspect. If you work at the local level, it is probably true there too, and the idea of maybe knocking on doors for a candidate you once bitterly fought against seems unthinkable. I understand those feelings. They are the natural human responses to competition. It is the same impulse that leads hockey teams into rivalries; and, the truth be known, the same impulse that leads hockey dads and soccer moms to think dark thoughts about that big, or swift, or chippy eleven year old on the other team. But as Liberals I am sure that, with a little concentration, you can probably think of a few big-mouths on your own side that might inspire similar loathing among New Democrats. The question is, how important should those partisan feelings be?

How important?

I want you to think about two things. First, what would be best for the people the Liberal party represents? What would be the best way to advance *their* political interests? Would it be to see you locked in a multi-election death-struggle with New Democrats, which inevitably would give the Conservatives an unearned advantage in our electoral system? Or would it be better to move now to create a new party with a realistic hope of achieving power soon, and implementing the policies that Liberal supporters have voted for?

Second, I want you to think back to what brought you into politics: the desire to make a difference. We have lost a sense of possibility in our politics, a sense of hope. You know that better than anyone, because you've been there, in the trenches, struggling against the sullen indifference of so many voters. Here's a chance to bring the idea of *progress,* economic progress, social progress, and environmental progress, back into our politics. And to do it so quickly that the Harper Conservatives won't know what hit them.

TO THE NEW DEMOCRATS

Some of you got into politics because you couldn't stand the Liberals. You don't like them because they make themselves look enough like New Democrats at election time to take your votes, but then head the other way once they are elected. You don't like them because they are a corporate-sponsored and corporate-staffed party that disguises its shape when appealing to voters. You don't like the Liberals because they steal New Democrat ideas, and then implement them—if at all—in watered-down form. And they don't just steal the ideas; they steal the NDP's thunder and sap its force. And now, at the very moment, the historic moment, when you have displaced them in parliament, and find yourself on the threshold of government, some people are coming along and saying you should give it all up and welcome these people into the fold.

I hear you. But I want to remind you of something else. That is the strangeness of election night in 2011. You probably felt euphoric. It was an undreamed-of result, even a few weeks earlier. And Quebec: who could have imagined Quebec? It was not just the Liberals you had vanquished, but the Bloc Québécois—a feat that even some Liberals and Conservatives acknowledge. It was a wonderful, wonderful night. But I imagine that, like a lot of other New Democrats, you had another experience, perhaps late that night, perhaps the next day. Maybe your partner, or a friend, remarked on the Harper majority. That was a bit unexpected, too. Four years of Harper government, now unleashed from a minority parliament. It was like awakening from a pleasant dream. You knew that it was a wonderful New Democrat victory and yet a terrible progressive defeat.

And then came Jack's cruel death. It was a tragedy not just for the party, but for the country, as the reaction of Canadians so vividly showed. Jack's enthusiasm, his energy, and his commitment had helped break through the membrane that had so long held many Canadians back from supporting the NDP, especially in Quebec, but not only there. He took over a party that looked like a decrepit relic of an earlier age and turned it into something dynamic and modern: presenting an image of the future that many Canadians felt they shared. He also made a virtue of what many people feel is sorely lacking in Canadian politics: collaboration. In minority parliaments he made deals, practical deals that made a difference for people, even when there was a Conservative government in power. His was the inspiring spirit behind the bid to create a progressive coalition in 2008, and his hand was

clear in the progressive policy document that would have been
its charter. He campaigned on a theme of "working together"—
part of his critique of the BQ. When Michael Ignatieff ruled out
a future coalition under political pressure, Jack proudly refused
to do any such thing. After the 2011 election in which he had led
the NDP to unforeseen heights, he was not about to go begging to
the Liberal party that had been so humbled. But parse his words
carefully. He was always open to overtures should they come. His
strategic stance for many years had been to cooperate with the
Liberals if they were willing, but to compete unrelentingly if they
were not.

Now it's time for others to make those decisions, of course.
The party has strategic and substantive options. You can migrate
towards the centre, occupy the space once dominated by the Liberals, and hope to extinguish them—maybe even winning over
the odd Conservative voter as you do so. In a world where parties
were nothing but power-machines, this might seem like the sen-
sible thing to do. But very few New Democrats I know see this as
an option. Most of them didn't get into politics just to win, but
to change things, and this isn't the way to do it. I agree. I think it
would be pretty strange in 2015—at a time when the flaws in the
market ideology of the past thirty years had become so obvious,
in terms of inequality, financial crises, personal insecurity, and
climate change—for New Democrats to abandon their hopes and
ideals. A second option is to reassert traditional social democratic
principles. This has the advantage of authenticity. It would also
present voters with a set of ideas and policies that contrast with
those of the Conservatives. But there are dangers. Not the least
would be the temptation to refight the battles of the past—battles
that were lost. The Conservatives would like nothing better than
to portray the NDP as enemies of trade, of enterprise, and of
property, and as the advocates of nationalization, bloated bureaucracy, and a socialized underclass. Unfortunately, while the

NDP is none of those things, the failure of the Rae government in Ontario during the recession of the early nineties has been fixed into a powerful narrative of the party's incompetence and impracticality. What I am saying is that the NDP is ripe for caricature, and faces an opponent which has that bent. You can see it every time the Conservatives gin up some battle with organized labour, trying to distract the voters of today with the controversies of thirty years ago.

I am not saying that these challenges would be impossible for the NDP to overcome. NDPers have a proud history of competent, practical, humane, and generous government in the West and now in the East. The federal party too has shown that it is capable of re-examining its policies in the light of time and circumstance. A serious examination of the party's policies on trade, on business, on budgets, taxes, and social policy does not lend credence to the image of ideological socialists that the Conservatives would like to present. It is certainly possible that the NDP can overcome these stereotypes. It just won't be easy. And it is very unlikely to be quick.

What I am suggesting is another option: a merger with the Liberal party. In a narrow political sense, I think the advantages are pretty obvious. You would join with your principal competitors for the allegiance of that 60 per cent of Canadians who haven't voted for the Harper Conservatives. The effort and resources you expend now on fighting the Liberals could be redirected towards the Conservative government and its policies. Besides anything else, this would be a huge favour to the progressive-minded voters that you and the Liberals have been fighting over for as long as your party has existed.

What worries you, I think, are the issues and the people. There are differences between the Liberal and New Democratic Party traditions, to be sure. The Liberals have been more concerned with individual than with collective rights. They have felt less strongly about equality and more strongly about equality of opportunity. They have sometimes reflexively preferred market solutions, whereas many New Democrats are reflexively skeptical about the social outcomes of markets. That having been said, the differences are far from absolute. Most New Democrats strongly believe in individual rights. Most Liberals have always believed poverty is a problem and are coming to see the current level of inequality as a problem, too. Liberals have never been market absolutists, and New Democrats are much more business-friendly than their stereotype conveys, as you can see at the provincial level. The differences between the two parties' election platforms have actually not been very dramatic in the twenty-first century. Moreover, the parties have a long history of collaboration on programs such as medicare and unemployment insurance in the twentieth. When there was a coalition in prospect in 2008, the negotiations were tough, but neither party needed to hold its nose while supporting the policy document that resulted.

Many of the problems you have with Liberals come down to not trusting them to do in government what they say in their election platforms. There's been a history of that, I agree. But there are several things I want you to consider. Many of the true blue Liberals, of whom there are quite a few in the party's back-rooms, are likely to be left behind when a new progressive party is formed. Many tell me they aren't progressives, and if they drift out of politics or over to the Conservatives, so be it. The truth is that, even in the absence of a merger, the influence of big business is diminishing in the Liberal party. Big business cares about winners, but has much less interest in third parties of any political complexion. Moreover, the new party-financing rules make all the parties more dependent on many small contributors rather than a few big ones.

Of course, there are the issues, too, of individual personalities. Every partisan New Democrat will have come to dislike specific Liberals—a Scott Brison or a David Herle, for example—for their ideology, their partisanship or their tactics. Get over it. That is not a reason to deny Canadians the choice they want to make in election 2015. If it helps, fantasize instead of Ken Dryden, Glen Pearson, and Carolyn Bennett. I think most of you would be proud to share a stage with these people, even if you haven't agreed with everything they have ever said.

There are some of you who will object to a merger on deeper, ideological grounds. You may have felt that Jack had already compromised the party's socialist heritage too much and had been too willing to work with the Liberals and Conservatives. The fact is that your view of the NDP, while it may be closer to the ideas of the founders of the CCF and even of the NDP, has long since ceased to be an accurate reflection of the party that others inhabit, or, indeed, that so many Canadians vote for. For a very long time now, you have remained in the NDP because you felt that you could better promote your ideas inside the party than from outside on your own. There's no reason why that can't hold true in a larger, progressive party. Some of you, I know, would quit, rather than be part of a merged party. But I would urge you to stay and see whether you can't have an influence on it, as you did on the NDP. If you can't, then I understand.

To all New Democrats, I say this is an important moment. Important to be generous to like-minded people in other parties and to be determined in opposing your true political foes. More than thirty years ago there was a paradigm shift in politics, led by Margaret Thatcher and Ronald Reagan—a shift so profound that its ideas live on in the Harper Conservatives. We may be on the verge of another such shift, but we need to seize the moment. Thatcher and Reagan won the day, not just because of the turmoil of the moment and the strength of their convictions, but because they harnessed the political institutions at their disposal. Our moment is now.

TO PROGRESSIVES

Most of you fall into one of two camps. Like many Canadians, you may have wished for something better from our parties and our politicians, but essentially despaired. Of course, you troop dutifully to the polls on election day, and cast your vote for a Liberal, a New Democrat, or a Green. But the truth is you don't expect that much from your vote. Either because you don't think the people you elect will carry through with their promises, or that they won't get close enough to power to do so anyway. So you grumble at the summer barbecue, but you have essentially retired from party politics, if it ever tempted you at all. You are much more likely to attend a meeting of your community association or the parent-teacher group at your kids' school than attend a party meeting, much less join a party or knock on doors at election time. You're on the sidelines.

Or you may have gone another way. Rather than waste your time on phony party bickering, you've got involved in a charity, your union, your church, a student group, an environmental or anti-globalization group. You sign petitions, go to meetings or demonstrations, contribute to the causes you care about and raise money from others when you can. You are active on behalf of the causes you believe in.

If you are in either camp, I want to urge you to think again. The 2011 election has enormously changed our politics. It has installed the most conservative government we have ever had in Canada, and though it might just fall of its own weight in 2015, that isn't likely. In fact, given the divided opposition, it is quite possible that Harper's Conservatives can stay in power for quite a while, just as Jean Chrétien's Liberals were able to do in similar circumstances. What that means is that the inequality in our society will continue to grow and, far from combatting climate change, our government will in effect promote it through overly rapid development of the tar sands. The only way to change that is by another party or combination of parties defeating the Conservatives. At the same time, all the progressive parties, and I will include the Greens here, are in a period of great ferment. Each of them faces an entirely new situation and must make important decisions about how to go forward. This is a particular moment in history, when you can be part of critical debates about the future of our politics and our country. Parties welcome new members, and the Liberals have decided that you don't even have to join to participate in choosing their new leader.

I am not asking you to transform your life. But if you haven't always voted, make sure you do next time. If you usually vote, why not put a sign up on your front lawn at election time? And if you already do that, maybe help distribute them on your block? If you are someone who is already politically engaged, working on environmental causes, perhaps, or with the poor, remember that while parties may not have the purity of purpose that other movements and organizations do, they have a unique capacity to effect change if they get into government.

So get involved, join a party, become part of a movement for hope and progressive change. If you are persuaded that a merger would be a good thing, as I have argued here, then push for it from inside. Support candidates for party office and leadership who support or sympathize with that view. But if a merger doesn't happen, don't feel disappointed and run away. Progressive parties need your help to pursue progressive change however the next few years unfold.

And here's something really important. The changes to the party fundraising laws under Chrétien and Harper eliminated much of the direct financial influence of corporations and unions, and eventually even of large individual donors. They have raised up a new class of political influentials in this country: the small donors. You can see it all the time in the behaviour of the Harper Conservatives, who have been most successful in this new regime. Many of their policies and much of their rhetoric is aimed not at the "swing" voter but at the energized base, who provide the party's backbone with ten, fifty, and one hundred dollar donations, often in response to narrow issues that make them hot under the collar, such as gun control or hostility to the CBC.

Now is the time for ordinary progressive-minded people like you to wield that same weapon. The next time you are writing a cheque to the cancer society or buying a lottery ticket for the children's hospital fundraiser, send a hundred dollars to one of the parties as well—you get most of it back through a tax credit anyway. And give your money strategically. Donate to a candidate who is supporting a common progressive option. Let the parties know you want them to work together by including a note with your donation. If the NDP tries raising money from you by attacking the Liberals, give some money to the Liberals instead and sent the NDP an email explaining what you've done and why. And visa versa. If the parties begin to feel that hyper-partisanship is hurting fundraising, and that working together helps, they will change their tune, and you will have been part of that.

We are at a moment of crisis, whether we all recognize it or not. An environmental crisis and a rumbling financial crisis that simply will not go away. Conservatives have become masters at exploiting crises—natural and humanmade—to reshape our societies to look more as they would like them to look. They've done it again and again during the last three decades by having a set of policies they believe in and waiting for the propitious moments to spring. They've remade our governments, our economies, and even, to a degree, our minds. It is time for progressives to show the same resolve.

ENDNOTES

CHAPTER 1 – WHY PROGRESSIVES DON'T WIN

1 Neil Reynolds, "Canada's Conservatives Should Ease Up on Harper," *Globe and Mail*, May 9, 2011. The only exception in this period, according to Reynolds, was the short-lived Martin government.

2 Conference Board of Canada report on world inequality, September 2011, http://www.conferenceboard.ca/hcp/hot-topics/worldinequality.aspx.

3 EKOS Research Associates, April 28, 2010.

4 1984: 47 per cent; 1988: 52 per cent; 1993: 48 per cent; 1997: 50 per cent; 2000: 49 per cent; 2004: 52 per cent; 2006: 48 per cent; 2008: 51 per cent; 2011: 53 per cent.

5 2011 Manning Centre Barometer.

6 Environics poll for the CBC, June 1, 2011.

7 Nik Nanos, "Canadians Strongly Support Immigration but Don't Want Current Levels Increased," *Policy Options* 31, no. 7 (July–August 2010).

8 Citizen Society Research Lab, Lethbridge College, *Albertans' Opinion Structure on Six Policy Issues*, Fall 2011.

9 EKOS Research Associates, April 1, 2010.

10 EKOS Research Associates, May 2010.

11 Neil Nevitte and Christopher Cochrane, "Value Change and the Dynamics of the Canadian Partisan Landscape," in *Canadian Parties in Transition*, 3rd ed., ed. Alain-G. Gagnon and A. Brian Tanguay (Broadview Press, 2007).

12 They included Michael Decter and George Ford, who would go on to prominent roles as senior bureaucrats under NDP governments in Ontario and British Columbia.

13 The combined total of Canadian Alliance and Progressive Conservative votes in the 2000 election was 45 per cent. The new united Conservative party won 30 per cent in 2004, 36 per cent in 2006, 38 per cent in 2008, and 40 per cent in 2011.

CHAPTER 2 – WHY NOW IS THE TIME

1 Conference Board of Canada reports on inequality, July and September 2011.

2 Conference Board. To be absolutely clear, the net effect of taxes and transfers remains redistributive, but less so.

3 Cited in the Canadian Index of Wellbeing, "Living Standards," 2011.

4 Ibid., p. 43.

5 Richard Nixon echoed the phrase in 1971 (even as he began to unravel the postwar monetary system created at Bretton Woods).

6 I am oversimplifying a bit here. Friedman was himself a disciple of Friedrich Hayek, the expatriate Austrian philosopher and economist who taught at the London School of Economics and later the University of Chicago. Hayek's direct influence on conservative thinking was relatively greater in the UK, while mediated to a larger extent in the US through Friedman and other members of the "Chicago School." On one occasion, Mrs. Thatcher is said to have slapped a copy of one of Hayek's books on a table and declared, "This is what we believe." However, it was Thatcher who first and most aggressively adopted Friedman's theories of monetarism.

7 Most British wage workers at the time were paid in cash. In some industries, the "pay packets" were handed to what we would call shop stewards, who distributed them to the individual workers.

8 Robert Skidelsky, *Keynes, The Return of the Master,* Penguin 2009

9 James Laxer, *Beyond the Bubble: Imagining a New Canadian Economy*Between the Lines, 2009), pp. 53–55.

10 Emphasis in original.

11 My friend's doctorate related to Sen's groundbreaking work in social choice theory, which was only loosely related to the issues I am discussing here.

12 Jon Gertner, "The Rise and Fall of the GDP," *New York Times Magazine,* May 10, 2010.

13 See, for example, Richard Wilkinson and Kate Pickett, *The Spirit Level: Why Greater Equality Makes Societies Stronger* (Bloomsbury, 2009). The University of British Columbia economist John Helliwell has contributed extensively to this literature. Also, see the Canadian Index of Wellbeing, produced by the Wellbeing Institute at the University of Waterloo.

14 Yoram Bauman, "The Dismal Education," *New York Times,* December 16, 2011.

15 Daniel Kahneman and Amos Tversky, "Prospect Theory: An Analysis of Decision under Risk," *Econometrica* 47 (1979), pp. 263–91.

16 For an entertaining romp through the findings of behavioural economics, see Dan Ariely, *Predictably Irrational: The Hidden Forces that Shape Our Decisions* (HarperCollins, 2009).

17 I wrote this passage before the publication of Daniel Kahneman's wonderful book *Thinking, Fast and Slow* (Farrar, Strauss and Giroux, 2011), in which he offers an almost identical example.

18 Amos Tversky died prior to the awarding of the Nobel Prize to Kahneman in 2002.

19 Both the Obama administration and the Cameron government in Britain have set up units in the public service aimed at adapting the insights of behavioural economics into public policy—inspired in large part by the work of the American behavioural economist Richard Thaler. Thaler is the co-author with Cass Sunstein of the best-seller Nudge: Improving Decisions About Health, Wealth and Happiness (Yale University Press, 2008).

20 Bernard Harcourt, T*he Illusion of Free Markets: Punishment and the Myth of Natural Order* (Harvard University Press, 2011).

21 There is some irony, nonetheless, that Greenspan's surprise at what happened in the subprime crisis was rooted in his failure to grasp that the financial institutions in which he placed so much trust were undermined in part by a system of financial incentives that encouraged the people working in the institutions to take risks with other people's money that were not in the interests of the companies or their shareholders. This is the radically individualist philosophy of Ayn Rand—of which Greenspan was a celebrated admirer—turned on itself.

22 Thomas S. Kuhn, *The Structure of Scientific Revolutions* (University of Chicago Press, 1962).

CHAPTER 3 – WHY CONSERVATIVES WIN

1 See "Harper says Conservatives Must Reach Out to Quebec", *cbc.ca,* July 10, 2011.

2 Environics Research Group, *2011 Post-election Issues Survey,* http://www.environics.ca/uploads/File/Environics---2011-Post-Election-Survey---Summary-Report---June-3-2011.pdf.

3 Reform was initially critical of Mulroney's policies on trade as well, though that angle of attack was destroyed, of course, with the negotiation of the Free Trade Agreement (FTA) with the United States in the run-up to

the 1988 election. In fact, the FTA, which was very popular on the Prairies, was almost certainly responsible for dashing Manning's hopes for a Reform breakthrough in the 1988 election.

4 Manning initially hesitated in opposing Charlottetown, influenced, perhaps, by his close advisor Rick Anderson, who supported the Accord. However, Manning eventually was at the forefront of the populist campaign against it, particularly in the West. Anderson separated from the Manning camp for a time over the issue.

5 Paul Wells, *Right Side Up* (McClelland and Stewart, 2006), p. 142. Wells's book, along with Tom Flanagan's insider's book, *Harper's Team* (McGill-Queen's University Press, 2007), provides fascinating detail on how Harper fashioned the newly united party.

6 I've avoided the term "libertarian" here because it suggests a greater degree of stringency than Harper has exhibited in his career as prime minister. Harper is not Ron Paul. However, his decision to kill the mandatory long-form census questionnaire certainly seems to reflect the libertarian streak in his thinking.

7 See, for example, *"Police-reported Crime Statistics,"* Statistics Canada, July 21, 2011. This survey suggested that crime was at its lowest level in forty years. It can be found at http://www.statcan.gc.ca/daily-quotidien/110721/dq110721b-eng.htm.

8 Chantal Hébert, *French Kiss* (Alfred A. Knopf, 2007).

9 The NDP sweep of Quebec in 2011 reduced the Conservatives' total to five seats.

10 Thomas Frank, *What's the Matter with Kansas* (Picador, 2005), p. 5. Frank's thesis has been strongly disputed. See Larry M. Bartles, "What's the Matter with What's the Matter with Kansas," *Quarterly Journal of Political Science* 1, no. 2 (2006), 201–26.

11 See Darrell Bricker and Keren Gottfried, "The New Tectonics of Canadian Politics," *Policy Options* (October 2011). Unless otherwise mentioned, the numbers in this section are drawn from the enormous Ipsos Reid post-election survey.

12 Tom Flanagan, *Harper's Team*, pp. 223–24.

13 Though it is worth noting that the Conservatives had found that parents like my wife and me with two children were less likely to be available to them than people like Steve and Heather who had three (or more) children.

14 Named after the American journalist Michael Kinsley, who defined a gaffe as a politician's accidentally telling the truth.

15 Discussions in this area are bedevilled with definitional problems. We all have an ethnicity, of course, even if we are White Anglo-Saxon Protestants, which is why some people object to the use of the term "ethnic voter." "New Canadians" doesn't do either, since some communities, including Jews, for example, fall mostly outside this category. Typically, the underlying question analysts are trying to get at is whether people who have an identity other than simply English- or French-Canadian vote along distinctive lines and how that may be changing. Sometimes apparent disagreements about changing voting patterns, however, turn out to be based on different operational assumptions. That is, if you look at people who are "foreign-born," you will exclude many Jews and second- and third-generation visible minorities, while including people who have immigrated from Anglo-Saxon countries and do not form a distinctive voting community.

16 It caused a controversy in part because it was attached to a party fundraising letter written on the parliamentary letterhead of the minister of immigration, Jason Kenney, by one of his aides.

17 That was a reference to the practice of some English landowners of leading their farmworkers to the polls, where they would promptly vote the landowner's wishes.

18 This kind of scene has increasingly been a feature also of Conservative nomination meetings, itself an indication of the shift in the politics of minority communities.

19 The candidate was John Beck.

20 Joe Friesen, "Jason Kenney: The 'Smiling Buddha' and His Multicultural Charms," *Globe and Mail,* January 29, 2010.

21 The large Ipsos Reid post-election poll suggested that a majority of Jewish voters supported the Conservatives in 2011. Although the sample size was small even in this massive poll, the result is consistent with other surveys, anecdotal evidence, and vote swings in seats where there are large Jewish communities.

22 Democratic party presidential candidates Al Gore, John Kerry, and Barack Obama each carried the Jewish vote in the mid- to high-70 per cent range. Although Jewish support for Obama flagged after his election in 2008, in part because of his willingness to apply some rhetorical pressure on the Netanyahu government, it remained higher than among the general population. In Canada, now, Jewish voters support the Conservatives by a substantially higher margin than do the general population.

23 Tonda MacCharles, "Travelling Tory Woos Ethnic Voters," *Toronto Star,* February 23, 2008.

24 The best summary of what was known about ethnic, new Canadian, and visible minority voting in the 2011 at the time this book went to print was in Pundits' Guide to Canadian Federal Elections, *Who Really Won the Ethnic Vote in the May Election,* (undated, but accessible from http://www. punditsguide.ca/2011/09/).

25 Tom Flanagan, *Harper's Team,* p. 85.

26 Mark Brownlee, "Liberals Try to Catch Up with Tories on Voter Identification Database System," *Hill Times,* January 10, 2011.

27 During the 2011 election campaign, Harper made a further commitment to move the deadline for eliminating the deficit up a year, to the 2014–15 fiscal year. However, within a few months of the election, his finance minister, Jim Flaherty, seemed to cool on that objective.

28 Ipsos Reid post-election survey, May 2011.

29 See Paul Martin, *Hell or High Water: My Life In and Out of Politics* (Emblem, 2009; Douglas Gibson Books, 2008), pp. 179–84.

30 There's evidence that in recent elections polls have tended to underestimate Conservative strength, most likely because that party's supporters have a greater propensity to turn out to vote than those of other parties.

CHAPTER 4 – WHY THE NEW DEMOCRATS BROKE OUT

1 The Liberals, in contrast, who had run first or second in 200 seats in 2008, now fell to 110. Calculations by www.punditsguide.ca.

2 June Rowlands was a partisan Liberal but ran on a conservative platform.

3 The formerly common practice of union organizers being seconded to the NDP machine during campaigns is now regarded as an in-kind contribution to the party, which is included in election expenses, making it more efficient for the unions to pursue parallel campaigns.

4 It's worth noting, however, that the party spent far less than its limit at the local level in 2008, and less in this respect than the other national parties, in part because it was not competitive in much of the country. This situation improved somewhat in 2011, though to what extent was not yet clear at the time of writing.

5 Petti Fong, "Welcome to Crowfoot, Alberta. Now Vote for Stephen Harper," *Toronto Star,* April 25, 2011.

6 Ryan Flanagan, "Alberteen Spence Running for Greens," *Thompson Citizen,* April 8, 2011.

7 Chantal Hébert, *French Kiss* (Knopf Canada, 2007), pp. 170ff.

8 Jean-Herman Guay, "L'après-Jack : l'avenir du NPD au Québec," *Policy Options* (October 2011), p. 35.

9 Ensight Canada, *Mind Your Majority, Eh? A Report Based on Canada's Only Genuine Exit Poll,* May 2011.

10 Jean-Herman Guay, "L'après-Jack," p. 34.

11 Leger online survey conducted for the Association of Canadian Studies, May 3–5, 2011.

12 Éric Bélanger and Richard Nadeau, "The Bloc Québécois Capsized by the Orange Wave," in *The Canadian Federal Election of 2011,* ed. Jon Pammett and Christopher Dornan (Dundurn, 2011). They drew this conclusion from "preliminary results" of the Canadian Election Survey of 2011.

13 Elly Alboim, "The NDP Numbers: Some Random Thoughts," *Political Perspectives* (April 21, 2011), www.cusjc.ca.

14 The turnout for the one-member, one-vote leadership selection in March 2012 was about 50.7 per cent nationally. There's no reason to suppose that Quebec's would have been higher than the national average.

15 www.cbc.ca/thenational/indepthanalysis/story/2011/04/18/national-jacklaytoninterview.html.

16 He had been more explicit, for example, in the 2006 election, when he asked Liberals turned off with the sponsorship affair to "lend us your vote"—a clever attempt to separate residual partisan loyalty from vote choice.

17 Linda Diebel, "What Really Sunk Michael Ignatieff and the Liberals," *Toronto Star,* May 7, 2011.

18 The Liberal gain, in Winnipeg North, a storied NDP seat, had first come in a by-election in 2010, and was narrowly held—by just forty-four votes—in 2011.

19 Innovative Research Group online poll conducted for the Historica Dominion Institute, May 3–8, 2011. The NDP was particularly strong among young people in Quebec.

20 "*'Splits' Decisions: A Closer Look at Vote Splits in Greater Toronto,*" www.punditsguide.ca/2011/05/splits-decisions-a-closer-look-at-vote-shifts-in-greater-toronto/. Also, Ken Boessenkool and Brian Topp, "Who Really Benefited from Vote Splits This Election?" May 9, 2011, www.theglobeandmail.com/news/politics/second-reading/brian-topp/who-really-benefited-from-vote-splits-this-election/article2015619/.

21 John Ibbitson, "Onetime Parliamentary Page Returns to the Hill as a Tory

MP," *Globe and Mail,* May 11, 2011.

22 The NDP lost one of the 103 MPs they elected in 2011 when Lise St-Denis crossed to become a Liberal early in 2012.

23 This seat might be one of the genuine examples of "vote-splitting," where the NDP gain in votes did reduce the Liberals' support sufficiently to cede the seat to the Conservatives.

CHAPTER 5 – WHY THE LIBERALS' STRANGE DECLINE

1 In his book *When the Gods Changed: The Death of Liberal Canada* (Random House Canada, 2011), Peter C. Newman attributes the phrase to Jack Pickersgill, but I have been unable to confirm this, and Newman does not give a reference.

2 Andrew Mayeda, "Liberals Should Stop Seeing Themselves as the 'Natural' Governing Party: Ignatieff," *National Post,* January 19, 2010.

3 Simon Doyle, "Canada Has Had 'No Natural Governing Party since the 1950's': Russell," *Hill Times,* May 12, 2008.

4 The exception was 1921, when the Progressives took 21 per cent, but that was a short-lived aberration. The Progressives were, in the main, subsequently absorbed into the Liberal party.

5 This figure does not include Reform, which won the second-largest number of votes in 1993.

6 The 2011 election marked a modest deviation from this pattern, with the Liberals, Bloc, and Greens pulling just 28 per cent of the vote, though this remains a much higher level than in earlier years.

7 In 1953, the Liberals won twenty-four seats, compared with twenty-one for the CCF, fifteen for Social Credit, and nine for the PCs.

8 At least three of those four seats, Hedy Fry's, Ralph Goodale's, and Kevin Lamoureux's, were arguably personal, not party, wins.

9 This transformation reflected to a degree the taxonomy of parties laid out in Maurice Duverger's classic work, *Political Parties* (1951). Basing his theories mostly on European experience, he argued that elite, parliamentary-based parties react to the emergence of mass-based parties by developing higher levels of internal organization, including local chapters.

10 Christina McCall-Newman, *Grits: An Intimate Portrait of the Liberal Party* (Macmillan of Canada, 1983), p. 42.

11 See John English, *Just Watch Me: The Life of Pierre Elliott Trudeau: 1968–2000* (Knopf Canada, 2009).

12 Eddie Goldenberg, *The Way It Works* (Douglas Gibson Books, 2006), pp. 17–18.

13 Paul Adams, "Liberals, a Party of Power Looking for a Way Back," *Policy Options* (May 2010).

14 It is testimony to Trudeau's rivals' success in mythologizing the event that even today journalists and historians will casually refer to the circumstances in which the deal was done as "the Night of the Long Knives"—in what should be a repugnant allusion to Hitler's murder of his Nazi party rivals in 1934.

15 Lapierre had originally been elected to parliament as a Liberal, and supported Martin for the party leadership against Chrétien in 1990. When Martin lost, he quit, subsequently joining the BQ. Lapierre quit politics in 1992, and worked as a radio host until Martin recruited him again in 2003.

16 Along with former Ontario cabinet minister Chaviva Hošek.

17 Alan Frizell, Jon Pammett, and Anthony Westell, eds., *The Canadian General Election of 1993* (Carleton University Press, 1994), pp. 144–45.

18 André Bernard in *The Canadian General Election of 1993*, p. 85.

19 John Turner also remained on the last ballot. Although he would eventually be seen as a business Liberal, he was not identified strongly as such in 1968.

20 Paul Martin, *Hell or High Water: My Life In and Out of Politics* (Douglas Gibson Books, 2008), pp. 128–32.

21 Paul Martin, *Hell or High Water,* p. 150.

22 Jean Chrétien, *My Years as Prime Minister* (Knopf Canada, 2007), pp. 66–67.

23 Sheila Copps went further, resigning and running in a by-election, because she had promised to do so if the tax were not "scrapped."

24 John Turner's crusade against free trade had helped dry up corporate support for the Liberal party. See Stephen Clarkson in *The Canadian General Election of 1993*, p. 29.

25 Brian Topp once remarked to me that if you keep repeating a campaign message it is typically less successful each time out. Voters get used to it and opponents are prepared for it.

26 Just a few days before the 1998 budget, one of Martin's aides summoned me on short notice to meet with the minister. Martin asked me whether I wanted to talk on or off the record and I suggested we talk off the record at first so he could be frank, but then go on the record so I could get some clips for my radio story. It was a bad idea. Martin spoke very candidly about

the fifty-fifty formula when we were off the record, but when I turned my tape machine on he wouldn't repeat a word of it. At best he gave tepid hints at what he had said earlier. To this day, I am not sure whether I did the right thing, but I used his on-the-record clips and then presented them with a heavy interpretative gloss suggesting that the fifty-fifty formula had played absolutely no role in the formulation of his budget. There was some controversy for Martin in the House the next day, but it quickly blew over.

27 See, for example, Preston Manning, *Think Big: My Life in Politics* (McClelland and Stewart, 2003).

28 The other element was an appeal to "soft sovereigntists," based on Martin's less-centralist vision of Canada, marked by his support for Meech Lake and coolness to the *Clarity Act*. As it happened, however, he abandoned this appeal, too, in Quebec mid-campaign, calling the arch-federalist Stéphane Dion off the backbench to which he had been relegated to help shore up the party's federalist core in the province.

29 *Every Voter Counts: The 308 Riding Strategy, Report of the Special Committee on Party Renewal* (Liberal Party of Canada, 2008).

30 Interview with Tom Flanagan, 2010.

31 Steven MacKinnon, "After Dion, A Time for Liberals to Rebuild," *Policy Options* (November 2008).

32 The work of Daniel Kahneman and Amos Tversky, the forerunners of behavioural economics, is relevant here. They've established how risk-averse most of us are. What that means is that when a policy proposes to give with one hand and take with the other, we focus much more heavily on the loss than the gain. What looks to the policy wonks as "revenue neutral" looks to regular humans like a bad deal.

33 Jack Layton, similarly, claimed that the NDP's costing of its election promises would be unaffected by the financial crisis.

34 Ignatieff had taken the refrain from another song, Bruce Springsteen's "My City of Ruins."

35 The ad referred to 2005, presumably meaning the non-confidence motion that defeated the Martin government and killed his government's agenda.

36 Ian Davey, "Five Things the Liberals Must Do to Win the Next Election," *National Post*, June 2, 2010.

37 Ensight Canada, *Mind Your Majority, Eh? A Report Based on Canada's Only Genuine Exit Poll*, May 2011.

38 www.punditsguide.ca, May 11, 2011.

39 Historica Dominion Institute, "Youth Voter Turnout," May 10, 2011.

40 Online survey of 36,000 Canadians by Ipsos Reid, reported by the Canadian Press, May 9, 2011.

41 "What a Liberal Riding Looks Like Before and After the Election," *Globe and Mail*, May 15, 2011.

42 Éric Grenier, "Just How Big an Electoral Challenge Do the Liberals Face in 2015?" *Globe and Mail*, January 23, 2012.

CHAPTER 6 – WHY WORKING TOGETHER IS HARD

1 See, for example, Laura Peyton, "NDP MP Lise St-Denis Jumps to Liberals," posted January 10, 2012, www.cbc.ca/news/politics/story/2012/01/10/pol-lib-rae-coderre.html.

2 Michael Ignatieff, remember, foreswore a coalition in the early days of the 2011 campaign, to avoid incoming fire from the Conservatives. Thomas Mulcair made a similar pledge in the course of his race for the NDP leadership.

3 Thanks to Jamey Heath, who made this observation in the course of a conversation on the two parties.

4 Darrell Bricker and Keren Gottfried, "The New Tectonics of Canadian Politics," *Policy Options* (October 2011). The survey examined broad social, political, and economic attitudes rather than specific policies.

5 Jamey Heath, *Dead Centre, Hope, Possibility and Unity for Canadian Progressives* (John Wiley and Sons, 2007).

6 Apps, incidentally, or perhaps not, was one of the small group of young Liberals, along with Terrie O'Leary and Peter Donolo, said to have recruited Paul Martin into active politics a decade and a half earlier.

7 Martha Hall Findlay, "Not Left, Not Right—Whither the Liberal Party," *Policy Options* (October 2011).

8 See Éric Grenier, "Conservative Fundraising: Lead on Other Parties Narrows," *Huffington Post*, February 3, 2012, www.huffingtonpost.ca/2012/02/03/conservative-fundraising-canada_n_1251144.html. The Conservatives had a relatively poor fourth quarter, but at $4.1 million still far outstripped the other parties, though it is perhaps worth noting that the Liberal and NDP combined total was higher than the Conservative total for the first time in many years.

9 Brian Topp, *How We Almost Gave the Tories the Boot: The Inside Story Behind the Coalition* (James Lorimer and Company, 2010).

10 John Turner's Liberals had been reduced to just forty seats in 1984, compared with Dion's seventy-seven, but he had won 28 per cent of the popular vote, compared with just 26 per cent for Dion's Liberals.

11 The original subsidy, introduced by the Chrétien government in 2003 when it also eliminated union and corporate contributions to political parties, had been $1.75 per vote, but was structured to be adjusted for inflation.

12 By the time the opportunity for a coalition emerged, Dion had already announced his resignation and was serving as interim leader until a replacement was chosen.

13 Less than three years later, during the 2011 election, many media outlets would repeat the mendacious Harper version as fact.

14 *Hot Air* is Jeffrey Simpson and Mark Jaccard's excellent book on the failures of Canadian government policy on climate change. Jeffrey Simpson, Mark Jaccard, and Nic Rivers, *Hot Air: Meeting Canada's Climate Change Challenge* (Douglas Gibson Books, 2007).

15 Brian Topp, "Two Down, One to Go," *Policy Options* (June 2011).

16 Jim Stanford, "The History of the New Politics Initiative: Movement and Party, Then and Now," *rabble.ca*, November 29, 2011.

17 See, for example, Adrian Morrow, "CAW Chief Lewenza Urges NDP to Consider Merger with the Liberals," *Globe and Mail,* September 2, 2011.

18 A number of surveys suggested that, unlike the rest of Canada, the NDP's support in Quebec did not skew towards those with lower incomes.

19 Interview with Althia Raj, *Huffington Post*, March 10, 2012.

20 He was also one of a minority of MPs who had broken ranks with Layton by supporting the abolition of the gun registry—changing his vote only after launching his leadership campaign.

21 The *Pundits' Guide* offered an exhaustive list of legal and administrative pitfalls, "Pros and Cons of the Cullen Plan: A Sceptic's Guide to Electoral Coalitions in Canada" (undated), www.punditsguide.ca/2011/12/pros-and-cons-of-the-cullen-plan-a-sceptics-guide-to-electoral-coalitions-in-canada/.

22 This option was also available to party members who did not attend the convention, who could vote in real time over the Internet, but relatively few availed themselves of this option, perhaps because it was not well understood.

23 See "Cullen Narrowly Won Convention, but Mulcair Victory Already Assured," *Pundits' Guide* (undated), www.punditsguide.ca/2012/04/cullen-narrowly-won-convention-but-mulcair-victory-already-assured/.

24 David Herle, "Go Big or Go Home," *Policy Options* (March 2012).

CHAPTER 7 – WHY CHANGE IS NOW POSSIBLE

1 Joseph E. Stiglitz, *Freefall: America, Free Markets, and the Sinking of the World Economy* (Norton, 2010), p. 219.

2 See David Frum, "When Did the GOP Lose Touch with Reality," *New York Magazine*, November 20, 2011.

3 Jeffrey D. Sachs, *The Price of Civilization* (Random House, 2011).

4 Thomas Philippon, "The Future of the Financial Industry," *Stern on Finance*, October 16, 2008, http://sternfinance.blogspot.ca/2008/10/future-of-financial-industry-thomas.html.

5 See Jim Stanford, *Having Their Cake and Eating It Too* (Canadian Centre for Policy Alternatives, April 2011), available at http://www.policyalternatives.ca/publications/reports/having-their-cake-and-eating-it-too.

6 Tom Kent, *The Social Democracy of Canadian Federalism* (Broadbent Institute, 2011).

7 http://www.energy.gov.ab.ca/OurBusiness/oilsands.asp.

8 "The energy security benefits of robust Canadian oil sands production are real, but, because oil is essentially traded on a global market, not as large as some might intuitively assume." Michael A. Levi, *The Canadian Oils Sands: Energy Security vs. Climate Change* (Council on Foreign Relations, May 2009), p. 22.

9 Ibid., p. 23.

10 This benchmark has been used by the Stern Commission; the governments of Ontario, California, and several European nations; and the UN Framework Convention on Climate Change, among others, as an achievable and responsible goal. Harper has set a more modest goal for Canada: to reach 60 per cent by 2050.

11 Arguably more, since Obama pursued a more aggressive policy through his executive powers than the Harper government has pursued.

12 Ezra Levant, *Ethical Oil* (McClelland and Stewart, 2011).

13 Oil is a fungible commodity, and sourcing oil from Canada would not affect the price for Americans, even in a crisis. It is almost impossible to imagine Levant's "unethical" suppliers ganging up on the United States, but in that unlikely event it is possible that Canadian oil supplies—guaranteed to a degree by NAFTA—would indeed be somewhat more secure from an American perspective, albeit at a price.

14 *The Climate Change Performance Index,* available at http://germanwatch.org/en/3528.

15 Jean Chrétien, *My Years as Prime Minister* (Alfred A. Knopf, 2007), pp. 382–389.

16 Ibid., p. 388.

17 In their book *Hot Air,* the best account of the policy failures of these years, columnist Jeffrey Simpson and leading environmental scientist Mark Jaccard put it this way: "Without consulting cabinet, Chrétien had changed Canada's negotiating position…From that moment on, guided almost entirely by political optics, Chrétien set Canada on a climate change policy course whereby the government accepted onerous obligations without knowing how to fulfill them. Every day from Chrétien's fateful call to Kyoto to the end of his years as prime minister, and every day since he left office, Canada has moved steadily father from meeting its Kyoto targets, compiling the worst climate change record of any major country that signed the Kyoto Protocol on global warming" (pp. 33-34).

18 Jean Chrétien, *My Years as Prime Minister,* p. 388.

19 Brian Topp, *How We Almost Gave the Tories the Boot* (James Lorimer and Company, 2010), pp. 44–45.

20 Chris Bataille et al., *Exploration of Two Canadian Greenhouse Gas Emissions Targets: 25% below 1990 and 20% below 2006 Levels by 2020* (Pembina Institute and Suzuki Foundation, 2009).

21 Joseph E. Stiglitz, *Freefall,* p. 196.

22 Armine Yalnizyan, *The Rise of Canada's Richest 1%* (Centre for Policy Alternatives, December 2010).

23 The Conference Board of Canada, *Hot Topic: Canadian Income Inequality,* July 2011, http://www.conferenceboard.ca/hcp/hot-topics/canInequality.aspx.

24 Brian Murphy, Paul Roberts, and Michael Wolfson, *High Income Canadians* (Statistics Canada, September 2007).

25 KPMG, *Competitive Alternatives, 2010 Special Report: Focus on Taxes.*

Taking the United States as 100, Canada was given a 63.9, the UK 88.0, Germany 124.1, and France 181.4. The study included provincial as well as federal taxes, as well as payroll taxes such as employment insurance and CPP.

26 Jim Stanford, *Having Their Cake and Eating It Too*, p. 3

27 As I write, the forecast for the British structural deficit has *increased* by £22 billion, notwithstanding, or rather because of, the UK's severe austerity program, "requiring" further cuts. See Robert Skidelsky, "The Wages of Economic Ignorance," *Project Syndicate*, Nov. 21, 2011, available at http://www.project-syndicate.org/commentary/the-wages-of-economic-ignorance.

28 See Alex Himelfarb, "Tax is Not a Four-Letter Word," *Alex's Blog*, October 15, 2011, http://afhimelfarb.wordpress.com/2011/10/15/tax-is-not-a-four-letter-word/. A shorter version appeared in the *Globe and Mail* the previous day.

29 Brian Topp, "Bringing Balance and Fairness to Canada's Tax System," *rabble.ca*, November 28, 2011. http://rabble.ca/.

30 Jeffrey D. Sachs, *The Price of Civilization*, pp. 222–23.

31 The idea that the Canadian banks did not get a government bailout is an outright myth. A Report for the Canadian Centre for Policy Alternatives, *The Big Banks' Big Secret: Estimating Government Support for Canadian Banks During the Financial Crisis*, released in the spring of 2012, calculated that the Canadian banks had in fact received in the neighbourhood of $114 billion in cash and loan support to weather the financial crisis.

32 OECD, Rodolfo García Zamora, *Society at a Glance 2011– OECD Social Indicators* (OECD Publishing, 2011).

CHAPTER 8 – WHY WE SHOULD HAVE HOPE

1 Dan Lett, "He Didn't Just Win Their Votes, He Won Their Hearts," *Winnipeg Free Press*, November 5, 2011. I've drawn mainly on Lett's account for this paragraph.

2 Harold Myerson, "Make It Personal," *American Prospect*, June 19, 2008.

3 See Henry Milner, "The Problem of Political Drop-Outs: Canada in Comparative Perspective," in *Canadian Parties in Transition*, ed. Alain-G. Gagnon and Brian Tanguay (Broadview Press, 2007).

4 Paul Howe, *The Electoral Participation of Young People* (Elections Canada, 2007), p. 437.

5 Robert D. Putnam, *Bowling Alone* (Simon and Schuster, 2010).

6 The best performers were Borden in 1917 and Diefenbaker in 1958.

7 Paul Howe, *Citizens Adrift* (UBC Press, 2010), p. 21.

8 Lawrence Leduc et al., *Dynasties and Interludes* (Dundurn Press, 2010), p. 543.

9 See for example, Carolyn Bennett, "Voter Suppression" (April 7, 2011), http://carolynbennett.liberal.ca/blog/voter-suppression-2/ and Warren Kinsella, "Voter Suppression" (undated), http://warrenkinsella.com/articles/vote-suppression/.

10 See, for example, Frank Graves, *The 41st Election:A Polling Retrospective; Implications for Methodology and Democracy,* http://www.ekospolitics.com/wp-content/uploads/41st_election.pdf.

11 Michael Adams, *Fire and Ice, Canada and the Myth of Converging Values* (Penguin, 2003), pp. 31–33.

12 Paul Howe, *Citizens Adrift,* p. 28.

13 Ibid., pp. 209–30.

14 Of course, most professors were at the top of their own classes as students—not at the median—which may partially account for this cognitive delusion.

15 Amber Hidebrandt, "'Vote Mobs' Shake Up Election," *cbc.ca,* April 6, 2011, http://www.cbc.ca/news/politics/canadavotes2011/story/2011/04/06/cv-election-flash-vote-mobs.html.

16 This account is drawn substantially from David Remnick, *The Bridge: The Life and Rise of Barack Obama* (Alfred A. Knopf, 2010).

17 The best account of the Obama strategy and organization is that of his campaign manager, David Plouffe, *The Audacity to Win* (Viking, 2009).

18 David Plouffe, *The Audacity to Win,* pp. 66–67, 161.

19 One lively account of the Obama's e-campaign with lots of vivid detail was written by a young Canadian volunteer, though her book is marred somewhat by the attempt to turn her experience into a marketing manual. Rahaf Harfoush, *Yes We Did: An Inside Look at How Social Media Built the Obama Brand* (New Riders, 2010).

ACKNOWLEDGEMENTS

Thanks first of all to my publisher, James Lorimer, and editor, Diane Young, for seeing the value and potential of this book. Canada needs a vigorous publishing industry to promote a robust public debate.

It was Brian Topp, who had previously written about the 2008 coalition bid for Lorimer, who suggested that I get in touch with James and Diane. I am indebted to him for that, as well as for making time for me over several years to discuss the substance of this project, which evolved considerably from its beginning as an examination of the decline of the Liberal party. Thanks to Brian, as well as to Nathan Cullen, Paul Dewar, and Peggy Nash, each of whom agreed to long interviews during their race for the NDP leadership, when they had more pressing demands on their time than those from an author who would not publish until long after the votes were counted. Bob Rae also gave generously of his time, as did several other Liberal MPs and candidates.

In the research for this book, I conducted in the neighbourhood of eighty formal interviews with MPs, candidates, strategists, and party activists from the Liberals, NDP, and to a lesser extent the Greens, and a similar number of less formal, but no less illuminating, extended conversations over coffee, lunch, or drinks and at conferences and conventions. I have quoted sparingly from these interviews and conversations, many of which were not for attribution, but I am nonetheless grateful for the time so generously given. This book is critical of the current strategic views of many lifelong Liberal and NDP partisans. Let me make it clear, nonetheless, that I have great admiration for those who give so much of their lives and energies to the maintenance and vitality of our political parties in an age of general disengagement. I applaud, and in some ways envy you. Thanks so much for your help.

I am grateful to Carleton University, where I teach in the School of Journalism and Communication, and which granted me a sabbatical during which I completed the book.

Elly Alboim, an early journalistic mentor of mine and by now an old friend, was kind enough to read large portions of this book in draft though he did not, to say the least, agree with every word of it. I am enormously grateful to Paul Barber, who lent his scrupulous eye to large portions of the manuscript, steering me clear of some errors, guiding me towards useful scholarship, and offering many helpful suggestions. Doug Gibson, my editor on an earlier project, has a genius for resurrecting my spirits, allowing me to dispense with the hard drink on which I was once forced to rely. Laurie Miller did such a fine job of copy editing that I conceded the Oxford comma. Needless to say, none of these people, nor the others who saw bits and pieces of the manuscript, associate themselves with the thesis here. The book is mine, for better and for worse.

Finally, as anyone with the misfortune to have an author in the house knows, family bear an enormous and unsought share of the burden, in terms of time lost, energy displaced, and mysterious mood shifts associated with sticky passages and looming deadlines. To my wife Suzanne, thank you for your patience and support. I love you. And to my children, Alex and Sophia, I'm all yours (for a while). Sophia, I'll take you to Chipmunks now.

INDEX